Richard Sibbes

God's Spreading Goodness

R N Frost

Cor Deo Press

Vancouver, Washington

Cor Deo Press
P.O. Box 871983
Vancouver, WA 98687

www.spreadinggoodness.org

www.cordeo.org.uk

Email: ron@cordeo.org.uk

ISBN 978-1-105-46367-9

Contents

To Steve and Jean Hix

Abbreviations

ARH	*Archive for Reformation History*
CTJ	*Calvin Theological Journal*
CH	*Church History*
DNB	*Dictionary of National Biography*
EQ	*Evangelical Quarterly*
GBWW	*Great Books of the Western World*
HTR	*Harvard Theological Review*
JBS	*Journal of British Studies*
JEH	*Journal of Ecclesiastical History*
JRH	*Journal of Religious History*
MVHR	*Mississippi Valley Historical Review*
NEQ	*New England Quarterly*
NPNF	*Nicene and Post-Nicene Fathers*
PP	*Past and Present*
RTJ	*Reformed Theological Journal*
SJT	*Scottish Journal of Theology*
SCJ	*Sixteenth Century Journal*
WTJ	*Westminster Theological Journal*
WMQ	*William and Mary Quarterly*, 3rd series

Preface

This book was birthed by curiosity: I wanted to unpack some of the big differences in faith I found among my Christian friends. My own experience of faith might be called an evangelical pietism. My parents met and married in Illinois where my mother worked at Wheaton College and sang in vocal groups with the "preacher boys" led by Billy Graham. My father's family lived in Wheaton and when I was born he was an instructor pilot for Missionary Aviation Fellowship at the local airport. My conversion to a lively Christianity occurred at a Montana church camp when I was sixteen. Two men, Art and Sam, then coached me to enjoy bold Bible reading. I went on to earn a pair of bachelor degrees, one from a Bible School and the other from a Catholic University in Portland—with some obvious contrasts of faith involved there. But my curiosity was most stirred in my days as an Army draftee at Fort Myer, Virginia, just across the Potomac from Washington DC.

There I enjoyed fellowship with a church home group of Reformed Christians. My own theological heritage had been shaped by Dispensational and Keswick teachings so in basic doctrines I agreed with my new friends but we differed in framing the overall Bible narrative. Our lively conversations were alternately theological—where my Reformed friends were razor sharp—and biblical where I was better read. A later six-week internship at the *Christianity Today* magazine offered similar contrasts between the creedal keenness shared by the mostly Reformed editors and my own simple biblicism. I was intrigued by a number of tensions between what I found in face value

Bible readings and the theological sophistication of my friends and mentors.

Those experiences were context for a dawning that came as I attended divinity school. My studies in church history included a course on the Puritans that touched on the New England Antinomian Controversy (1636-1638). That debate centered on tensions that were in many ways parallel to my Washington DC conversations. Intrigued, I examined the competing versions of salvation in the Controversy as an MA thesis. In that study I found that one side, led by a Boston minister, John Cotton, held that saving faith is a person's assurance of God's love as revealed by Bible promises and personally affirmed by the Spirit. The other group, led by Peter Bulkeley and Thomas Shepard, dismissed such assurance. They held, instead, that faith is a supernaturally aided act of the will that also includes an ongoing capacity to obey God's moral laws.

Now my curiosity was alive: what accounted for this difference? The ministers on both sides of the Boston conflict had trained at Cambridge University and in some cases had been friendly colleagues. Yet the debate was sharp and the divisions deep. My own sympathies in the debate were more with Cotton than with his foes. His more experiential theology was supported by what I found in my own reading of the Bible and even in my reading of John Calvin. Yet works by some theological historians in the Reformed tradition treated Cotton as a near heretic.[1] Another point in Cotton's story also intrigued me: he professed an adult conversion to faith *after* he was already a trained and lauded Puritan preacher. This was a surprising turn to say the least.

Cotton reported that a sermon by Richard Sibbes opened his eyes. Who was this Sibbes, I wondered, and what did he teach? The question led me to take up Sibbes as my subject in a doctoral program. There I found him to be a winsome and influential figure—a man well regarded by every brand of Puritan. He was strongly Trinitarian and affective in his spirituality—similar at many points to Calvin—and he emphasized the Spirit's role in stirring faith and guiding practice. His admirers included some high profile ministers—Thomas Goodwin, Jeremiah Burroughs, and Philip Nye, among others—who worked together to collect and publish most of his sermons posthumously.

What was intriguing is that these same friends were also known as the Dissenting Brethren at the Westminster Assembly where they promoted Congregationalism in the face of the majority preference for Presbyterianism. Sibbes died five years before that gathering yet his views may help account for their dissent—though he was not a Congregationalist himself.

Like Sibbes the dissenters were Trinitarian: treating God's Triune, relational love as an explanation for creation and God's engagement with humanity. This in turn offered the context for the dissenters' shared emphasis on affective themes in the Bible. Did such beliefs make any difference in applied ministry? Yes. In John Cotton's case there was a lively welcome accorded to his portrayal of God's Triune love in both Bostons—first in old England and then in New England. Yet the themes also proved to be disruptive when certain colonial activists celebrated Cotton's preaching while treating most other regional preaching as unsound.

His unhappy colleagues then confronted Cotton with what amounted to a trial just two years before the Westminster Assembly gathered—and this would have made the Westminster dissenters aware that alignment with Cotton's theology would be viewed with suspicion or hostility as word of the debate spread. Because the Parliament had indicated that the Assembly was not to be a forum for theological debates the ministers were silent about why they preferred a given polity. But it is plausible if not probable that the dissenters wanted a polity with space for disagreements to exist. And the dissenters knew from the New England episode that if a Presbyterian polity became the law of the land the resulting synods were likely to suppress preachers who were aligned with Cotton's affective spirituality. Most Presbyterians, by contrast to Cotton, embraced the growing hegemony of Federal theology that featured the rather disaffected spirituality of legal obedience.[2] A looser Congregational polity, by contrast, would more readily allow for such theological differences to exist among preachers.

Acknowledgements

Before we move to the study itself I want to express some appreciation here for the help I received in writing the dissertation that stands behind this work. Mark E. Dever had just concluded his own doctoral study of Sibbes when I arrived in England for my research. For months—until he left England—Dever offered me leads to some important sources. Although my reading of Sibbes' theology differs from Dever's, his biographical work on our shared Puritan was convincing. My doctoral supervisor, Susan Hardman Moore, was also helpful in pointing me to many key resources and in offering critical feedback—though she is certainly not responsible for any oversights or missteps that remain. The late Colin Gunton and colleagues of his Institute for Theological Research at King's College London helped me to see that Sibbes—a Trinitarian theologian—has many present-day counterparts.

A golden moment in my research came when Paul Blackham, a fellow student, noted the strong similarities between Sibbes' work and that of Martin Luther as best expressed in Philip Melanchthon's 1521 *Loci Communes Theologici*. Luther, I realized, played a key role in forming Sibbes' mature theology. This insight was pivotal to my research.

Some brief extensions of this project have been published and may be of interest to readers.[3] I am also aware of ongoing contributions—including important works by David R. Como, Tim Cooper, and Michael P. Winship, among others—that touch on the Puritans and Puritan concerns with salvation and sanctification. I know, too, that some of the dissertations I discuss here have since been published as books and my work should be updated accordingly. In fact an engagement of all such works is called for but to do it here would only overextend my already too-long delay in going to print. My particular contribution—the matter of how Augustine's Trinitarian and affective reading of the New Testament divided Puritans—needs to be considered sooner rather than later.

Finally, the deeper question of this study is more about the competing portrayals of God they offered rather than the beliefs of the English Puritans as ends in themselves. Sibbes' view is arguably more winsome: God is portrayed as offering his heart to his creation with an invitation for all to respond to his love. The other version of God is more formal and imposing:

his power, demands, and self-concern are treated as defining qualities. In the latter vision humans are called to a more contractual obedience with all the duties such an arrangement entails. The debate divided the Puritans, and even today those differences still stir debates among evangelical Christian communities.

Sibbes' pleasure in God—and his celebration of God's "spreading goodness"—began with his appreciation of the social dimensions of the Godhead. His sermons were widely read and significantly embraced by the lay public and by later ministers including, among many others, Richard Baxter, John Wesley, and Jonathan Edwards.[4]

This book offers Sibbes as an important contributor to the question of what constituted the early Reformed tradition in England. His was a leading voice among the Puritans who looked to the Augustinian tradition for inspiration in their ongoing conversation about sin and salvation; and of God's grace as the basis for saving faith.

Camas—January 2012

Introduction

What is Grace?

William Erbery (1604-1654), an antinomian, wrote of God's blessing on the English church. In Erbery's view a happy progression was evident among leading Puritan preachers who opposed a moralistic law-based theology and favored, instead, a theology of free grace through union with Christ.[5]

> I observed four great steps of God's glorious appearance in men's preaching. First, how low and legal were their teachings as they learned the way of preaching from Mr. Perkins, Bolton, Byfield and Dod and Dike . . . Next the doctrine of free grace came forth, but with less success or fruit of conversion by Doctor Preston, Sibs, [&] Crisp. . . . Thirdly the letter of scripture, and flesh of Christ hath been highly set up by both the famous Goodwins: . . . [Thomas] excels in spiritual discourses of Christ's death, resurrection, ascension, and intercession, yet much according to the flesh, for he meddles not with the mystery of Christ in us . . . . [The fourth step] is the knowledge of Christ in the Spirit . . . .[6]

This identification of Richard Sibbes (1577-1635) as part of a free grace movement that led away from the theology of William Perkins (1558-1602), among others, is consistent with studies by Michael Schuldiner and Janice Knight in pointing to a divide among early seventeenth century English Reformed ministers.[7] The Puritan house was divided not just over church polity differences—about which friends could disagree—but over the crucial and more contentious doctrine of grace.

For Erbery to place, with some accuracy, such theologically moderate figures as Sibbes, John Preston (1587-1628), and Thomas Goodwin (1600-1680) in line with his more radical antinomianism is a notable contemporary claim: it underscored an ongoing dispute over the meaning of divine grace. The question of grace had been at the heart of the divide between the Calvinists and the Arminians—the Puritans and the anti-Puritans. It also divided Puritans as seen in the Antinomian Controversy of New England (1636-1638); and the issue continued to stir divisions among English Protestants during the Civil War, into the Interregnum, and beyond. The doctrine of grace was one of the most unsettled and unsettling issues of Christendom.

Why did it stir such strong and persistent debate? Because grace was the basis for faith and faith gave access to eternal life. Salvation was the sought-after end as in the apostle Paul's statement: "For by grace you have been saved through faith" (Ephesians 2:8). Given this conceptual priority of grace pastors could and would express fierce devotion to their own creedal system—of how they defined grace, faith, and salvation—in order to assure parishioners that their teaching offered the proper keys to God's kingdom.

Sibbes in context

Sibbes' emphasis on God's free grace invites special notice. He held two posts at once—as Preacher at Gray's Inn, London, and Master of St Catharine's Hall of Cambridge University. The period of Sibbes' adult ministry—from 1595 to his death in 1635—saw a movement in the Stuart era toward a more Arminian theology among English church leaders, a shift that helped lead to the Civil War. This dynamic period in England's religious history forced ministers to take sides in sometimes dangerous ways. Sibbes, however, was notably irenic amid the doctrinal battles of his day yet without being passive. He was devoted to Church history. This, no doubt, accounts for some shifts in his theology over time as he traced the thinking of early Reformation theologians back to their own sources and to Augustine of Hippo (354-430) in particular.

Many of the shifts reflected turns away from William Perkins. Perkins was a major presence at Cambridge during Sibbes' education and was widely known through his preaching, teaching and publications as Sibbes first arrived at the University. Perkins' works represented a post-Reformation scholasticism that looked to Thomas Aquinas (1224-1275) more than to Augustinian themes that first sparked Protestantism many decades earlier. Perkins' *Works*—a three-volume folio publication—was among the most extensive and prominent systematic theologies available to the Puritans and drew widespread attention. Yet in time the younger man—by almost twenty years—distanced himself from many of Perkins views on sin, grace, and salvation.

Because Perkins' theology offers an important context and counterpoint to Sibbes' mature teaching he is given almost as much notice as Sibbes in our study. The constant comparisons of their views that follow here raise a question: did Sibbes have any direct meetings with Perkins? If they did meet there is no record of it. Yet we can assume they crossed paths in the course of preaching and teaching at the University because their periods of Cambridge residence overlapped from 1595 to 1602 and they shared Puritan sympathies. Sibbes was a bright and affable student who was becoming an educator; Perkins was a noted theologian whose role it was to instruct men like Sibbes.

Biography

Sibbes was an important transitional leader in the middle era of Puritanism. He was born in 1577 to a wheelwright in Tostock and proved to be an able student.[8] He gained patronage for placement at St. John's College, Cambridge, in 1595 and completed his Bachelors and Masters degrees there in 1602.[9] In 1601 he was made a fellow of the college with regular tutoring duties and in time he gained greater responsibility and status. In 1610 he was granted the Bachelor of Divinity degree and in 1627 a Doctor of Divinity. He also flourished as a preacher and served as the Lecturer at Holy Trinity Church, Cambridge, from 1610 to 1615. In 1617 he was called to preach at Gray's Inn—one of the prestigious London Inns of Court—which offered him a platform to speak to many of London's major politicians.

As a churchman Sibbes was a moderate—able to conform to the requirements of ecclesiastical uniformity—yet on two occasions he drew the unhappy attention of William Laud, later Archbishop of Canterbury.[10] One episode involved his efforts to raise financial support for Protestant refugees in Germany and Bohemia (1627). In the other he was confronted for his role in raising money for teaching posts—"lectureships"—to be held by Puritan preachers among parish churches (1632). Sibbes submitted in both cases and neither event diminished his freedom to preach.[11] In 1626 he was made Master of St Catharine Hall, a post he held to the end of his life along with his role as preacher at Gray's Inn.[12]

Perkins' place among English ministers is examined in Ian Breward's extended introduction to the abridged edition of Perkins' *Works*.[13]

Sibbes' prayer

A prayer offered by Sibbes captured the main elements and priorities of his theology. It was published with his final sermons and offers an order for this study. Some of the sequential excerpts from his prayer, here in highlights, will be used as chapter headings and will define the chapter themes.

> *Gracious and holy Father!* which hast sanctified this day for thy own service and worship, and for the furthering of us in the way of salvation . . . so sanctify our hearts by thy Holy Spirit at this time that we may perform these holy services as shall be most to thy glory and our own comfort. *Unworthy we are* in ourselves to appear in thy most holy presence, both *by reason of the sins of our nature, and the sins of our lives* . . . . But thou are a gracious and merciful Father unto us in Jesus Christ, in the abundance of thy love and mercy. . . . And then we

> beseech thee to *speak peace unto us in thy Christ, and* say to our souls *by thy Holy Spirit,* that thou are our salvation. And for clearer evidence that we are in thy favour, let us find the blessed work of thy Holy Spirit *opening our understandings, clearing our judgments, kindling our affections, discovering our corruptions, framing us every way to be such as thou mayest take pleasure and delight in.* . . . And grant, we beseech thee, that now at this time out of it [the word] we may learn thy holy will; and then labour to frame our lives thereafter, as may be most to thy glory and our own comfort, and that for Jesus Christ his sake thine only Son, and our blessed Saviour. Amen.[14]

Sibbes' theology will thus be allowed to define both the substance and the order of the topics addressed in this study. The first chapter sets out both the contemporary and modern issues in debate. The second chapter examines Perkins' and Sibbes' separate views of God's predestinarian purpose. Perkins' theology is portrayed in relief, representing the emerging orthodoxy of late sixteenth century Cambridge Puritanism as Sibbes would have learned it, and from which he departed at important points. Conflicting traditions of nature and grace, starting with Augustine versus Pelagius, offer context for their opposed views. Definitions of grace are shown in chapter three to be linked to different versions of sin—treated either as privation or as concupiscence. In chapter four we trace differing views of how Gods' covenant sets up salvation. Perkins and Sibbes also explained the soul in different ways, so in chapter five we consider how a soul receives saving grace—with separate versions of grace corresponding to those differences. Chapter six examines the relationship of God's initiative in his promises and the believers' assurance of salvation—the point where Sibbes' theology shows its greatest inconsistency.

Continuity and discontinuity

In this study I emphasize theological differences that separated Sibbes and Perkins. But first I need to acknowledge their superficial similarity: both men preached to lay audiences in very affective terms, portraying God's love in winsome terms. Yet, as we will see, this shared pastoral rhetoric is misleading. Perkins' academic works—published in Latin for scholars to read—displayed a very different trajectory to the direction Sibbes would take.

With an eye for this discontinuity we must also raise a seeming problem of inconsistency in Sibbes. At important points among his sermon series he exhibited jarring inconsistencies. To use Perkins' theology as a point of reference, Sibbes agreed with him in some sermons and disagreed with him in others. At times, for instance, Sibbes used the moral laws of the Bible to exhort believers to seek spiritual self-improvement—a common theme in Perkins—but he denied such an approach elsewhere. He also affirmed a privative definition of sin in one place but dismissed it elsewhere.[15] What accounts for these shifts? The most likely answer is that he moved away from his early, student era, acceptance of Perkins' teachings as he read more widely in his maturity.

This brings us to a problem with chronology: Sibbes' works are mostly undated. He left no collections of papers and most of his sermons—published posthumously—lack any reference to when they were offered. It could be argued, of course, that Sibbes was an inconsistent thinker but there are good reasons to dismiss that prospect. One is the clarity of his expression and coherence within a given sermon series. Another is the standing he had among some very able scholars in his day that afforded him the positions he held at Cambridge and Gray's Inn—a status not likely to be granted to a careless thinker. Any inconsistencies are better explained by assuming that he changed his mind over time.

We know that Sibbes read widely throughout his career—a habit displayed in his range of cited sources when he preached—and this offers a likely basis for his changes. So here we will treat his inconsistencies as signals of a trajectory away from positions he received in his early Cambridge studies to views more aligned with figures such as Augustine, Luther, and Calvin. To support this premise we find that on the questions of sin and salvation—where he can be read in separate places as both for and against a Perkinsonian position—his teachings that most differed from Perkins' view were well aligned with John Cotton's New England views—noticed below—that were aired soon after Sibbes died. In other words, Cotton reflected Sibbes' mature views in the New England controversy; and Cotton's opponents held views Sibbes once held but later discarded.

One additional question should be asked. Did Sibbes challenge Perkins or his system by name? No. Despite his willingness to dismiss certain theological assumptions with clarity and courage, Sibbes was irenic enough to avoid naming those whose positions he opposed. So although he certainly understood Perkins' Federalism and disagreed with it, Sibbes only mentions Perkins once.[16] This indirection helps account for the shared view of two doctoral studies on Sibbes (Dever's and another by Stephen P. Beck) that present him as aligned with Perkins' Federalism.[17]

Finally, this study addresses matters of continuity and discontinuity from an extended historical frame of reference. Some historians, including Dever and Beck, have read Sibbes in light of their own commitment to modern Reformed dogmatics. Others scholars, as will be seen, use a sociological and political lens to examine the effects of Sibbes' heightened Pneumatology in the English church. Still others, led by Richard A. Muller, see Thomas Aquinas in his twelfth-century synthesis of faith and reason to be the proper scale for measuring seventeenth-century Reformed theology—with the result that a figure like Perkins is seen as wholly orthodox.

This study, by contrast, looks much more to Augustine as a sound touchstone of orthodoxy. Augustine's mature—post-Pelagian-controversy—views of grace and faith were distinctive and well known by later theologians, including Martin Luther and John Calvin. Sibbes read these men and came to favor the Augustinian tradition as his own basis for understanding grace.

Chapter One

Divided by Grace

Early in 1637, New England ministers tried to cool the "hot contentions and paroxysms" among the region's churches by a written exchange of views with John Cotton, a minister in the Boston church. Cotton's sermon series on God's saving covenant triggered what has since been called the Antinomian Controversy. According to Cotton God's love as revealed in Scriptures and affirmed by his Spirit *is* his grace; and, given his love, faith is a person's response of reciprocal love and trust. Other ministers, however, held grace to be an infused capacity granted by God solely to the elect, a gift that enables them to meet the first duty of salvation: to believe.

Listeners were quick to take up the question this raised: is salvation a response or a responsibility? Does God draw and save his elect people through unsolicited self-disclosures? Or does he set out a requirement to believe and then enable his elect to supply an act of faith as their entry point to salvation? And, with such options, what assurance of salvation is available? Is faith and assurance the same thing—a response to God's loving self-disclosures? Or is it only gained as individuals discover an ability to meet God's call for lifelong obedience, an ability only found among the elect?

Cotton's parishioners for the most part sided with Cotton and began to press other churches to affirm their minister's stance. But most of the other local ministers would have none of it. One preacher even raised a concern about Cotton's orthodoxy: "You cannot be ignorant which way the stream of most divines, both of our own country, and others, runs."[1] This only invited Cotton's indignant counter-charge that some divines were more reliable than others:

> And seeing we all profess . . . to hold forth protestant doctrine, let us hold it forth in the language of Calvin and others [of] our best protestants, who speak of purity of life and growth in grace and all the works of sanctification as the effects and consequents of our assurance of faith . . . . And therefore if we will speak as protestants, we must not speak of good works as causes or ways of our first assurance. . . . [Y]et indeed you carry it otherwise. . . . Which, seeing it is disallowed by the chief protestant writers, if you contrary to them do hold it forth for protestant doctrine, that we may gather our first assurance of justification from our sanctification, it is not the change of words that will change the matter.[2]

Cotton's reference to Calvin was a fair response given Calvin's belief that faith *is* a person's assurance of salvation.

The question of assurance was central in the New England debate. Cotton's particular target was the "practical syllogism" by which other preachers promised an assurance of salvation based on a parishioner's moral and spiritual self-improvement: by their growing sanctification. Thus, in Cotton's "rejoynder" he built his case with frequent citations from John Calvin's works. He also cited Augustine against Pelagius: that without God's immediate presence and relational initiative humans can do nothing to succeed either in their salvation or in ongoing sanctification.[3]

Cotton also looked for support in Sibbes' writings. Cotton had come to an assured faith under Sibbes' preaching, a faith that displaced the "false hopes" of that which was "no true grace".[4] The preaching of William Perkins, in contrast to Sibbes' gracious sermons, had "laid siege to and beleaguer'd his heart".[5]

It is on the basis of this theological polarity over the basis of saving faith that Janice Knight challenges the "myth of consensus at the center" in seventeenth century Reformed Orthodoxy, a consensus she attributes to Perry Miller.[6] There was, she argues, a division among the Puritans in which Richard Sibbes' affective theology was pitted against the rationalistic and moralistic views of Perkins and his protégé William Ames. Those who followed Sibbes were committed to a "More emotional and even mystical" theology that "stressed divine benevolence over power. Emphasizing the love of God, they converted biblical metaphors of kingship into ones of kinship."[7]

Michael Schuldiner found the same division in New England. The Puritan faction who followed Cotton's affective theology reacted to the legalistic teaching of their opposites: "[A]fter Calvin's seminal presentation of spiritual growth, a dichotomy of views developed, some theologians emphasizing man's performance of the Law and some emphasizing the affective experience of the Spirit as the indication of the conversion and means of further spiritual growth."[8] Schuldiner presents Calvin's form of spirituality as one in which "the experience of the Spirit is primary. This experience, which stirs the heart and illumines the mind" offers assurance of salvation.[9]

This chapter provides context for all that follows in our study by identifying the main features of the divide. A related academic issue should be raised before moving ahead: how is it that this important division has received so little attention from historians?

Evidence for the Division

Knight engages the latter question—how has this facture escaped historians' notice? She answers by pointing to Perry Miller's pioneering work in the field. Most Puritan scholars have followed in Miller's wake by accepting his premise that Puritans shared a broad doctrinal consensus—one basic orthodoxy. This despite evidence noticed even in the 1930s—when Miller first published—that doctrinal differences among the Puritans were evident to historians. She notes, for instance, that in the same decade of Miller's first publication another historian, William Haller, portrayed many of the ministers noticed by Miller as lesser figures—as men known mainly for their New England ecclesiology. Haller, in turn, gave much greater standing to Sibbes, Cotton, John Preston, Thomas Goodwin, and Philip Nye. Knight's point is that Miller treated one wing of two competing Puritan orthodoxies as primary and Haller elevated the other.[10]

The problem of definition

The present study sets the division in a much broader theological context than we find in Knight or Schuldiner. This, in turn, modifies its significance. The competing New England camps were citing separate theological traditions—opposed to each other at many points—as they exchanged views. Their separate sources, whether acknowledged or not, signaled separate theological trajectories that still exist. Cotton, on the one hand, was explicit in citing Calvin and Sibbes, among others, as guides to his own salvation narrative. The other ministers remained silent in the face of Cotton's claims and failed to cite their own heritage.

The divide is not just an historical artifact but is present in current historiography as well. Historian William Stoever, for instance, portrayed Cotton as a crypto-sectarian for his affirmation of the Spirit's active presence in the soul.[11] Cotton's alignment with someone like Calvin on this claim sets up the contentious prospect that in some key issues current "Calvinists" are not aligned with Calvin himself.

The New England debate, when examined in this context, was not simply a local conflict but another stage of an ongoing debate over the relation of God to humanity—the question of nature-and-grace. The tension was present in the New Testament era—as seen in Paul's letter to the Galatians—and it became a well-defined polarity in the debate between Augustine and Pelagius. Most subsequent debates over grace display the reoccurrence of a '*response*-to-God' versus a '*responsibility*-to-God' dichotomy in explaining the saving application of grace. Battles over grace in the English church during the Tudor-Stuart era, when stripped of their specific embellishments, usually turned on that tension.

The separate definitions of grace used by Perkins and Sibbes displayed these enduring distinctions. Perkins elevated the importance of human initiative in a synthesis that relied on

Thomas Aquinas' theology while Sibbes' focus on God's initiative was aligned with Augustine's mature theology. Perkins' use of a Thomistic solution in his Federal theology was, arguably, the destabilizing factor that led to the Puritan division over grace.

This claim brings a scholarly tension to the fore. Many theological historians of this era come to the arena with a pre-commitment either for or against Thomas. Richard Muller, for instance, in *Christ and the Decree: Christology and Predestination in Reformed Theology from Calvin to Perkins*, argues that the Thomistic solution was positive as it helped to fill out and strengthen Reformed theology in the face of contemporary opposition. Muller will be cited as approving of the speculative creativity that generated the cooperative model of Federalism.

Stephen Strehle in *Calvinism, Federalism, and Scholasticism*, on the other hand, is critical of the return of Thomistic theology as expressed in English Federalism. In Perkins, in particular, Strehle notices the "voluntaristic penchant of the second generation of Protestants".[12] He also traces, in *The Catholic Roots of the Protestant Gospel*, a Protestant return to the medieval use of the law and the elevation of human initiative. This was in contrast to the strict Christocentricism of the first reformers:

> The antinomians attempted to restore much of this Christocentric vision of Luther against what they perceived as a reversion to the law of works and an inversion toward one's own piety. The practical syllogism and the bilateral covenant were thought to lead the believer away from Christ toward an egocentric analysis of the fruits of true election . . . all of which

were stained with depravity. One could not trust in Christ and oneself at the same time.[13]

In this study Sibbes' theology is presented as antinomian in the sense Strehle describes here and as a rejection of the version of grace offered by Perkins and Federal theology. As such Sibbes was a proponent of early Protestant theology—of positions associated with Luther and Calvin—in the face of a growing defection by many Puritans from Augustinian themes.

Debates over ecclesiology

The failure to notice this division may also be found, ironically, in the success of another field of Puritan studies: in the work of political and ecclesiastical historians. Such studies have identified, with increasing precision, groups of ministers on the basis of their polity, politics and levels of conformity. Yet in doing so researchers have often overstated the degree to which those groups agreed on matters of grace.

One of the enduring debates in the Tudor-Stuart era addressed the form and functions of the English church. There was a continuum between the opposed poles of Geneva-inspired Presbyterianism (with its minimized liturgy), and the more Catholic *via media* (as more liturgical and guided by Episcopalian hierarchy). Recent studies have discarded anachronistic notions of a simple polarity between Anglicans and Puritans yet it is clear that throughout the Tudor-early Stuart period the English church was divided by different responses to the Erastian requirements for uniformity.[14] If anything, the responses of Puritans to the *via media* represented something of a continuum. Whole-hearted conformists worked with moderates who worked with radicals, and so on. The question may be asked, however, whether a given individual's place in this continuum can be linked to a particular view about grace with any degree of confidence.

Some closer attention to the matter is called for, given the tendency of some to make the two doctrines virtually coterminous in such a way that a shared ecclesiology among individuals might well disguise their differing views of grace. There is little doubt that in the minds of many contemporary ministers as well as modern historians the affiliation between specific positions of ecclesiology and matters of grace were inseparable: Presbyterians were predestinarians and Episcopalian proponents of the *via media* were Arminians. Indeed, the vigorous and ongoing debate surrounding Nicholas Tyacke's thesis in *Anti-Calvinists: The Rise of English Arminianism, c. 1590-1640* points to the strength of this affiliation. He argues on the basis of such a linkage that the disruption of a consensual Calvinism in the English church by newly emergent Arminianism eventually led to the Civil War.[15] Yet the doctrine of the church, despite such evidence of continuity between grace and ecclesiology, must be differentiated from the doctrine of grace. The doctrines address separate issues that, in turn, make parallel affiliations possible but never necessary.

What, then, was the relationship of the church and grace for Puritans? The church was seen to be a product of grace but the reverse was not true: the church herself is not a source or distributor of saving grace. Such grace is solely and wholly a gift of God. In that respect grace has greater import than ecclesiology. A London craftsman, for instance, had suicidal thoughts as he questioned his own access to saving grace; and he was only an extreme example of the distress felt by many.[16]

It was a divisive issue as well. Calvinists, who believed that saving faith is not a result of human initiative, were prepared to break fellowship with their Arminian opponents over calls by the latter for moral effort in achieving salvation. In ecclesiastical matters, on the other hand, there was greater openness. Puritans in New England, for instance, were prepared to maintain contact with separatists, showing that issues of polity were at the level of *adiaphora*.

Puritans varied in their church-grace combinations. Some, including both Perkins and Sibbes, accepted Episcopalian polity and embraced predestination. Other predestinarians promoted Congregationalism (John Cotton and Thomas Goodwin), and others Presbyterianism (Edward Reynolds and Thomas Temple). And while virtually all Presbyterians were predestinarians, not all Arminians were Episcopalians—as in the case of John Goodwin.[17]

John Cotton also illustrates the separate nature of the issues when, soon after his sharp debate with New England critics over matters of grace, he was prepared to link arms with them in attending the Westminster Assembly to promote their shared ecclesiology.[18] Thus, alliances formed by ministers in the midst of one debate may seem anomalous if viewed in the context of the other. This created crossover relationships that puzzle modern researchers if the concurrent but differing issues of grace and ecclesiology are not separated.

Stephen Brachlow's helpful study of Puritan ecclesiology, *The Communion of Saints*, inadvertently illustrates this thesis by displaying the shared values among ministers in matters of grace (in covenantalism, saving faith and assurance) while acknowledging that the same participants disagreed over ecclesiastical matters (illustrated by the radical but non-separating Puritans and the separatists). The theological emphases among the various ministers Brachlow examines shifted depending on their purpose and audience in writing. Thus Brachlow's method, in displaying concurrent but separate issues, unravels some anomalous relationships.[19]

When the two debates are viewed together and compared in terms of key polarities, a set of options result. Conforming Puritans might agree in their polity but differ over the use of the law in sanctification (those in favor of the law, as will be seen, are identified as nomists; those opposed as antinomists). This was the case for Perkins and Sibbes. Conforming and nonconforming theologians could also be closely aligned by a shared commitment to the notion that grace is expressed by obedience to the law, as in the case of Perkins and Ames. This study demonstrates how differing views of grace divided individuals who, when measured by ecclesiastical commitments, were in full accord. We will see that disagreements over grace were deeply rooted and resulted in profoundly different visions of faith.

An undeveloped feature in this discussion is that William Laud's efforts to enforce ecclesiastical uniformity and political compliance on both moderate and non-conforming Puritans in England forced them together artificially. This pressure was strongest in the second and third decades of the seventeenth-century, just as Sibbes was beginning to display his opposition to the nomist model of grace. When proponents of Sibbes' views were freed from such external pressures, as in the case of Cotton in New England, the differences over grace quickly erupted in the Antinomian Controversy. Yet that dispute was a modest dust-up when compared to the explosive disagreements over related questions that erupted in England as the power of Charles I ended in the 1640s.

To understand Sibbes' position we need to look at Perkins as well. Their different assumptions about what grace is and how it serves as the basis of salvation call for close comparisons.

Principal Figures: William Perkins and Richard Sibbes

William Perkins' theology

What, then, was the shape of William Perkins' theology? His ecclesiology was moderate and unexceptional, but in matters of grace he was the chief proponent of English Federal theology for his generation. Ian Breward summarized Perkins' moderate episcopacy as aimed "to correct pastoral deficiencies" while always maintaining proper submission to the magistrate.[20]

Perkins' advocacy of the Federal model of predestinarian theology—a theology only recently adopted in England from continental sources—elevated the function of contract-like covenants to a coordinating role in all God's relations with humanity.[21] This claim of a mitigated quid-pro-quo basis for engaging God did much to roil the waters of the English church according to Peter Heylyn's contemporary report. Heylyn held that Perkins' writings were behind the 1595 predestinarian debate at Cambridge that generated the Calvinism versus Arminianism rift in the following decades. William Whitaker (Regius Professor of Divinity) was the main spokesman for predestinarian forces, but according to Heylyn it was the impact of Perkins' 1590 *Armilla Aurea* [*Golden Chaine*] that stirred William Barrett—sharing the views of Peter Baro—to preach a sermon that first triggered the controversy.[22]

The sequence of reaction against Perkins' writings began when Baro (then Lady Margaret Professor of Divinity) expressed his opposition to Perkins' view that God's arbitrary distribution of salvation also posited that Christ's atonement on the cross was meant only for the elect. Salvation, then, was not a real option for all humanity—to any who believed—but was meant solely for the elect. Baro insisted, instead, that God's grace is universal. His complaint—voiced by Barrett—was the basis for Whitaker's response in a public lecture on 27 February "against the advocates of universal grace".[23]

Perkins offered a second and more immediate target for Barrett in his publication in April of his *Exposition of the Symbol, or Creed of the Apostles*.[24] Barrett answered at the end of April with his sermon at St. Mary's Church that challenged Perkins' notions of assurance, gracious perseverance, and the belief that reprobation is arbitrary rather than a result of foreseen sin. In support of Heylyn's claim that Barrett's target was the *Golden Chaine*, the main positions opposed by Barrett were to be found in that work.

Perkins' writings became increasingly prominent during that period. His *Works* were an English Reformed *Summa Theologiæ*, being reprinted and widely distributed both in England and on the continent.[25] His *Golden Chaine*, along with the *Exposition of the Symbol*, promoted the theology he drew from Girolamo Zanchius (1516-1590) and Theodore Beza (1519-

1605), among others, that emphasized a predestinarian basis for all God's relations with humanity.[26]

Perkins and Calvin compared. Perkins—like Beza and John Calvin—followed the order of content found in the Apostles' Creed in his own ordering of *An Exposition of the Symbol.* Perkins' *Golden Chaine* also drew elements from Calvin's theology, but he departed from the Genevan mentor in his portrayal of God's purpose for the creation. This was part of an increasing appetite in Reformed circles for Aristotelian rationality and values. This led to the development of post-Reformation Scholasticism, a movement that Beza helped to facilitate at the Geneva Academy where he was both the administrator and a teacher from its founding in 1559.

Perkins, too, viewed God through an Aristotelian lens with monadic rather than Trinitarian features in the foreground. Where Perkins followed Aristotle in treating divine power as a self-explanatory reality—so that creation is a stage to display the glory of God's power—Calvin had followed Scriptures in portraying God as essentially relational: as a Triune lover. With this Calvin held God to be all-powerful as creator; but a creator motivated by an overflowing love to share with the creation the eternal Triune life of Father, Son, and Spirit.

Perkins, with this departure from Calvin and others, followed Aristotle's portrayal of God's ultimate concern by adopting a supralapsarian explanation of God's creation purposes.[27] God's glory, Perkins explained, comes in his display of ultimate and self-oriented powers. Perkins, as we will see, was following Beza's own movement toward a more Aristotelian—wholly disaffected—portrayal of God's creation purposes. Beza was the chief architect of "Calvinism" at Geneva in the decades after Calvin's death. Perkins, in England, followed him. Both, respectively, shepherded this move in Genevan and English theology after Calvin's passing.

Perkins' Aristotelian-Thomistic categories. Perkins assimilated the Thomistic or scholastic model of theological analysis and synthesis: reason, epitomized in Aristotle, was used to systematize biblical content. The Bible and Aristotle—"the prince of philosophers"—represented complementary authorities for Perkins: the supernatural and natural. The Bible, while ultimate in authority, was made accessible and applicable through categories and terminology supplied by the philosopher.[28] This confidence reflected the prominence of Aristotle's moral, natural and metaphysical philosophy in college curricula during Perkins' life. The philosopher's methods and many of his assumptions were essential to academic discourse.[29]

Students were first introduced to Aristotle in their undergraduate studies, with special attention given him in the final two years of the Bachelor of Arts degree. Careful study of the philosopher's works continued throughout subsequent studies as well. Lawrence Breeton, a later contemporary to Sibbes, and student at Queens' College, Cambridge, summarized Aristotle's status among most students of the period: "*vera et sana philosophia est vera Aristotelica*".[30] Calvin, by contrast, rejected in principle any use of expansive speculation, charging that such efforts are profoundly dangerous because of their inherent and proven tendencies to mislead.[31] Thus, while Calvin was philosophically alert but critical and reserved, Perkins drank freely at the Aristotelian well.

The system of philosophical analysis offered by Peter Ramus (1515-72) must also be noted for its impact on Perkins. Some preferred Ramus in place of Aristotle but most remained devoted to the latter—including Beza. Perkins, though, seems not to have felt any tension between the two systems and he regularly employed the Ramist device of setting out analytical dichotomies—with an elaborate set of opposed pairings that enlarged the Bezan polarity of reprobation and election—as just one example.[32]

Yet Perkins' interests were primarily pastoral rather than philosophical. The manner in which the two concerns interacted in his ministry should be noted. Heinrich Heppe identified Perkins as a "father of pietism" in his disposition to apply theology to life.[33] Yet even Perkins' pastoral applications were shaped by his commitment to a synthesis of reason and revelation. To this end he was the first of the Protestants to take up the Roman Catholic tradition of pastoral casuistry—providing manuals to prescribe proper moral conduct. His two casuistic works, *A Discourse of Conscience*, and *The Whole Treatise of Cases of Conscience*, displayed a confidence that rational persuasion produces moral development. As Norman Fiering has shown, this "Scholastic-Aristotelian approach" to ethical training was firmly in place at Puritan academic centers in 1650.[34]

Historians have argued over the implications of the restored devotion to Aristotle represented in Perkins and others. Basil Hall, for instance, charged that Calvin would have rejected subsequent Calvinism. The "successful repristination of Aristotle among Protestants", he argues, "led to the Reformed scholasticism that distorted the Calvinist synthesis".[35] R. T. Kendall argues that Perkins was the crucial figure in transmitting these views in England. Kendall's discussion includes other questions about Calvin's continuity with Calvinism, especially about the extent of the atonement and assurance of salvation. The latter issues drew critical responses from Paul Helm and Andrew Woolsey, among others.[36] These scholars, however, are relatively indifferent to the claims made about renewed Aristotelian thought in Calvinism. Their intention, instead, is to demonstrate an essential continuity between Calvin and English Reformed orthodoxy in covenantal matters.

Richard Muller, on the other hand, both supports and challenges the Hall-Kendall thesis. Muller freely acknowledges the reacquisition of Aristotle in Beza and Perkins—as claimed by Hall and Kendall—and he displays the logic of renewed Thomism among Reformed Protestants. Muller, however, implies that Hall and Kendall have chosen a faulty standard when they elevate Calvin. Calvin, Muller argues, failed to grasp "the causal priorities in the mind of God". Scholastic methods, with "speculative elaboration of the original doctrinal ground . . . and rationalization of dogmatic stance", were needed to lead later Protestants to the logical expression of God's creation purposes.[37]

Muller, in fact, suggests that the first reformers only represent a brief phase of adjustment in the longer and more significant development of orthodoxy that Thomistic theology offered:

> Whereas the Reformation is surely the formative event for Protestantism, it is also true that the Reformation, which took place during the first half of the sixteenth century, is the briefer phenomenon, enclosed as it were by the five-hundred-year history of scholasticism and

> Christian Aristotelianism. In approaching the continuities and discontinuities of Protestant scholasticism with the Middle Ages and the Reformation, the chief task is to assess the Protestant adjustment of traditional scholastic categories in the light of the Reformation and the patterns according to which it mediated that tradition, both positively and negatively, to future generations of Protestants.[38]

In challenging the Hall-Kendall interpretation Muller also displays the vulnerability of the Helm-Woolsey critique of Hall and Kendall by his exposition of the reentry of an Aristotelian-Thomistic presence in Reformed theology. This movement is shown to have acquired its central feature—the supralapsarian decree of predestination—only *after* Calvin's death. Muller seeks to show that this position is incipient in Calvin's thought but he finally admits, "Calvin never sought to develop this more speculative side of his doctrine".[39] Muller then points to differences on the matter between Calvin and some of his contemporaries as well as in Beza, his director of the Geneva Academy.

Muller thus recognizes a fundamental discontinuity in Calvin and later Protestant orthodoxy that Helm and Woolsey tried to dismiss on the basis of their own focus on covenantalism.[40] Muller's argument in turn raises a much larger question than Hall and Kendall's theses present. Is it possible that Calvin and others of the first reformers who rejected key aspects of Thomism were actually heterodoxical in their resistance?[41] Such a view is unconvincing for reasons that will be developed below.

Perkins, in Muller's view, was a premier figure in the return to Thomistic themes by English Protestants. This sets up a pair of questions for students of the sixteenth and seventeenth century history. First, what lenses are being used today to read the theology of that era—especially as one Reformed tradition is now considered normative and another is dismissed?

And, with that, have students today noticed and appreciated the well-informed contemporary resistance among many Puritans to Perkins' initiatives? As William Erbery's review suggested, Sibbes' theology and the "free grace" efforts by Cotton and others displayed a distinct theological counterpoint to Perkins' initiative. These dissenters believed they were being faithful to early Reformation themes. Given their claims any anachronistic readings of the debate must be avoided and closer attention should be given to the substance of their positions.

Perkins' supralapsarian theology. Perkins' second point of parting from Calvin is seen in his adoption of Beza's potent supralapsarian theology. Beza and Perkins, with others, elevated the doctrine of predestination to a unique prominence. As L. B. Tipson, Jr., notes, the belief that election and reprobation are hidden in God's secret counsel was nothing new, "But to derive God's entire plan of salvation logically from it was new, and Beza proceeded to do precisely that."[42] The supra and infralapsarian positions displayed differing perceptions of God's ultimate intention in creation and, more specifically, in his purpose for the divine-human relationship.[43] More will be said about this in the next chapter; here it will be enough to distinguish the Beza-Perkins' position from Calvin's. Both positions were drawn from the biblical imagery in Romans 9:21 of God as a potter and all of foreknown humanity viewed, collectively, as clay. In the supralapsarian view God begins by determining to create a single lump of humanity. He then decrees—before setting out the fall—that out of humanity there will be two groups: one elect and the other reprobate. Beza's reasoning was rooted in his concern for God's sovereignty:

> There is no doubt but God takes both the sorts out of the same lump, ordaining them to contrary ends. Yet do I say and plainly avow that Paul in the same similitude mounts up to the said sovereign ordinance whereunto even the very creation of mankind is submitted in order of causes, and therefore much less does the Apostle put the foreseen corruption of mankind before it. For first by the term Lump (*massae*) there is manifestly betokened a substance as yet unshapen, and only prepared to work upon afterward. Again in likening God to a potter and mankind to a lump of clay whereof vessels of wrath are made of that lump. For if that lump betokened men corrupted, then were they vessels of dishonor already, and the potter should not be said to make them, other than such as they had themselves already.[44]

Postfall theology, by contrast, makes the fall a matter prior to God's decree of election and reprobation—prior not in chronological time but in the logic of predestination. Thus the work of Christ is determined by humanity's need but his redeeming work is applicable only to those in the corrupt mass of humanity who are ordained to receive mercy. In this view God's elective mercy is elevated while his purpose for the fall remains a mystery.

Calvin, unlike Beza, held infralapsarian assumptions in discussing predestination: God's purpose is to engage humanity in light of the fall as a "corrupt mass" rather than as a morally neutral or "unshapen" lump as Beza presumed.

> Let all the sons of Adam come forward; let them quarrel and argue with their Creator that they were by his eternal providence bound over before their begetting to everlasting calamity. What clamor can they raise against this defense when God, on the contrary, will call them to their account before him? If all are drawn from a corrupt mass, no wonder they are subject to condemnation! Let them not accuse God of injustice if they are destined by his eternal judgment to death, to which they feel—whether they will or not—that they are led by their own nature of itself.[45]

Not only were the reprobates drawn out of this mass, so were the elect. But not for reasons found in themselves: "We admit the common guilt, but we say that God's mercy succors some. Let it succor all, they [opponents] say." Calvin then cited Augustine: "Augustine's statements most aptly accord with this: 'Since in the first man the whole mass of the race fell under condemnation . . . those vessels of it which are made unto honor are vessels not of their own righteousness . . . but of God's mercy, but that other vessels are made unto dishonor'".[46]

Perkins, following Beza, presented the supralapsarian model in his *Golden Chaine.* In the foreword Perkins made it clear that the purpose of his work was "to oppugn" three faulty views of predestination, the second of which was the Lutheran version of infralapsarianism:

> The second [group] who of some are termed lutherans, which teach that God foreseeing how all mankind being shut up under unbelief would therefore reject [the] grace offered, did hereupon purpose to choose some to salvation of his mere mercy without any respect of their faith and good works, and the rest to reject, being moved to do this because he did eternally foresee that they would reject his grace offered them in the gospel.[47]

For Perkins, as with Beza, God's glory defined the goals of supralapsarianism. He presented the decree of predestination as that which defines both the creation and the fall: "God . . . has ordained all men to a certain and everlasting estate, that is either to salvation or condemnation, for his own glory. The means of accomplishing God's predestination are twofold: the creation and the fall."[48] The work of Christ's saving mediation was expressed in election and displays "the glory of his grace." In turn, the punishment of the reprobate, who by God's laws are only and always unrighteousness, displays God's sovereign justice.[49] Thus it is God's volition alone—and not human will—that determines both immediate and ultimate matters.

In presenting his supralapsarianism Perkins effectively embedded all of God's communicable attributes within the divine will. The three attributes "which do manifest the operation of God towards his creatures" were listed as "his wisdom, will and omnipotence." Both wisdom and omnipotence, in this scheme, were simply the means by which the will is equipped to accomplish its role effectively. The conspicuous absence of such primary virtues as love and justice was remedied only by placing them in a list as differing modes by which will is expressed.

> The will of God is that by the which he, both most freely and justly with one act, willeth all things. God willeth that which is good by approving it, that which is evil, inasmuch as it is evil, by disallowing and forsaking it. And yet he voluntarily doth permit evil, because it is good that there should be evil. The will of God, by reasons of divers objects, hath divers names and is either called love and hatred, or grace and justice.[50]

Perkins was consistent in maintaining this arrangement throughout the *Chaine*, but by so doing he created tensions within other elements in his theological structure. Ian Breward has argued, for instance, that this theology weakened Perkins' Christology, which in turn weakened Christology among Puritans who relied on Perkins' model. This, Breward believes, opened the door to "the emergence of the God of the Deists or the Christ of the Socinians in the seventeenth century." Geoffrey Nuttall has affirmed and enlarged Breward's point by arguing that it also opened the door to the Quakers. Nuttall makes the point, apart from Perkins in particular, that "[I]t was insufficient to contemplate and adore God as the Creator, eternal but distant in the heavens. God must be found in direct personal experience".[51] Calvin, however, made the believer's personal experience of God the centerpiece of his theology.[52]

Perkins' moralistic assumptions. The Old Testament moral law was fully engaged with Perkins' supralapsarian theology. Obedience to the law served to display God's glory among the elect and God's glory is the goal to which every aspect of the supralapsarian model moves. In Perkins' view, a person's ability to achieve God's glory through obedience requires that the moral quality of every action should be well defined. To this end Perkins offered a taxonomy of sins in his *Treatise of the Vocations or Calling of Men* that looked to the Mosaic Decalogue.[53] A closer examination of the law as part of Perkins' theology of God awaits chapter two but some initial comments will introduce Perkins' place among English theologians who elevated the law.

Perkins' emphasis on the law was part of a broader movement among the Puritans. Jerald C. Brauer proposed four categories of Puritans: nomists, evangelicals, rationalists, and mystics. His attention was drawn to the smallest of the categories, the mystics, given his interest in Francis Rous.[54] Nevertheless his recognition of the two major groups, nomists and evangelicals, displays the same division among Puritans noted by Schuldiner, Knight and the present study. Brauer, in fact, identifies Sibbes as the Puritan who epitomized the evangelicals. Nomists, according to Brauer, "held the fundamental belief that the divine intention is to recreate obedient creatures who can now, though grace, fulfill the intent of God, namely, obedience."[55] Brauer's nomists include Thomas Cartwright, John Field, Walter Travers, John Penry,

John Udall, John Greenwood, William Pryn, and Samuel Rutherford. Perkins, overlooked in the list, must be included on the basis of the criteria that Brauer identifies. It was, in fact, Perkins' written expositions of Federal theology that did the most to promote the importance of obedience to the law for sanctification among Puritans in his era.

There was, however, another theological current feeding the status of the law in Reformed theology, namely, the pastoral use of the law to soften the conscience. Preaching which emphasized the penalties of law breaking, despite the obverse conviction that law keeping offers no hope of salvation, did much to anticipate and support the Federal emphases when they emerged. Tipson identifies proponents of this tradition in both Scotland and England. In Scotland John Knox was followed by John Craig in elevating the law to generate humility.[56] In England John Bradford, Thomas Wilcox, and Richard Greenham did the same.

Tipson links these men to Perkins' theology in arguing that they all represented a belief that conversion is a process that includes preliminary periods of moral struggle, and not as a distinct event in time. Bradford (b. 1510), who was often cited by Perkins, could insist for instance that those who failed to discover a "terror of conscience" or "their just damnation in the Law of God" could never "find sweetness in the Gospel of Christ." Thus it was the preacher's task to bring his listeners "even to the brim of despair" before sharing the gospel.[57] Greenham (1535?-1594?), although reputed to be a "comforting" pastor, also held that sinners should be stirred "by feeling of their sins, to seek after Christ".[58]

Given Tipson's premise that in virtually all early Reformed circles conversion was seen to come about through an extended period of moral despair, his thesis unintentionally displays Beza's role in the subsequent Puritan divide over how saving grace is given. That is, a conversion that features a distinctive inward change through a sense of spiritual encounter with Christ—as held by Cotton who was converted as an adult, after he had already trained for ministry—is very different to what many of his Puritan colleagues expected; namely a saving faith revealed in progressive behavioral changes. For Tipson even Calvin was liable to criticism for not fitting his thesis when he notices that the French reformer held a "harsh" view of fallen humanity, a view that called for a distinct conversion to faith. Beza, on the other hand, adopted an "emphasis on the fruits of faith that Calvin had avoided."[59]

The elevation of the law among the nomists elicited a reaction. This was most obvious in Cotton's teachings that generated the Antinomian Controversy. Cotton's antinomist—"anti-law"—theology was similar to Sibbes' views that were, in turn, aligned with Luther's skepticism in affirming the law. In light of this distinction, Sibbes, Cotton, and others who, like the young Luther, refused to treat the moral laws of the Old Testament as a guide to spirituality are labeled as antinomist—even though their moral conduct was wholly on par with the nomists.[60]

Sibbes' theology, then, must also be introduced in its fundamental aspects, some of which are virtually the opposite of the views affirmed by Perkins.

Sibbes' theology

Like Perkins, Sibbes was a moderate churchman who accepted the required episcopal polity of his day.[61] Mark Dever helped to clarify an enduring misperception of Sibbes as an ecclesiastical nonconformist who was deprived from his early Cambridge posts.[62] Sibbes, in fact, seems not to have been deprived and, in fact, subscribed to the articles of conformity, although with certain misgivings. Furthermore, he wrote a pastoral piece, *A Consolatory Letter to an afflicted Conscience*, urging an unnamed dissenting friend—Alexander Grosart suggests it was Thomas Goodwin—to maintain communion with the church.[63] That is not to say that Sibbes was reluctant to express points of profound dissatisfaction with the church. He was very critical of godless conduct among church leaders and derided "corrupted" ceremonialism as well. Still, to depart from the church was "a remedy worse than the disease".[64] Differences between Sibbes and Perkins, then, were not in matters of church polity but over matters of grace.[65] The first distinction is seen in Sibbes' view of the Spirit.

Sibbes' emphatic Pneumatology. Sibbes' Pneumatology was the centerpiece of his applied theology: God, by his Spirit, is locally present in the soul of every believer. Indeed, the mystery of the incarnation was almost matched, in Sibbes' view, by the "wonder at the love of the Holy Ghost, that will take up his residence in such defiled souls."[66] The Spirit, Sibbes held, is the agent of all grace through a real union with Christ: "As the union of [Christ's] human nature to the divine was the cause of all other graces of his human nature, so the Spirit of God, uniting us to Christ, is the cause of all grace in us."[67] This theme will be developed more fully at a later point. Here it is useful just to notice sources Sibbes used for his Pneumatology and to point out some confusion in recent discussions of Sibbes' views.

Sibbes' moderate mysticism showed his alignment with early church theologians who affirmed God's active presence in the soul. Sibbes, for example, used overtly mystical themes at times such as a metaphor from Gregory of Nazianzus that believers are like "wind instruments" by which "we yield music, but no further than we are touched by the Spirit of God."[68] Sibbes also cited Augustine regularly, and drew heavily from Bernard of Clairvaux's sermons on the Song of Songs.[69] It was Bernard, rather than Aquinas, who was Sibbes' favorite source among medieval theologians.[70] Sibbes shared the conviction of the earlier men that God's love is to be a believer's first point of spiritual reference, a love that the Spirit confirms to the heart. Sibbes' own sermons on the Song of Songs, as will be seen, offered the clearest expression of his affective theology. The Song provided Sibbes with an explanatory basis for the union and communion of a believer's relation to Christ.[71]

This sort of affective theology, however, raised hackles for many of Sibbes contemporaries as well as for some modern interpreters. Claims that the Spirit is overtly engaged in believers' lives were and are especially upsetting for some. William Stoever, for instance, argues that the covenantal structure—with the covenant described in disaffected contractual terms—"comprised widespread consensus" among English Reformed theologians. This consensus was said to include Sibbes, John Preston, and Thomas Shepard. But Stoever's inclusion of Sibbes and two of his close theological companions raises questions. Against Stoever's claim Sibbes affirmed the Spirit's active presence in believers as a signal of new life in Christ. But we should consider Stoever's concern in order to capture what he sees to be at stake.

He explains, "The prominence of the doctrine of the Holy Spirit in English Puritanism is well attested, as is the challenge to Puritan societies, both civil and ecclesiastical, by people . . . who claimed greater than usual intimacy with the Holy Spirit." Such pretensions of Spiritual intimacy—linked to radicalism—required restraint: "The Spirit might 'blow' when and where he listed; the person whom he encountered had less large a liberty."[72]

Stoever wants to warn readers against Cotton's affirmation of the Spirit's immediacy in the New England controversy: "Examined in relation to this material, the chief New England elders appear less radical . . . and John Cotton . . . more radical than sometimes supposed."[73] For Stoever Cotton's belief in the Spirit's palpable place in a believer's life—over against an indirect role—undermined the relative independence of human nature.

A measure of independence was axiomatic in the preference in Federal theology for a balance between nature and grace.[74] Stoever argues that the Spirit—properly understood—is always indirect in his activities.

> The thorough subordination of created nature to the operation of increated grace, advanced by English and New English antinomians, had sweeping implications not only for theology and ethics but also for physics and epistemology. Were these implications followed to their logical extremes, a great wedge would be driven between God and his creation, with disturbing

> consequences for human social and intellectual life. Reformed divines were quite unwilling to allow such a rupture between Creator and creatures, and they looked with suspicion on anyone whose passion for the gratuity of grace or yearning for intimacy with the Spirit tended in that direction.[75]

Stoever's claim, although overstated, reflects a sixteenth century shift by Beza away from Calvin on the Spirit's place in salvation. Beza replaced Calvin's belief that an assurance by the Spirit of God's benevolence toward him or her is the very substance of saving faith. Beza held, instead, to the practical syllogism—that assurance is separate from the act of believing and is based, instead, on a person's improving moral state. The Spirit, in this arrangement, disappears from view into the unfelt and unseen interior of the soul. Later Perkins would split the difference between Calvin and Beza by treating assurance of salvation by a direct witness of the Spirit as a possible but uncommon prospect. In practice the practical syllogism dominated Perkins' discussions. This shifting order of salvation helps account for Stoever's view that Federal theology must dismiss "intimacy with the Spirit" in order to protect the status of nature.[76]

In another appraisal of the Puritan emphasis on the Spirit, Stephen Foster, like Stoever, views the antinomian crisis in New England as a product of Cotton's Pneumatology. However, unlike Stoever who presumes a settled consensus among preachers in England, Foster properly sees the New England issues as imported from home: "The mushrooming controversy in New England in the late 1630s mirrored exactly the increasing volatility of the Puritan movement at home in England".[77] Foster traces differences between Puritan moderates and radical separatists back to their differing goals. The moderates were able to endure required ceremonialism for the sake of their larger goal, reaching "the mass of the unconverted . . . by powerful preaching . . ."

The radicals, on the other hand, needed a freer form of church governance—to have churches where the Spirit's felt works could be acknowledged without the suppression that Episcopalian oversight would likely entail. So radical ecclesiology was engendered by a spiritual theology: "the greatest internal danger to Puritanism on both sides of the Atlantic came from its own left wing, from groups that (in Perry Miller's words) 'came to their various opinions from a common belief that the union of the elect with the Holy Ghost is immediate and intimate.'"[78]

In both Stoever's and Foster's views the doctrine of the Spirit is a cause of theological upheaval in New England but the scholars differ in establishing their historical antecedents. Their separate interpretations are based on separate concerns. Stoever is focused on the theology of covenants and Foster is concerned with ecclesiology. In either case Sibbes upsets their respective views. He was a seminal figure in the Puritan elevation of the Spirit as he embraced the Spirit's active and felt presence in believers for both salvation and sanctification. Yet in Stoever's thesis Sibbes is a positive figure—portrayed as an advocate of Federal theology; and in Foster's thesis Sibbes (where he is largely ignored) would represent a conforming churchman despite his strong Pneumatology.

Sibbes' moderate mysticism. Sibbes regularly affirmed that believers should expect a palpable sense of the Spirit's immanence in their experience of faith. To that end Nuttall identifies the same kinds of movement among Puritans toward a more profound Pneumatology that Erbery identified in his seventeenth-century chronology. Nuttall suggests that Sibbes wielded "a large influence in directing the Puritans' attention to the doctrine of the Holy Spirit".[79] James Maclear followed Nuttall's lead both in exploring internal and logical elements of Puritan Pneumatology. He identifies biblicism, hidden rationalism, and mysticism as essential elements in such theology and he points to Sibbes as a leading proponent. Sibbes, "more than any other was responsible for this direction to Puritan piety in the second quarter of the [seventeenth] century."[80]

By mysticism, Maclear meant "the deep emotional longings for personal encounter and direct communion with God, in independence and contempt of all mediatory principles." Charles Cohen, in *God's Caress*, also gives Sibbes special prominence. However, unlike Nuttall and Maclear, Cohen does not present Sibbes as a seminal figure as much as a member of a small group of advocates for a theology which emphasized spiritual experience: "A few people closed with God more intensely, exhibiting elements of the mystical piety that surfaced in such Puritans as Sibbes, Preston, and Francis Rous."[81] Mark Dever, however, is unconvinced. Sibbes, he insists, is certainly affectionate but must not be mistaken for a mystic.[82] Yet this sort of reserve misses a key distinction that other scholars readily identify in Sibbes' theology: his certainty that the "motions" of the Spirit are requisite to a proper faith.

Jerald Brauer, like Dever, is also unwilling to identify Sibbes as a mystic, although he accepts the label for Rous. Both

Dever and Brauer are troubled by the definition of mysticism but Brauer examines the matter more closely than does Dever. Brauer acknowledges the increased fervency among many Puritans in Sibbes' era but separates "Puritan mystical thought and Puritan spiritualism". His former distinction includes Rous, Thomas Traherne (c. 1636-74) and Henry Vaughn (1622-95); the latter includes Sibbes and Lewis Bayly (d. 1631).[83]

Brauer's conclusions are drawn by his use of a more extreme, Neo-Platonic, Roman Catholic mysticism as a measure for using the term. Such mysticism seeks ineffable and ecstatic encounters with God as promised by Pseudo-Dionysius—an unidentified devotee to Plotinus whose works appeared and were widely accepted in the fifth century on the basis of his spurious self-identification as Paul's Athenian convert (see Acts 17:34).[84] His version of mysticism, if seen as a standard, can blind us to a moderate, biblical and affective mystical tradition promoted by Bernard of Clairvaux.

This distinction invites more attention. Mysticism has never been a creedal system with monolithic values or sharp distinctions. Yet there are identifiable trajectories that can be helpful in distinguishing forms of such experiential theology. Bernard McGinn, for instance, in *The Foundations of Mysticism* associates one wing of mysticism with a more cataphatic theology—drawn from positive or revealed portrayals of God—that looked mainly to Bernard and his followers. It was this tradition that Sibbes used to portray God with the sort of relational intensity Bernard found in the Bible Song of Songs. Origen, long before Bernard, had treated the Song allegorically—as speaking of the fervent love between Christ and the church, and Bernard was happy to follow that lead.

There was another wing, McGinn explains, that gave a nod to God's revealed qualities but much preferred a negative or apophatic mysticism that reveled in God's unknowable depths. Pseudo-Dionysius developed these positive and negative distinctions and preferred the later basis for approaching God. It was a pathway he took from the pagan Plotinus whose ambition it was to encounter the mysterious and non-discursive One.[85]

Heiko Oberman, addressing mysticism in the broader perspective of the early Reformation, and in Luther's theology in particular, also comments on the difficulty of defining mysticism. Radical mysticism, for instance, was represented in the apocalypticism of Thomas Müntzer, or by spiritual absorption which involves the "dissolution of the human person", a form which "crosses the extreme boundary of Christian mysticism". However these extremes must not rule out more viable forms that helped generate early Protestant spirituality:

> It is impossible to avoid the question of how mysticism and Reformation theology are related. Reformation scholarship has reached no consensus concerning whether or not Luther ought to be called a mystic. At least it is certain that without mystical theology there would have been no 'young Luther': without the experience of the mystical path from Augustine to Bernard of Clairvaux, Luther would not have developed his particular faith in Christ, vital and hungry for experience.[86]

In a similar vein, but in relation to Calvin, Judith Rossall argues that the reformer was heir to separate anthropological traditions, one scholastic and the other Augustinian. The former looked to Aquinas who had adapted Aristotle's assumption that God must be unmoved—hence a disaffected deity—to Christian faith.

This, by extension, dismissed human affections as a basis for engaging God; and it also elevated the mind and the will as the proper bases for human motivation. The Augustinian model, on the other hand, held that the will is dispositional—an instrument of the heart—that reveals a person's ultimate ambitions. This was reflected in Augustine's constellation of synonymous terms such as "love", "soul" and "heart".[87] Perkins' anthropology, as has been seen already, opted for the former and Sibbes, for the latter.

It will be useful, now, to return to the categories used in presenting Perkins to complete our introduction to Sibbes' theology.

Sibbes and Perkins compared. Sibbes displayed little appetite for any method that elevated Aristotelian categories or used Ramist bifurcations to analyze and synthesize theology. Sibbes, like other scholars at Cambridge, certainly recognized the legitimacy of the *scientia* of philosophers over against, and often complementing, the *sapientia* of theology.[88]

But Sibbes was skeptical about the value of systematic or synthetic theology as compared to biblical theology. While he could use the language of Aristotelian causation he preferred to use biblical rhetoric instead, taking the supernatural events of the Bible at face value. This was a proper environment for faith.[89] In this he anticipated a tension between biblical and systematic theology that became more formal in later centuries.[90] Calvin may have been his model here as Sibbes once cited the reformer as opposing speculative theology: "Calvin, as he was a very holy man, so out of his holiness he avoided curious questions as much as he might, therefore [he] gives an excellent answer . . . 'It is curious to search, it is rash to define'."[91]

Sibbes also justified his refusal to take up systematic theology on biblical and pragmatic grounds. He argued from experience that a person's raw intellect did nothing to ensure his or her theological integrity. Intellectual power could, in fact, be a spiritual liability if it is separated from sound faith. Such faith, he held, begins with the heart captured by Christ. That, in turn, directs the mind. He asked, for instance, why the most capable scholars are often those least alert to the role of love in a person's bond with God. He answered by blaming an overstated devotion to dialectical reasoning:

> But it may be asked again, as indeed we see it is true, what is the reason that sometime meaner Christians have more loving souls than great scholars, men of great parts? One would think that knowledge should increase love and affection? So it does, if it be clear knowledge; but great wits and pates and great scholars busy themselves about questions and intricacies, and so they are not much about the affections.[92]

He also held that Satan is presented in the Bible as one able to manipulate the intellect so that misguided reason is one of his chief devices. In Genesis 3 the serpent was presented as the most brilliant of creatures and, as such, he uses "the best wits"—those unbelievers who unwittingly "carry the devil in their brain".[93] Sibbes held Roman Catholic scholasticism to represent how the devil is able to use the mind to distort truth rather than to establish true faith.

> What is the reason, that in popery the schoolmen that were witty to distinguish, that there was little Spirit in them? They savoured not the gospel. They were wondrous quick in distinctions . . . They divided Christ, they knew him not; and dividing Christ, they wanted [lacked] the Spirit of Christ; and wanting that Spirit, they taught not Christ as they should. . . . These were the doctors of the church then, and Christ was hid and wrapped in a company of idle traditions and ceremonies of men; and that was the reason that things were obscure.[94]

A product of Sibbes' skepticism about the reliability of pure reason has been a criticism that he was "not a powerful theologian" and that his theology had a "disheveled" quality to it.[95] But this runs against evidence that he was highly regarded by some of the most capable people of his era. His skill in identifying crucial theological issues, rather than his analytical work, held his audience. Throughout his career he remained devoted to expositional theology, avoiding use of the systematic approach that, by its very nature, required speculative syntheses in areas where the Bible is relatively silent but where systemic completeness and coherence requires responses.

Sibbes, it must be said, was not anti-intellectual even given his critiques. He valued natural reason as an expression of God's image in humanity, "as a candle in the dark night of this world, to lead us in civil and in common actions".[96] But natural reason—in addressing matters of faith—only extends a person's distance from God when that person is separate from him: "'All things are impure to him that is impure, even his very light is darkness,' Tit. 1:15; Mat. 6:23."

The problem with reason, Sibbes held, is its *autonomous* use—the function of thinking apart from faith. In his exposition of Paul's discussion of spiritual and carnal wisdom in 1 Corinthians 1, Sibbes cited Luther to make his point.

> Not that the light of nature and that reason which is a part of the image of God is in itself evil. It is good in itself, but the vessel taints it. Those that have great parts of learning, that have great wits, and helps of learning as much as may be, what do they? They trust in them, and so they stain them. Therefore, Luther was wont to say, "Good works are good, but to trust in good works is damnable".[97]

So while autonomous intellectualism carries a devilish unreliability, reliable knowledge is to be found in "the word of God . . . the Spirit of God . . . [and] the grace of God". Believers "are wise still, but they are wise by a supernatural light, they are wise in supernatural things." Reason must always be informed and redirected by grace.

Sibbes was, it seems, responsive to the Perkinsonian view of the law in his early ministry. Indeed, he appears to have moved significantly on the role of the law during his lifetime. This assumes, given the internal variation in his corpus, that he began his career at Cambridge with a position that conformed to the views of most of his mentors. In his sermons, *The Christian Work*, Sibbes at first displays the main values found among the nomists and the Arminian, John Goodwin, introduced the work. In it Sibbes called for seekers of God to work "to be wrought upon by God's Spirit." Furthermore, he argued that the life of faith is to be lived in obedience to "all God's laws, for partial obedience is no obedience."[98]

But later in the sermon Sibbes also argued that this work is God's operation within the soul, as God changes the dispositions of the heart.[99] At this stage in his teaching he had aligned himself with the idea that the moral law of the Old Testament provides the primary tool for achieving genuine spirituality.

Similarly, Sibbes spoke in another sermon of the "spiritualness and purity of the law" that leads Christians "to consider the purity and holiness of God".[100] However, such views that gave an important place to the law, while never rejected, were later displaced by another emphasis that was far more common throughout his works.

Sibbes offered his more characteristic view of the law in *The Hidden Life* in which he argued that a person's affections are drawn to Christ in the regenerated life so that a Christian becomes functionally dead to the law. A person is not to look for salvation or even "comfort" from the use of the "moral law".[101] In his making the point that salvation is not found in keeping the moral law Sibbes was simply repeating an orthodoxy shared by the nomists. The context in which he placed the point is the distinctive element. He held that Christ's communion with a believer is a felt reality. It comes as a spontaneous affection for Christ that displaces the law as a motive for conduct. As in a marriage—one that prospers in love rather than by regulations—union with Christ unfolds as love rather than by law. Properly speaking Christian behavior is shaped by a person's devotion to Christ as cultivated by the Spirit.

This theme of communion through union with Christ will be addressed in all that follows. Suffice it to say for now that the law is the point where, despite some early points of agreement, Sibbes' divergence from Perkins and his alignment with other earlier reformers becomes most evident.

Schuldiner, for instance, argues that Perkins departed from Calvin by identifying the law as the "means" of salvation and the Spirit as its "cause". "For Calvin", Schuldiner points out, "the Spirit was the cause and means of salvation, working directly within the believer throughout the course of his development."[102] Sibbes, according to Schuldiner, is the primary figure among the Puritans who maintained Calvin's model against the legalism that Perkins' scheme bred.

The nomists traced the moral law as a continuous thread shared by both the Old and New Testaments as the basis for God's work of sanctification in believers. Sibbes, however, came to see the law as obsolete after the coming of Christ. He explained the basic discontinuity of the two testaments in his aptly titled sermon series, *The Excellency of the Gospel Above the Law*. It is this principle—that the Spirit's work in the New

Testament displaced the Old Testament law—that characterized antinomists, a group that now included Sibbes. His literal reading of 2 Corinthians 3:17-18 was crucial, a text that spoke of the Mosaic era as inferior to the new era of the Gospel.[103] Sibbes honored the law as revealing features of God's character but not as the basis for faith.

Sibbes also held an infralapsarian theology of grace rather than the supralapsarianism gaining traction among Puritans at Cambridge under the tutelage of Perkins and others. One promoter of supralapsarianism was Paul Bayne whose preaching had converted Sibbes. Given Bayne's view Sibbes was put in an awkward position when he was asked to write a foreword for Bayne's posthumous work, the supralapsarian *Commentary on the 1st Chapter of Ephesians*.[104] Sibbes deftly avoided a direct confrontation of Bayne's view by affirming three assumptions he shared with Bayne: that God's eternal purposes include sin's divisiveness; that such an arrangement displays God's sovereignty by not making predestination contingent on a foreknowledge of human choice; and finally, that final damnation is therefore just. To say more, Sibbes concluded, is "unnecessary intermeddling".

It is likely that Sibbes' first exposure to scholarly wrangling over infra and supralapsarian views came early in his formal studies. Sibbes began his Cambridge education at St John's College in 1595 either during or soon after the upheaval began between Whitaker and Barrett. The debates continued during his first year at the college and, given the broad student attendance at university sermons, Sibbes probably attended the service on 12 January 1596 where Baro challenged the Lambeth articles.[105]

His sermon is notable in relationship to Sibbes in that the latter's mature theology shared an important assumption with Baro about the fall. The French theologian insisted that God, by his antecedent will, would never determine that certain humans be created strictly to destruction as the supralapsarian doctrine of reprobation would have it. Instead, reprobation must be seen as an act of the consequent will of God, resulting from a person's sin: "Men shut themselves out of heaven, not God."[106] Baro also held that saving grace is given based on God's foreknowledge of those who would respond to it—a view later held by Arminius. This Sibbes rejected.

Nevertheless, Sibbes' infralapsarian position was similar to Baro's on the former point. The elevation of these matters through the Cambridge controversy (whether Sibbes heard Baro's sermon or not) certainly forced members of the university to think about the issues involved.

Baro's challenge displayed a stark alternative: either God created humanity in order to display his sovereignty through arbitrary choice; or he created humanity with a purpose to allow sin to spoil the whole and then to rescue a certain number from their sin by his mercy. Baro adopted the latter option and further mitigated any charges against God's character by his view that God's choice to offer mercy is based on the foreseen results of grace in individual lives.

Sibbes, like Calvin, held that God determined, but did not cause sin; and that he chooses to rescue some from sin because of his sovereign and gratuitous mercy but allows others to remain in sin by their own choosing. A branch layout offers the competing options including the two added possibilities of infralapsarianism.

God's creation purpose is ***either***:

Supralapsarian	***or***	*Infralapsarian*
to display his will in arbitrary election & reprobation (Perkins)		to display his goodness, despite the advent of sin, through ***either***:

gratuitous mercy (Calvin & Sibbes)	***or***	mercy based on foreknowledge (Baro & Arminius)

Sibbes' primary premises in holding the infralapsarian view were that God's purpose in creation reflects: 1) his goodness, and 2) that God's mercy is expressed by the incarnation of Christ whose coming is a response to the fall. The theologians who discussed the order of God's decision-making understood that they were making statements about God's theological priorities and not about a presumed temporal sequence in God's thoughts. Their constructs described varied perceptions of God's values and intentions for the creation.

In Bayne's book, for instance, Sibbes acknowledged that the validity of such discussions is limited by "the difficulty of understanding how God conceives things, which differs in the whole kind from ours, he conceiving of things altogether and at once without discourse, [but] we one thing after another and by another."[107] Why, then, did Sibbes—who avoided speculative theology—enter the fray by disagreeing with Perkins and Bayne?

Sibbes' answer, in his sermon *The Privileges of the Faithful*, came in his discussion of theodicy—"how all ill things can work together for the best to God's children."[108] He answered by pointing to the incarnation as *the* ultimate expression of goodness, a goodness that resulted from the fall. The answer assumed God's positive relational intention in creation, an assumption that will be developed in the next chapter. Given this positive purpose Christ's coming was a necessary response to the fall, meant to reestablish the divine-human relationship. By extension the incarnation would not have occurred apart from the fall.

> The first sin of all, which hath gone over whole mankind, and is spread abroad in every one of us, this by God's mercy and our repentance proves to all believers a transcendent good; for the fall and sin of the first Adam caused the birth and death of the 'second Adam,' Christ Jesus; who, notwithstanding he was God, took upon him the nature of man, and hath made us by his coming far more happy than if we had never fallen. Neither would God have suffered Adam to have fallen but for his own further glory in manifestation of his justice and mercy, and for the greater felicity of his servants in Christ their mediator.[109]

Sibbes, then, shared Calvin's assumption that the mass of humanity, the "whole mankind", was viewed in God's predestinarian purposes as fallen. The benefits of Christ's coming results in "far more" happiness than if the fall had never occurred. Later in his sermon, and elsewhere in his corpus, Sibbes justified his assumption that the outcome of sin was superior to a hypothetical state of sin never appearing. His reason? Sin—by its resolution—called for a union between God and his elect humanity. God overcomes sin by drawing believers into his own eternal life. This eternal communion with God is greater than Adam's standing before the fall: "He doth not only overcome evil *for* us, but also overcometh evil *in* us, and gives us his Spirit, which unites us to himself; whereby we have ground to expect good out of every ill, as knowing that whatsoever Christ wrought for the good of mankind, he did it for us in particular."[110]

Conclusion

This chapter began by examining evidence of a division over grace among English Reformed theologians. Richard Sibbes' affective theology was set against the moralistic Federal theology of William Perkins, reflecting tensions in the basic question of human initiative in salvation. Indeed, Sibbes came to differ from Perkins over: a) the validity of Thomistic theology, b) the matter of infra and supralapsarian theology in defining God's purpose in creation, and c) the use of the law in defining spirituality. God's intentions were construed in very different ways. Yet each of these issues a competing portrayal of God's grace in allowing—or in inaugurating—and treating sin was at stake.

The chapter also pointed to the need for historians of theology to enlarge the framework by which the division of Puritan theology must be evaluated. If the Puritans were merely divided over issues of Pneumatology, as Stoever and Foster assume, then figures such as Sibbes and Cotton are easily marginalized in the face of a monological covenant theology as posited by Miller. If, however, a broader framework is used—as illustrated by Muller's use of Thomistic theology as the measure of orthodoxy—then a new set of questions emerge.

This study assumes an even wider frame of reference, by referring to the Augustinian-Pelagian dispute. This chapter applied that broader context by referring to an enduring historical opposition of response versus responsibility in the application of grace in salvation. With that framework Sibbes may be presented as a representative of one side of a polarity, reacting to the promotion of the alternative position. When the affective tradition of Augustine is used as a standard, the moralistic theology of Thomas and, later, Perkins, is to be seen as disruptive. Knight's proposal that there were two orthodoxies in Massachusetts may be seen, then, as both helpful and as misleading because it suggests the presence of a pluralistic religious environment in the seventeenth century. Such was not the case as ensuing fights revealed.

Another development of this chapter, that will not be further pursued, is the call for much greater discrimination in modern historiography on questions of grace. The Puritan division over grace—largely overlooked by modern scholars—was certainly a source of contention for contemporary figures, as evidenced in the Antinomian Controversy and in the Civil War. Political and ecclesiastical issues were important as well, but the battles between conformists and nonconformists, "Calvinists" and "anti-Calvinists", must include much more nuanced examinations of the doctrines of grace held by participants. The Tudor-early Stuart era was enormously complex and unsettled, and the unsettled doctrine of grace is one of the major threads needing to be unraveled by modern researchers with much greater care.

The broad assertions of this chapter invite closer examination of specific claims. The claim by Schuldiner, Knight, and the present study, that Sibbes represented an affectionate theology, rooted in Calvin and Augustine before him, as against the moralistic theology of Perkins' system, is the subject of the next chapter.

Chapter Two

An Affectionate God

"Gracious and holy Father!"

God, in Christ, was the focus of Richard Sibbes' faith. The chief end of man, he said, is "to look to Christ". This is a goal with two aspects: "The one, that [God] might be glorified; the other, that we might be happy. And both these are attained by honoring and serving him."[1] Was Sibbes anticipating the "chief end of man" question of the Westminster Assembly Catechisms, published just a few years later?

Yes and no. There is a shared concern for God's glory in each case. But Sibbes looked to the relational starting point within God himself: that it is a believer's delight in Christ that brings glory to God the Father. And some of the divines of Westminster certainly shared Sibbes' emphatic love of God—the defining quality of Augustine's affective theology—but there was also a more detached and disaffected version of glory offered by others, with the academic works of William Perkins offering the main example of a superficially affective God, while still viewing him as necessarily disaffected.

Holmes Rolston points out that God's love—the basis of Augustine's affective theology—was not a guiding value at Westminster.[2] In its place was a devotion to the Old Testament moral law that the participating ministers held to be "a rule of life, informing them of the will of God and their duty . . ."[3]

What Sibbes offered as an alternative view of God and his saving plan was that the elect would be "swallowed up in the love of Christ." These different portrayals of God—of his nature and his ends—divided English Reformed theologians at the most basic level possible.[4] Two competing versions of God were at stake.

Predestinarian theology—a theology defined by its intended outcomes—served the Puritans as a hermeneutical key for understanding any particular life narrative. As such Christian teleology engages every event in history: God is either a creator who rules, or a lover who creates.[5] In the former he is seen as pragmatic and demanding and in the latter he is first a lover and then a creator—and the creation then provides a setting where his love is present. Given the latter God's purpose is to extend his inherent relations. Either option offers an *inclusio* of originating decree and final outcome to explain God's works in every moment; and the final judgment measures everything on the basis of God's ultimate purpose, a purpose embedded in the first decree.[6]

Thus, providence, salvation, sanctification, and God's very character were read within a teleological grid. God's glory was seen by every Puritan to be the outcome of creation, but the question remained: what *is* God's ultimate glory? Is it relational—the glory of his immanent and overflowing love as expressed in John 17:24? Or is it glory as a commodity—the concrete displays of his brilliance and power expressed in his rule over the creation?

Boston in New England was not the first place where this sort of division led to controversy. The collision between Thomistic moralism and Augustinian affective theology accounts for Luther's earliest activism, as seen in his *Disputation Against Scholastic Theology* of 1517 and the Heidelberg disputation of May, 1518.[7] By way of context, Heiko Oberman notes that in the fourteenth century there existed a "suspicion of speculation" and a "programmatic call for an affective theology in its place".[8] Luther, reflecting this disposition, was confident that the time for change had come when, in 1517, he wrote that Augustine's theology was beginning to spread while Aristotle's status was declining.[9] Luther's optimism, however, was misplaced. The philosopher's presence continued among English Protestants as a product of the Cambridge University curriculum. Thus, during the Perkins-Sibbes era, many of the guiding assumptions for ethics and anthropology were thoroughly Aristotelian.

God's grace and the human will

Ethics and human choices are linked in Reformed anthropologies. All held that people are accountable for their choices. But the debate was in the definitions: while righteous choices are a product of God's regenerating grace, is that grace an event in spiritual illumination or a gift of enablement? One option portrays faith as response, the other as responsibility; one is unilateral, the other cooperative.

Aristotle, Aquinas and cooperative theology. An underlying assumption of the cooperative position was expressed in Aristotle's *Nicomachean Ethics*: morality is defined by a freedom to either choose or refuse the good apart from any external constraint or compulsion. In his definition Aristotle specifically rejected any reference to the passions ("By passions I mean appetite, anger, fear, confidence, envy, joy, friendly feeling, hatred, longings," etc.) because they are "neither praised nor blamed"—that is, they fall outside the categories of merit. As such, the system is anthropocentric in that it identifies all behaviors as either elevating or reducing the value of the person.[10]

Aquinas assimilated Aristotle's ethical assumptions but struggled to formulate them in terms suited to Augustinianism. Luther believed that he failed in the effort. Oberman points to the main target of Luther's criticism: Aquinas and most medieval theologians assumed that a gap exists between the presence of grace or love in a soul—the *iustitia Christi*—and a demand for full righteousness when that soul is examined on judgment day—the *iustitia Dei.* According to Aquinas Christians move from one status to the other over their lifetime by supplying a faith formed by love—*fides caritate formata.* Love in this arrangement is a responsibility or obligation to be met rather than the reciprocal of response to God's love. The soul must continue to grow in love through ongoing choices.

Aquinas, then, presumed love to be a function of the will—a self-generated event—and as an act of the will it carries a moral benefit. By Aristotelian standards it is a good and therefore meritorious: the one who loves is good for having made a good choice. As reconfigured by Aquinas love is a mitigated good because all who choose to love supply that love as a capacity of the will that God himself first supplied as an infused grace. God nevertheless crowns such grace-enabled efforts with merit.

Luther dismissed such reasoning. He insisted instead that a new believer possesses both the *iustitia Christi* and the *iustitia Dei* by faith—so there is no need for a human effort to progress from one status to the other over time. Luther based this on the legal principle of shared marital ownership of goods, a principle made applicable to believers by marriage to Christ.[11]

Luther's basis for salvation differed from the Thomistic portrayal of grace as a quality infused in the soul and the difference was critical feature for the Protestant reformer. Oberman's discussion also sheds more light on Aquinas' perception of love. He treated love as a human effort able to achieve greater spiritual benefits. In the *Summa Theologiæ*, addressing the new law (*lex nova*), Aquinas portrayed faith working through love—*fide per dilectionem operante*—as a property of grace. The grace is delivered through the effective power of the sacraments and by an instinct of inward grace. The benefit of the new law, as against the old, is its relative freedom (*lex libertatis*) from specific demands.

When Aquinas placed this in the Aristotelian moral framework to either do well or badly in the act of choosing—with an associated merit—he adopted the philosopher's premise that a soul requires freedom in order to be a true moral agent. Aquinas anchored this point by citing Aristotle directly: "the free man is one who is his own cause".[12] In sum Aquinas thought he needed and found the volitional space for free choices, as enabled by grace, to accomplish good. Yet all this was only a limited autonomy—limited because it exists only by divine permission within the realm of God's greater will. And also because the soul relies on the Spirit for the enabling grace needed to produce a decision to love.

This was a critical point in building his version of salvation. God creates grace but the grace is a separate entity from God. This was a hypostatic version of grace: something brought into being by God. The alternative portrayal of grace was to see it as God's love being expressed to a soul by the presence of the Spirit himself. In his favor Aquinas knew that for ages grace had been treated as a distinct entity in the Eucharist—with the elements graciously transformed into Christ's body and blood. This set up a free-standing grace: "Since therefore the grace of the Holy Spirit is a kind of interior disposition infused into us which inclines us to act rightly, it makes us do freely whatever is in accordance with grace, and avoid whatever is contrary to it."[13] The shorthand designation for this dispositional grace was "habit"—or *habitus*.

The notion of *habitus*, a key to Aristotle's anthropology and psychology, is examined more closely in later chapters. Here it is useful to be alerted to its significance: *habitus* is the principal meeting point of nature and grace in Aquinas' spirituality, the gift of grace that supernaturally enhances nature to bear the duties of faith (*aliquid inditum homini quasi naturæ superadditum per gratiæ donum*).[14] Thus Aquinas' view of grace combined an anthropocentric responsibility with theocentric enablement: a cooperative model of faith.

Love, here, must be part of the will in order to be crowned with merit, rather than an affection. If, by contrast, love is an affective response—something God stirs in the soul—it would be non-meritorious to the person who loves.

But this is not the case for Aquinas: his theology turned on a disaffected version of love. With love seen as a choice, even though enabled by a God-given *habitus*, his premise that salvation comes through a faith formed by love set up a progressive model of justification.[15]

Cornelius Ernst rightly identified this cooperative model as semi-Pelagian.[16] Aquinas held, with Pelagius, that human culpability requires that moral decisions be made freely. But, like Augustine, and against Pelagius, he held that original sin destroys any human ability to choose well. Restoration comes only by God's grace. This led to the conundrum that morality requires free will, but original sin precludes it. Semi-Pelagians offered a solution: God provides an assisting grace that enables but does not compel the will to choose the good. Culpability is then based on the failure to apply God's gracious enablement.

This solution, however, identifies a false conundrum, namely, that God's direct intervention implies a compulsion of the human will; and that the opposed alternative is an unassisted human initiative. This invites a brief excursus.

Neither of these assumptions was operative in Augustine's debate with Pelagius. Both men held that faith depends on grace.[17] The debate actually addressed the Pelagian premise that grace exists as a quality *separate* from God himself. For Pelagius grace is twofold: the moral knowledge gained through the law and a gift of human volition that allows for moral choices. A person then makes an informed choice to either obey the law, meriting salvation, or to deny it.

Augustine rejected this anthropocentric scheme. To affirm it makes nature autonomous by holding that goodness is a self-made quality rather than a full dependence on God who alone is good. Augustine, against this Pelagian version of goodness and grace, recognized grace to be relational: the expression of God's love. Thus, Pelagianism and semi-Pelagianism, by his measure, rely on faulty definitions of grace—making grace into a commodity-like quality that humans can engage and apply. Augustine, by treating grace as an affective bond—God's love—neither assigned any merit to love nor any compulsion to God's work in the soul. He held, instead, that the soul gains faith in God in an affective transaction: God's love elicits a human response. Thus there is no extrinsic compulsion when love is birthed by love.

Augustine on the will

Augustine's doctrine of grace presumed the Spirit's work of illumination that elicits an obedient love for God. Thus, like Pelagius, he affirmed a link between grace and obedience. In the *Treatise on Grace and Free Will*, an anti-Pelagian work, he affirmed "the free choice of the human will" and the merits of obedience: "Indeed, a work is then to be pronounced a good one when a person does it willingly; then too, may the reward of a good work be hoped for from [God]".[18] What, then, were the specific elements of Augustine's view of the will in his conflict with Pelagius? Three issues are evident.

The heart is the core of the soul. Augustine developed his argument in stages, all of which assumed a "heart" conversion. Thus, while Augustine accepted the reality of a free will, he portrayed it as useless, "perverse and opposed to faith", until the heart, that includes the will, is replaced in the terms of Ezekiel 11:19-

20, "I will give them another heart", replacing a stone-like heart which "has no feeling", for one "which possesses feeling". God himself is the only proper object of these feelings. Thus, he warned that free will with a hard heart only leads to accountability; but God transforms some hearts: "For what does it profit us if we will what we are unable to do, or else do not will what we are able to do?"[19] The heart for Augustine, sometimes called love or will, is the inclusive faculty of the soul in relationship to God.[20]

Every choice is motivated by an affection. A question must be raised about the relationship of the will and love in light of Augustine's interchangeable use of the words. Is love a work of the autonomous—self-moved—will? Or does the will gain its priorities through the affections? Augustine held the latter position, a crucial point that both Aquinas and Perkins either missed or ignored. Instead they accepted Aristotle's separation of morality from the affections. When applied to Christian ethics, in which love is the ground of morality, it required that love be seen as a work of the disaffected will. This, in turn, led to their use of a cooperative model in which God enables the disaffected—and therefore free—will to determine its own destiny.[21]

Augustine seemed to support this synthesis but only if read carelessly. The bishop, in fact, spoke freely of God enabling the will in his *Treatise* as if accepting the key contention of the Pelagians that "God would not command what he knew could not be done by man".[22] Augustine first made a case for human ability to choose well before turning to attack what he perceived as its flawed logic. He noted Philippians 2:13 ("It is

God who works in you, even to will!"): "It is certain that it is we that act when we act; but it is He who makes us act, by applying efficacious powers to our will", and, "Make or enable me, O Lord [to obey]." Furthermore, God is "He who prepares the will, and perfects by His cooperation what He initiates by his operation".[23]

Augustine's intention, however, was not to affirm Pelagian confidence in a self-moved will, but to deny it after first noticing the biblical texts that seem to support the premise. Having set up the Pelagians, he overturned their argument by asserting the primacy of the affections as they guide the act of choosing: "When the martyrs did the great commandments which they obeyed, they acted by a great will—*that is, with great love.*"[24]

He then supported the crucial role of love with a litany of verses on its power, including the call to follow Christ's example: "Greater love hath no man than this, that a man lay down his life for his friends." Similarly, it was a "small and imperfect love" that God's cooperation promised to assist in supporting "what He initiates by His operation". Augustine's point, unless he had been suddenly converted to the Pelagian position, is that love—seen as will *and* affections—is the motive center of the soul. Thus, it is through the illumination of the soul by God's love that the soul moves, by response, out of its imprisonment of self-love. It is this *absolute* linkage of affections to choices that characterized the will for Augustine, as summarized in his paraphrase of 1 John 4:19, ". . . we should not love God unless He first loved us."[25]

In *The Spirit and the Letter*, also written against the Pelagians, Augustine presented the Spirit as the source of the love that shapes the believer's response: “For it would not be within us, to whatever extent soever it is in us, if it were not diffused in our hearts by the Holy Ghost who is given to us. Now ‘the love of God’ is said to be shed abroad in our hearts, not because He loves us, but because He makes us lovers of Himself.”[26] Thus, the Spirit's presence in believers provides the sanctifying force of faith.

Love and obedience operate unidirectionally. In Augustine's acceptance of a linkage between the will and obedience he denied the correlative assumption that a decision to love God can be achieved by the self-moved will. The assumption that the will is able to move itself when aided by infused will power was, in fact, the foundation of the cooperative model. Augustine denied its key premise and in doing so he exposed in three steps the single direction of travel in the love-obedience nexus: 1) love generates obedience; 2) but certain types of obedience may be achieved without love; 3) therefore obedience does not assure the presence of love.

He thus challenged the critical Pelagian assumption that "Love comes to us of our own selves".[27] That is, the premise that love is an independent activity or choice of a free will rather than a response of the heart to another heart. Augustine used a literal Bible reading to make his case against the Pelagians. Since, as found in 1 Corinthians 2:12, the Spirit teaches "the things that are freely given to us of God", and, from 1 John 4:16, that "God is love", then the knowledge of God as love comes only by the Spirit. Augustine challenged the Pelagians for their credulity in identifying grace with law and not with God's love:

> And thus the Pelagians affirm that they actually have God Himself, not from God, but from their own selves! and although they allow that we have knowledge of the law from God, they will yet have it that love is from our very selves. Nor do they listen to the apostle when he says, "Knowledge puffs up, but love edifies." Now what can be more absurd, nay, what more insane . . ?[28]

Augustine extended his point by arguing that love has primacy over knowledge in that the latter generates pride while the former retains humility in its devotion to others.

Luther, Melanchthon, Calvin and the affective tradition

Luther's early disputations. Luther recognized the issues involved in Augustine's critique of the Pelagians, including an awareness that their dispute centered on definitions of sin, will and grace. To this end his targets in the *Disputation against Scholastic Theology* are revealing. Luther charged that Aristotle's categories and definitions were a primary source of heterodoxy. In sending the *Disputation* to Jodokus Trutfetter, Luther commented:

> Should Aristotle not have been a man of flesh and blood, I would not hesitate to assert that he was the Devil himself. My wish would be for Usingen [Bartholomaeus Arnoldi] and Trutfetter to give up their teaching, indeed stop publishing altogether. I have a full arsenal of arguments against their writings, which I now recognize as a waste of time.[29]

What, then, were these arguments? In both the *Disputation* and the *Heidelberg Disputation* Luther relied on Augustine's fundamental argument against Pelagius: the will is enslaved by self-love that defies God.[30] The enslavement is only overcome in the elect by the regenerating disclosure of God's love and goodness.[31] Aristotle, in Luther's debates, was transposed into the role of heresiarch in place of Augustine's Pelagius. Luther believed he could demonstrate an identity in definitions of the will between Pelagius, a confirmed heretic, and Aristotle. By this means any part of the scholastic tradition that assimilated this definition was subject to challenge. Luther's approach displays three assumptions.

Sin as enslavement through concupiscence. The *Disputation* opened with three theses that emphasized the polarity between Pelagius and Augustine by denying that Augustine's opposition to the "Pelagians and all heretics" is "exaggerated". The fourth and fifth theses expressed the heart of Luther's case: "4. It is therefore true that man, being a bad tree, can only will and do evil. 5. It is false to state that man's inclination is free to choose between either of two opposites. Indeed, the inclination is not free, but captive. This is said in opposition to common opinion."[32] The reason for this captivity is a paradoxical conflict taken from Augustine: "nothing is so much in the power of the will as the will itself".[33] This implied that the more intense purposes of the will always dominate lesser purposes. What, then, guides the will? Luther argued that sin is misapplied devotion: "Man is by nature unable to want God to be God. Indeed he himself wants to be God, and does not want God to be God".[34] The idea that nature, of its own accord, will love God above all else is a fantasy.[35] Thus, Luther used Augustine's definition of sin: "No act is done according to nature that is not an act of concupiscence against God" and, "Every act of concupiscence against God is evil and a fornication of the spirit."[36] This view of self-deceiving sin—labeled as pride—was further developed in the *Heidelberg Disputation*. Luther argued in that debate that Christian leaders display their self-love whenever they displace a Christocentric theology with anthropocentric folly.[37]

The inside-out pathway of moral behaviors. Luther, like Augustine, held an intentional and relational definition of sin rather than a behavioral standard such as law-breaking. This radicalized sin. Even "good" actions as measured by behavioral standards are useless if the underlying motives are wrong: "Every deed of the law without the grace of God appears good outwardly, but inwardly it is sin". This set up Luther's early rejection of the law, "even the Decalogue itself".

Why this extreme? Because even if the soul hates any imposition of the law it can still subvert the law for selfish ends, so that if "the will desires the imposition of the law it does so out of love of self". In any case the will is hostile to the law's goodness because "everyone's natural will is iniquitous and bad."[38]

These assumptions set up Luther's most important opposition between an Aristotelian-based scholastic theology and his own emerging faith. The deceptiveness of sin means that all behaviors, no matter how attractive outwardly, only witness to sin's pollution *unless* the soul is led to those behaviors by the Spirit's grace. Only in being loved by God—revealing his grace—is the soul able to love in return: "The grace of God is given for the purpose of directing the will, lest it err even in loving God" and "without it no act of love is performed".[39]

Aristotle's *Nicomachean Ethics* by contrast held that goodness is both intrinsic and extrinsic: rooted in habits (*habitus*) and displayed in actions (*actus*). Merit, in turn, is located only in the *actus*—the outward activity of the will.[40] While this intrinsic-extrinsic arrangement suggested a wholism in which the dual aspects of volition are fully meshed, *actus* is actually primary because it forms *habitus*. That is, doing virtuous activities forms virtues so that ethical transformation is generated from the outside-in rather than inside-out.

> Again, of all the things that come to us by nature we first acquire the potentiality and later exhibit the activity [as in physical functions] . . . but the virtues we get by first exercising them, as also happens in the case of the arts as well. For the things we have to learn before we can do them, we learn by doing them, e.g. men become builders by building and lyre-players by playing the lyre; so too we become just by doing just acts, temperate by doing temperate acts, brave by doing brave acts.[41]

Luther responded directly and pointedly: "We do not become righteous by doing righteous deeds but, having been made righteous, we do righteous deeds", and "Virtually the entire *Ethics* of Aristotle is the worst enemy of grace."[42]

Thus the radical polarization expressed in Luther's inaugural disputations—his pitting Augustine's affectionate theology against the Aristotelian intellectual-volitional model—was critical to the emergence of the Protestant Reformation.[43]

Melanchthon's Loci Communes Theologici (1521)

Melanchthon's earliest theological primer expanded many of the concerns offered in Luther's theses.[44] Luther praised the *Loci* as did Calvin who displays agreement with many of the fundamental contentions made in it.[45] The underlying assumption of the *Loci* is that the Spirit reveals God's transforming attractiveness to the elect. As Luther had before him, Melanchthon attacked Aristotle's presence in medieval-scholastic theology.[46] He insisted that the affections have primacy over the will in describing faith; and he defined grace as God's immediate favor as opposed to those who held it to be an intermediary and created quality.

The primacy of the affections. Melanchthon rejected the assumption that morality is defined by the human exercise of freely choosing either good or evil: "The term 'free will' [*arbitrium*] was used, a term most incongruous with Scripture and the sense and judgment of the Spirit, and a term that often offended holy men."[47] The scholastic elevation of the will, in Melanchthon's view, meant that the church had "embraced Aristotle instead of Christ".[48] Instead, Melanchthon held, the soul consists of cognition and inclination.[49] The former operates through reason and the latter through "appetition" or will.

> We divide man into only two parts. For there is in him a cognitive faculty, and there is also a faculty by which

> he either follows or flees the things he has come to know. The cognitive faculty is that by which we discern through the senses, understand, think, compare, and deduce. The faculty from which affections (*affectus*) arise is that by which we either turn away from or pursue the things known, and this faculty is sometimes called "will" (*voluntas*), sometimes "affection," and sometimes "appetite" . . . . in which are love, hate, hope, fear, sorrow, anger, and the feeling which arise from these.[50]

Experience shows, Melanchthon argued, that while the will can be informed by the intellect it is easily overcome by the affections.

He used the analogy of ancient Roman politics: despotic rulers often dismissed the reasoned deliberations of the senate. This displays the greater power of the affections *not* as a property external to the will but as the defining quality of the will: "the will [as in the political analogy] casts knowledge out and is borne along by its own affection". Thus in a critical distinction he relabeled the critical faculties of the soul as "the 'cognitive faculty' and the 'faculty subject to the affections'".[51]

Given this redefinition, Melanchthon was prepared to address the main question of the scholastics, "whether the will (*voluntas*) is free and to what extent it is free." He concluded from biblical evidence: "Since all things that happen, happen necessarily according to divine predestination, our will has no liberty."[52] The determinism of predestination is the point where, Melanchthon insisted, reason in the hands of Aristotelian theologians always violates scriptures because of their belief that good conduct arising from a self-moved will is the basis of morality (Aristotle's *eupraxia*).[53] Melanchthon addressed this tension by pointing to the controlling power of the affections as God's instrument for change. This allows a "certain freedom in outward works" but only within the limited range of the ruling affections of the heart.

The question of morality, then, is centered in the affections and not the behaviors. The "outward works" merely disclose the nature of the affections.

> The would-be philosophers who have attributed freedom to the will (*voluntas*) have fixed their eyes upon this contingency of external works. But Scripture tells nothing of that kind of freedom, since God looks not at external works but at the inner disposition of the heart. . . . By contrast [to external works], internal affections are not in our power, for by experience and habit we find that the will (*voluntas*) cannot in itself control love, hate, or similar affection, but affection is overcome by affection.[54]

The key principle—that "affection is overcome by affection"—captured Augustine's affective solution to perceived tensions between God's will and human will. He wrote: "[Let the soul seek God's mercy] that [God] may, by inspiring into it the sweetness of his grace through his Holy Spirit, cause the soul to delight more in he teaches it than it delights in what opposes his instruction."[55]

Thus for Melanchthon if sin is "a depraved affection", so that "the dominant affection of man's nature is love of self", then the solution to sin must come through an even greater affection that can eclipse the affections of sin.[56] God alone elicits such an affection as he is revealed to the heart by the Spirit: "For unless the Spirit teaches you, you cannot know what it is to love God, that is, unless you actually experience it inflamed by the Spirit himself."[57]

Grace as Christ's shared life and love. Melanchthon also challenged the medieval belief that grace can be construed as a quality that equips a human to cooperate in salvation. Melanchthon identified two opposed options on the way spiritual life is tied to God as giver. A gift may be seen either as an immediate and ongoing benefit of God's benevolence to a person through the Spirit's presence; or alternatively as something imparted by God yet independent from him—a newly created quality.

In the second option God is seen to impart a righteous disposition. When the capacity is given the recipient owns it so that it is not a function of God's presence. This second option was developed by Aquinas to establish a framework for cooperative salvation. A physical analogy for this is the motion imparted to a stone that, once free of the hand that throws it, is a continuing effect of the thrower; but given its freedom from the hand it is independent. Melanchthon, however, rejected such options as "Aristotelian figments".[58]

Instead Melanchthon held that the Bible treats saving grace as God's love or favor; and to make grace "a quality in the souls of the saints" is a shameful misuse. He went on: "The worst of all offenders are the Thomists who have placed the quality of 'grace' in the nature of the soul, and faith, hope, and love in the powers of the soul."[59] Melanchthon, in rejecting this Aristotelian notion of grace as imparted energy, turned to an affective basis for the proper understanding of grace: "But the gift of God is the Holy Spirit himself, whom God has poured out into their hearts. John 20:22: 'He breathed on them, and said to them, "Receive the Holy Spirit."'"[60] It is only by God's presence based on his benevolence and accomplished by the Spirit that a person is saved. His focus was on the giver rather than on the gift by itself.

Calvin on the affections and the will

What, then, of Calvin? He knew of Melanchthon's view that the affections guide the will but he seemed to cast his own lot with the rational-volitional anthropology of the Greeks.[61] This stance, in turn, set aside any lead role for the affections.

> [T]he understanding is . . . the leader and governor of the soul; and . . . the will is always mindful of the bidding of the understanding and in its own desires awaits the judgment of the understanding. For this reason, Aristotle himself truly teaches the same: that shunning or seeking out in the appetite corresponds to affirming or denying in the mind. Indeed, in another place [2.2.1-26] we shall see how firmly the understanding now governs the direction of the will; here we wish to say only this, that no power can be found in the soul that does not duly have reference to one or the other of these members.[62]

Gavin McGrath also notices some evidence in Calvin's anthropology that might support the enabled-will (cooperative) model of faith.[63] McGrath is alert to the role of the affections in shaping the views of Luther and Melanchthon about the impotency of the will, but he views the issue as a continuum rather than an opposition. Thus Calvin differed from the Lutherans not in kind but in degree. That is McGrath attributed to Calvin a belief that conversion comes through the grace-enabled will. This gave a major role to human initiative—something Luther dismissed.

The question was whether the event of conversion is a response or a responsibility. Not all would insist on a distinct moment of conversion but McGrath sees that feature in Calvin's faith so the question comes: how is faith birthed? He answers that Calvin took up the Thomistic answer: a person chooses to respond. With this McGrath assumed that Calvin used Aristotle's anthropology of moral choice. Taken in combination Calvin is portrayed as a moralist.

Judith Rossall, however, has a different reading of Calvin's anthropology. She agrees that Calvin formally affirmed Aristotle's description of the soul but she then shows that Calvin's actual teaching was Augustinian rather than Aristotelian. That is, Calvin resolved the question of salvation by consistently arguing from Augustinian assumptions. He held, for instance, that the orientation of the will determines salvation; that any desire for God in the elect is a response to the presence of the Spirit; and that the terminology of will and heart are interchangeable. Furthermore, his affinity to the Lutheran position in this respect is illustrated by his use of an analogy found in Luther's *The Bondage of the Will*.[64]

> Somewhere Augustine compares man's will to a horse awaiting its rider's command, and God and the devil to its riders. "If God sits astride it," he says, "then as a moderate and skilled rider, he guides it properly . . . . But if the devil saddles it, he violently drives it far from the trail . . . ."[65]

Augustine had rejected the Pelagian notion that God and humanity cooperate in accomplishing salvation—that grace initiates and nature reciprocates in acts of meritorious choosing. Calvin agreed. He argued, with Augustine, that believers are fully dependent on grace.

> [Augustine] strongly challenges the view that subsequent grace is given for men's merits because by not rejecting the first grace they render themselves worthy. For he would have Pelagius admit that grace is necessary for our every action and is not in payment for our works, in order that it may truly be grace.[66]

Calvin, like Augustine, saw the opposed positions as irreconcilable: "The human will does not obtain grace by freedom, but obtains freedom by grace". This grace works through transformed affections: "[W]hen the feeling of delight has been imparted through the same grace, the human will is formed to endure; it is strengthened with unconquerable fortitude; controlled by grace, it never will perish . . . ."

God's goodness—his benevolence—was for Calvin the explanatory basis for a living faith: "It is not enough simply to hold that God is one who should be worshipped and adored by all, unless we are persuaded also that he is the fountain of all good, so that we should seek nothing anywhere else but in him."[67] This confidence in God's goodness discloses a converted heart. Without the Spirit "the greatest geniuses are blinder than moles!" The unregenerate mind is darkened toward God not by an inability to process information but by the absence of "assurance of God's benevolence toward us (without which man's understanding can only be filled with boundless confusion)".[68] Thus, "the way to the Kingdom of God is open only to him whose mind has been made new by the illumination of the Holy Spirit."[69]

This illumination functions in both the mind and the will. For the mind it is *not* the external grace of knowledge, as Pelagius argued, but the capacity to see one's own sin: "For the natural man refuses to be led to recognize the diseases of his lusts."[70] Calvin argued that the "philosophers" identify sin as behaviors that "are outward and manifested by grosser signs. They take no account of the evil desires that gently tickle the mind."[71] These "lusts" and "evil desires" belong to the will.[72]

In summary, the separate traditions evident in this section—the affective theology of Augustine, and the moralist tradition of Aquinas—provided contexts for markedly different conceptions of grace and salvation. They were not, however, set in terms of the teleological *inclusio* that characterized Perkins' predestinarianism. Nevertheless the emphasis of the early reformers on God's benevolence, and the semi-Pelagian assumptions of Aquinas provided the primary context for the debates about grace in English Reformed theology.

Perkins and Sibbes: God, Grace and Predestination

Varied views of God's creation purpose shaped Puritan theologies. Perkins' predestinarian focus was on God's will and transcendence. He also affirmed the moralist's solution to the apparent conundrum of free will and original sin. Sibbes, however, portrayed God as affective and immanent. In doing so, he challenged the teleological emphasis of Federal theology. He also accepted the Augustinian view of conversion and portrayed grace as God's continuous benevolence through Christ.

Perkins on predestination

The Federal model of predestination came to England from continental sources in 1585.[73] The *Golden Chaine* was Perkins' exposition of that theology. The doctrine came to be widely accepted and achieved confessional status in 1647 in the Westminster *Confession of Faith*. While this approach to faith held broad continuity with earlier models of covenant theology it also contained new assumptions that stirred a reaction.[74] The Barrett-Baro episode, for instance, revealed a reconsideration of the otherwise dormant doctrine of election by foreknowledge. Until Perkins promoted the teleology of Federalism as a framework for justification the respected Baro had not promoted a doctrine of contingent predestination. His reaction suggests that the questions Perkins raised about God's creation purposes stirred Baro more than Baro's desire to promote contingent predestination.[75]

The sixty-two year period between the coming of Federalism until the Westminster Assembly also gave Sibbes time to reflect—along with others who where alert to the Cambridge controversy. Because the doctrine was not yet fully established Sibbes was not breaking an established orthodoxy when he questioned Perkins' views. As such Sibbes represented a reaction to the new scheme—a growing disquiet shared by at least some other Puritans.

Predestination and the human will. In the first chapters of the *Golden Chaine* Perkins made God's will the first point of reference in creation—all other qualities and actions by God are explained by his will. This will, expressed in God's original decree: "as it concerneth man, [it] is called predestination".[76] Perkins wrote the *Golden Chaine* to "oppugn as erroneous" three views of predestination, and to affirm the supralapsarian view as orthodox.[77] The common feature among the positions he rejected, including the "Lutheran" infralapsarianism, is any role for human choice in either receiving or rejecting grace for salvation. This, he believed, would make God's choice contingent on "foreseen" decisions. The Pelagians and semi-Pelagians built salvation on a foreseen decision to follow God by the elect; or the rejection of God by reprobates. The infralapsarian view assumes a foreseen rejection of God by the full mass of humanity.

Against these views, Perkins' supralapsarianism made God's will prior to *any* human morality, thus avoiding contingency. God's will shapes the *Golden Chaine* so that salvation and reprobation converge at "Gods Glorie" as the ultimate purpose of history.[78] God's purpose, then, must be seen to be wholly arbitrary: "the decree and eternal counsel of God concerning [the elect and the reprobate] both hath not any cause *beside his will and pleasure.*"[79]

This will-centered glory presumed God's nature to be simple—non-composite—and thus unchanging as prescribed by Aristotle.[80] The changelessness of God's will was a critical piece in Perkins' exposition: "God's immutability of nature is that by which he is void of all composition, division and change."[81] The Bible does presume God's essential unity and his changeless stability. But should this unity be read in terms of Aristotle's vision of a monadic God? Perkins thought so. Yet the Bible narratives collectively portray God's will to be located in the active relations of his Triune being—and therefore eternally stable in God's essential harmony of will. In Sibbes' view the latter view offers eternal stability within an active relationship: God as a lover is eternally faithful within a dynamic and reciprocal love.

Aristotle's premise, on the other hand, precludes relationality. How so? Because power is the defining quality of a monadic, unmoved God. And for his power to be absolute he must be free of any contingency, hence he is relationally detached as measured by any human relational connections.

Sibbes felt he had the Bible in his favor. A common prooftext for Perkins' sort of portrayal of an immutable God, for instance, was Malachi 3:6—"For I, the LORD, do not change; therefore you, O sons of Israel, are not consumed". This text, however, illustrates a problem of such proof-texting: in it God is hardly an unmoved, disaffected ruler. Instead he is relational and affective: a faithful, loving promise-keeper who endures the faithlessness of his people.[82]

Love and the will. In speaking of God, apart from any one of the triad of persons, Perkins identified a primary essence that is "void and free from all passion".[83] Love, if seen as essentially affective, would include an element of contingency, namely, God's *desire* that his creation respond to his love as the complement to his own love. If, however, love is a component of the will, God merely *requires* such a response.[84] In the *Golden Chaine*, then, love is striking in its absence as a motivation in God. This despite the primacy of divine love as expressed in the Bible.[85] In a published layout of the *Chaine* love is placed below Christ's mediatorial work, not above it.[86]

Perkins also believed that if God's love is perceived as an inherent motivation (that is, as an affection) it would suggest a universal salvation. He raised an "objection" in the *Golden Chaine* to make the point, although he immediately qualified it with an unexplained ambiguity:

> *Object.* Election is nothing else but dilection or love; but this we know, that God loves all his creatures. Therefore he elects all his creatures.
>
> *Answer.* I. I deny that to elect is to love, but to ordain and appoint to love.
>
> II. God does love all his creatures, yet not all equally, but every one in their place.[87]

This reflected Perkins' synthetic definition of God's love. In his *Treatise of God's Free Grace and Man's Free Will*, Perkins posed the question "whether there be such an affection of love in God, as is in man and beast."

> I answer that affections of the creature are not properly incident unto God, because they make many changes, and God is without change. And therefore all affections, and the love that is in man and beast is ascribed to God by figure.[88]

Thus God expresses himself immutably by doing "the same things that love makes the creature do" yet without any feeling in his choices. This anthropopathic premise—that God uses the language and functions of human love to achieve his eternal purposes while he is actually unmoved by any sort of human-like feelings—explained how God's pure will must be assumed even in the Bible's use of affective language to describe God's motives: "Because his will is his essence or Godhead indeed."[89] As such God's love language has nothing to do with the emotional love of humans—only the words are the same.

God's purposes are identified in the second pole of Perkins' teleological system. The outcome, God's glory, discloses God's reflexive or self-concerned purpose: "The *end* of the counsel of God" he argued, "is the manifestation of his own glory, partly in his mercy, and partly in his justice."[90] God's love is revealed only in the mediatorial work of Christ. However, even after conversion the elect need to be "well practiced in repentance". It is difficult to be fully assured of God's love since it is "the greatest measure of faith"—a level of faith apparently achieved by only a few.[91]

Dual agents: God and humanity. Perkins also needed to resolve the central tension of predestination: if God's will is absolute, how does the human will have meaning? He found a solution in scholastic theology, positing a cooperation of dual agents. In *God's Free Grace and Man's Free-Will* he attributed this crucial assumption to Aquinas.[92] Aquinas' concern, as was true of Perkins, was to maintain a cause-effect relationship between God and his creation: "We must therefore understand that God works in things in such a manner that things nevertheless have their proper operation." Aquinas concluded: "One action does not proceed from two agents of the same order. But nothing hinders the same action from proceeding from a primary and a secondary agent." Thus, in dual agency God is the primary agent. He supplies grace to the believer who applies it as a secondary agent. Grace, then, is God's enablement granted as an intermediary gift to assist the human will.

The Spirit, then, was seen by Perkins to be the agent of union, "whereby Christ and his church are joined together, for the very same Spirit of God that dwells in the manhood of Christ and fills it with all graces above measure, is derived thence and dwells in all true members of the church, and fills them with the like graces in measure".[93] In Perkins' understanding of the Trinity the Father rules and the Son offers "administration of every outward action". The Spirit is the agent by which that administration is accomplished.[94]

In this subordinate role the Spirit is "the bond of conjunction". He achieves creation, communication, illumination, and empowerment but somehow lacks a personal will. This is a logical concomitant to Perkins' emphasis on the directive will of the Father. It also helps to explain the ambiguity of the Spirit's role in sanctification where at times he appears to be bullied by humans who can "drive away [the Spirit] . . . from his own house".[95]

Theodicy. Why would Perkins want this arrangement? Because it explained why God allows evil to exist—the concern of theodicy. To do this he posited a limited place for moral neutrality in the human soul: a volitional space where neither goodness nor evil rules the will so that the self-moving function of choice can operate. Any extrinsic spiritual presence, whether of God or Satan, needs to be absent or inactive in order for this to occur. The elect person then chooses God by means of enabling grace; and the reprobate, without enabling grace, chooses evil.

God chose the arrangement for the sake of his own morality. "God", Perkins held, "voluntarily doth permit evil, because it is good that there should be evil." This is God's permissive will in which he "permitteth evil by a certain voluntary permission, in that he forsaketh the second cause in working evil." God, by withholding grace in a person, permits sin without causing it: "he forsaketh his creature either by detracting the grace it had, or not bestowing that which it wanteth." The human agent thus initiates his or her fallen choices and is condemned accordingly while God uses the results of the sin for his own good purposes.[96] This privative model of sin will be examined in a later chapter.

Perkins also described conversion as a cooperative exercise between two moral agents: God offers the promise of salvation to an elect person who—as enabled by grace—reciprocates God's action by offering the act of faith back to God. That faith is then authenticated by obedience. This assisted bilateralism set up the theological context for preparationism—the pursuit of moral sensitivity and obedience before conversion—in the hope of being elect. It also anchored the practical syllogism as an effort to demonstrate election through obedience—all in the pursuit of assurance that one is saved. And it invited casuistic ethics—the discrimination between biblical good and evil in order to recognize and achieve the good. Janice Knight summarized a reversal of the Reformation view of divine and human roles that resulted: "This . . . activism . . . implicitly undermines prevenience in favor of consequent moralism."[97]

Sibbes on predestination

What, then, were Sibbes' views concerning predestination? He both accepted it and, for the most part, ignored it in the practice of ministry. To be specific, he accepted the duality of election and reprobation, "that Christ justifieth us by his righteousness and merit, and sanctifies us by his Spirit, and hath predestinated and elected us, and refused others . . ."[98] He also rejected any notion that "Christ's death is of larger extent than his intercession": the range of God's election and the efficacy are identical.[99]

Sibbes' sermon, *The Faithful Covenanter*, also displayed some use of Federal language in his covenant theology. There he argued that the "communion and fellowship of man with God was first founded on a covenant of works made with Adam in paradise. If he did obey, and did not eat of the forbidden fruit, he should have life both for himself and his posterity".[100] Nevertheless, Sibbes' difference with Perkins over issues of the fall, including their infra- and supralapsarian views, point to their fundamentally different approaches to predestinarian salvation.

An assessment of Sibbes' model of predestination, then, begins with a puzzle: why does he ignore the doctrine in ministry while still affirming it? Modern scholars, in noticing this, have responded with guesses but offer no particular evidence. R. T. Kendall, for instance, comments that Sibbes gave such "small attention to the doctrine of predestination" that it "leads one to suspect that he would almost prefer that men forget about [it] . . ." Kendall attributes the neglect to pastoral concerns, but having said this he also describes Sibbes as a predestinarian "squarely within Perkins's mould".[101] Mark Dever says something similar by asserting that Sibbes was "reluctant to discuss the doctrine explicitly".[102] Sibbes, however, had explained his resistance to saying much about predestination. It came from his perception of God as an affectionate being.

God as loving. The goal of Sibbes' theology—his teleology—was relational. The conclusion of creation is defined by the reality of God's love. God created the universe on the basis of his inherent social nature as three-in-one:

> If God had not a communicative, spreading goodness, he would never have created the world. The Father, Son, and Holy Ghost were happy in themselves, and enjoyed one another before the world was. But that God delights to communicate and spread his goodness, there had never been a creation nor a redemption.[103]

In identifying the second pole of this pairing Sibbes turned to Augustine's theology: "As Saint Augustine says, 'Thou hast made us for thee, and our hearts rest not till we come to thee." It is the nature of a believer, Sibbes held, "to look principally to that which is his last and best and main end, which is God, and union and communion with God in Christ, who is God in our nature . . ."[104] This premise that God created humanity in order to offer himself affectively in Christ as a uniting and communing presence in human form shaped all of Sibbes' theology.

Sibbes' broader theology, in comparison to Perkins' formal writings, reveals differences in tone and substance. Sibbes emphasized God's mercy and insisted that communion with God is an immediate prospect, not a distant possibility. Dever, in fact, summarizes Sibbes' theology and ministry in just such terms: "For Sibbes, Christianity was a love story." Indeed, among the most common contemporary epithets for Sibbes were "affectionate" and "heavenly", both reflecting his cataphatic and affective theology.[105] The Father is the author of salvation: "Christ besides his abasement, he was a servant of state, he was an ambassador sent from the great God . . . to do a piece of service . . . to bring God and man together again".[106]

God's motive in offering the covenant of grace is one of paternal care: "Now in the covenant of grace, God would be known by the sweet name of Father, by the attributes of mercy and love."[107] This view affirmed the juridical issues of salvation in the same terms used by Sibbes' nomistic colleagues, but Sibbes placed justice in the larger context of God's love: "What stirred [God] to reconcile justice and mercy, but love, that loves us in Christ therefore, and only in Christ; because in Christ only his wrath is satisfied."[108]

Sibbes' alternative covenantalism. Sibbes, as we noted already, spoke agreeably of covenant theology. Yet he dismissed its substance by reinterpreting a central feature: the Federal commitment to mutuality—of maintaining both human and divine initiatives in salvation.

Let me begin by noting Perkins' position as a point of comparison. He suggested a strong continuity of the Old and New Testaments: "This covenant is also named a testament, for it hath partly the nature and properties of a testament or will." While the Old and New Testaments are distinct in certain functions, he explained, they are "one in substance."[109] His concern was to maintain some measure of continued mutuality between nature and grace as the function of a covenant. Yet he also affirmed the unilateral work of Christ whose completed work of salvation is a fulfilled testament or will. More will be said about these distinctions in a later chapter. The issue here is that the Federal model maintained the necessity of human initiative in conversion, albeit by means of enabling grace. By maintaining the perpetuity of the covenant of grace faith is construed as a responsibility: the *quid pro quo* to God's offer of salvation in Christ. This was the very heart of Perkins cooperative system of dual agents.

Sibbes, however, rejected this arrangement and instead characterized four "periods" of God's renewed covenant. He argued that with Christ's death the covenant reverted to a testament which "is a covenant sealed by death." As such it rules out any reciprocity. Therefore the initiative is God's alone, and his motive is love: "A testament *bequeatheth good things merely of love*" while a "covenant requireth something to be done."[110] Sibbes thus placed his own covenant theology on a foundation of love-and-response in contrast to the foundation of duty and obedience in Perkins' version. Yet Sibbes also maintained the predestinarian commitment of Calvin and others by affirming that this love is limited to "a certain company whom he foreknew to everlasting life". By this means all of God's attributes, including justice, "might fully be satisfied; but especially that his mercy and love might triumph."[111]

Sibbes' affective view of salvation. As Luther and Melanchthon before him, Sibbes recognized the relationship of the affections to the will. Sibbes also established his discussion of salvation within an affective and infralapsarian framework. Given the reality of the fall, God, within his Triune communion, determined to send the Son to "woo" listeners to himself.

> So, then, the whole evangelical truth is a mystery. . . . Because it was hid and concealed from all men, till God brought it out of his own bosom: first to Adam in paradise, after the fall; and still more clearly afterwards to the Jews; and in Christ's time more fully to Jews and Gentiles. It was hid in the breast of God. . . . After man was fallen to that cursed state, this plot, of saving man by Christ, came not into the head of any creature, to satisfy justice by infinite mercy; to send Christ to die, that justice might be no loser. It could come from no other breast but God's. . . . Therefore it was a plot devised by the blessed Trinity, the Father, Son, and Holy Ghost. It was hid in the secret closet of God's breast. Christ brought it out of the bosom of his Father.[112]

Sibbes believed that the obstacle to salvation is a caricature of God: he is unattractive apart from the illuminating work of the Spirit. For the elect, however, the "veil was lifted" and God is seen as lovely. Thus in both salvation and sanctification God draws hearts to himself in morally accurate and satisfying terms:

> By this we have communion with the Father, Son, and Holy Ghost. This incarnation of Christ, it brings us into fellowship with the blessed Trinity; and it teacheth us what conceits we should have of God, to have loving thoughts of him. Whence is that that we can call God Father? From this, "God manifest in the flesh." The second person, to take away enmity, was "manifest in the flesh." Hence it is that I can call God Father, that I can boldly go to God, that I can conceive of God as gracious and lovely. And whence is it that our person are become lovely to God? From this, that God hath taken our nature upon him. Our nature is become lovely to him, and his is sweet and fatherly to us.[113]

Sibbes sought to convince his listeners that the love of the Father had been guaranteed to them by the unity of love found within the Godhead—presented in John 17—so that the elect, once united with Christ, can be assured of God's eternal love.

> Is it possible that he should delight in the head, and refuse the members? that he should love the husband, and mislike the spouse? O no; with the same love that God loves Christ, he loves all his. He delights in Christ

> and all his, with the same delight. There is difference in the degree, "that Christ in all things may have the pre-eminence," Col. 1:18, but it is the same love; . . . [Christ] desires "that same love wherewith his Father loved him may be in them that are his," John 17:20 . . . This is our comfort and our confidence, that God accepts us, because he accepts his beloved; and when he shall cease to love Christ, he shall cease to love the members of Christ. They and Christ make one mystical Christ.[114]

Thus, Sibbes sought to remove the burden felt by believers about their inability to maintain the conduct appropriate to regeneration. Mystical union with Christ assured the elect of their salvation. The crucial imagery of marital union in achieving this will be the subject of chapter four.

God as Immanent in the Spirit. Sibbes' theology of a real union helps solve the puzzle of Sibbes' apparent disinterest in predestination. As already noted, he emphasized present experience in his theology and avoided broader speculations. In a sermon he challenged talk about creation decrees in seeking assurance of salvation. In doing so he reversed the common direction of travel for theological explorations: he concluded that efforts to extrapolate primary doctrines from the decrees or to build a theology around them were flawed.[115] Instead the ministry of the Spirit is the proper concern of applied theology because the Spirit represents God to believers in the most immediate and effective manner possible.[116]

> In that grand inquiry about our condition, there is a great miscarriage when men will begin with the first work of the Father in election, then pass to redemption by Christ: I am God's, and Christ hath redeemed me; and never think of the action of the third person in sanctification, which is the nearest action upon the soul, as the third person himself is nearest unto us; and so fetch their first rise where they should set up their last rest. Whereas we should begin our inquiry in the work of the third person, which is next unto us; and then upon good grounds we may know our redemption and election.[117]

Sibbes reaffirmed and emphasized the point even more strongly in his final supervised publication—its foreword prepared in the week of his death—*The Soul's Conflict.*

> [S]ome . . . proceed by *a false method and order* in judging their estates. They will begin with election, which is the highest step of the ladder; whereas they should begin from a work of grace wrought within their hearts, from God's calling them by his Spirit, and their answer to his call, and so raise themselves upwards to know their election by their answer to God's calling. [he cites 2 Peter 1:10] God descends down unto us from election to calling, and so to sanctification; we must ascend to him, beginning where he ends. Otherwise it is as great folly as in removing a pile of wood, to begin at the lowest first, and so . . . to be in danger to have the rest to fall upon our heads. Which, besides ignorance,

> argues pride, . . . in this, that they would bring God to their conceits, and be at an end of their work before they begin.[118]

Sibbes thus objected to the application of predestinarian thought in a pastoral setting. His concern was with the logic of the main question of predestination, "Am I God's?" Sibbes believed that the nerve of spiritual growth would be cut if the Christian life were reduced to finding an answer to that question by use of the practical syllogism. That is, if assurance were achieved by looking to the issues of election and legal standing before God, rather than in enjoying communion with God by his Spirit, the real point of sanctification would be lost. Assurance, he argued, is best gained by the activity of God within, and not by the use of potentially deceptive rationalism: "People out of self-love will have conceits of the Father's and Son's love severed from the work of the Spirit upon their hearts, which will prove a dangerous illusion."[119]

Thus Sibbes' resistance to the pastoral use of predestination was conscious and explicit. He opposed it because he saw a tendency among its exponents to elevate the doctrines of justification and assurance to the point that they obviated adequate attention being given to sanctification and glorification, about which the Bible had so much to say.

An attendant concern for Sibbes was the likely loss of motivation to pursue God in love, and with it the moral benefit which came from seeking a holy God. If confidence in gaining redemption was the chief theological concern of Christians, without a concomitant emphasis on the Spirit's work of sanctification, then, in Sibbes' view, moral corruption in the church was inevitable. The church would suffer through false and "powerless" notions of what God is like by failing to promote the Spirit's ministry.

> Although the whole work of grace by the Spirit arise from the Father's and Son's love, witnessed by the Spirit, yet the proof of the Father's love to us in particular, ariseth from some knowledge of the work of the Spirit. The error is not in thinking of the Father's and Son's love, but in a strengthening themselves by a pleasing powerless thought of it against the work of grace by the Spirit, which their corruption withstands. So they will carve out of the work of the Trinity what they think agreeable to their lusts, whereas otherwise, if their heart were upright, they would for this very end think of God's love and Christ's, to quicken them to duty and to arm them against corruption.[120]

Thus Sibbes left behind no mystery about his relative silence on predestination; he was committed to a theology of the Spirit's work in salvation and sanctification, as against a theology dominated by implications of predestinarian decrees of election. It was a theology that affirmed the affective tradition of Augustine and Luther by identifying God's initiative of love expressed continually through the Spirit to the elect. This is the cause of all changes in the nature-grace nexus. Thus, salvation is a response of the illuminated affections rather than a responsibility of the enabled will.

Conclusion

The collision of two competing views of salvation led to Luther's earliest protests in the Protestant Reformation. He challenged the widespread Aristotelian-scholastic themes of his era and instead defended the affective tradition of Augustine. Yet by the time of Perkins Protestants had reacquired the older Greek themes. Two matters were critical. First, Perkins' teleological emphasis along with his Aristotelian understanding of God's immutability set the context for his cooperative model of faith. His concern to avoid any contingency in God while maintaining human free will and original sin left him with a Thomistic solution. He seems not to have entertained the Augustinian alternative. Second, love was set out as a subsidiary rather than primary characteristic of God—and as a quality meant only for the elect. This supralapsarian interpretation of the creation was absolute and arbitrary: God is transcendent as the cosmic ruler whose decree is to accomplish his own glory.

Sibbes, on the other hand, rejected the cooperative solution. This rejection, as just seen, solves the puzzle about Sibbes' relative disinterest in predestination. He recognized that any approach to sanctification by way of predestination produces a self-deceiving introspection: professing believers would be left to search for signs of their election in their conduct. The stubborn anthropocentricism this reveals also distracts from the primacy of God's initiating love; and from the human response to that love as the true basis for sanctification. By taking this position Sibbes stood squarely within the affective tradition. He viewed grace as God's love by which the Spirit accomplishes a real union with the elect. The following comparisons of Perkins and Sibbes sharpen the point.

Pelagian, Thomistic, & Federal theologies are cooperative. The assumptions found in the Pelagian view of grace and salvation, which Augustine and the late-patriarchal church rejected, were seen by Luther and his followers to have been revived in the Aristotelian-scholastic synthesis of Aquinas. A summary sets out the main polarities:

The Augustinian-Lutheran position	The Scholastic-Federal position
the heart has primacy over the instruments of mind & will	affections are unreliable & must be ruled by the mind and will
morality is defined by the soul's of most-loved object: God or self	morality is defined by choices of the free will
grace is God's love expressed by the Spirit	grace is a created capacity to choose well
nature depends wholly on grace	nature has mutuality with grace
moral change is only 'inside-out' through divine transformation	moral change is 'outside-in' as initiated by human effort

The Augustinian model dismisses cooperative assumptions. Luther, Melanchthon, and Calvin all accepted Augustine's assumption that the will is guided by desire. In matters of faith a sinner's desires are stirred and sustained by the Spirit's gracious and direct disclosure of God's captivating love. The Augustinians did not make improved morality an entry ticket for salvation or the defining factor in ongoing faith. They held, instead, that sin is an obstacle to a person's perception of God's love but not an obstacle in itself. That is, the promises of his love in the Bible are present for all to read but are viewed with insurmountable skepticism by unbelievers who hold that behavioral morality determines salvation. The Spirit overcomes this skepticism by his presence as he offers loving illumination. Sibbes was, in this sense, consciously Augustinian.

It has been important to notice how concepts of grace, covenant, love and will were viewed from within differing and competing frameworks. The main question throughout has been one of initiative: is conversion an act of the assisted will; or the response of the will as formed by its driving affection? Another implicit question has also been present throughout: what *is* sin?

Chapter Three

Defining the Problem: What *is* Sin?

"Unworthy we are . . . by reason of the sins of our nature, and the sins of our lives"

Why do some people dismiss or hate God while others love and follow him? Richard Sibbes answered much as Philip Melanchthon had in 1521: "The affections" are "the feet of the soul, whereby we walk with, and before God."[1] The affections, once ordered by faith, are the basis for a person's communion with God. Sin, on the other hand, reveals a soul's disaffection:

> God hath made the soul for a communion with himself, which communion is especially placed in the affections which are the springs of all spiritual worship. The affections are well ordered, when we are fit to have communion with God, to love, joy, trust, to delight in him above all things. The affections are the inward movings of the soul, which then move best when they move us to God, not from him.[2]

Here Sibbes also assumes a disease-and-cure symmetry between sin and grace: individuals move either "to God" by grace or "from him" in sin. The key to this symmetry for Sibbes is heart-based—"the affections which are the springs of all spiritual worship".

This affective portrayal of spirituality helped to explain sin for Sibbes. But it was not an explanation all Puritans would share. The problem-solution symmetry of Puritan nomists was, instead, volition-based. They held the will to be a self-moved faculty of the soul that finally makes every decision. Given this primacy of the will Adam's sin was a volitional event: it was his free-will decision to break God's law by eating the forbidden fruit. Given the symmetry of sin and salvation this act of law breaking is logically resolved only by renewed law keeping. And in human history only Christ met this legal demand by his full obedience to the law. So he alone has a legal righteousness that allows him to offer his own righteousness to others in the transaction of salvation.

To be saved, then, all others have one necessary choice to make: believe in Christ. Salvation on this basis is both law-based and Christ-focused: Jesus is the divine-human law-keeper who provides his righteousness by forensic imputation to the elect once they, by God's grace, supply their personal act of faith.

This is only a snapshot of the issues of sin and salvation in Sibbes' era. To probe his view and the alternative view of his moralist friends a larger question comes into view: what is evil? Is evil, as the ground of sin, best described as a negative: the absence of goodness? Or is it a positive reality: a malignancy that actively opposes goodness? This pairing emerged in Augustine's debate with Pelagius. It also distinguished Perkins from Sibbes. Another related question also separated Sibbes from Perkins: does God accomplish an ultimate good by allowing evil? Perkins offered one answer and Sibbes another.

Adam's Sin: Privative or Positive?

Was Adam's fall caused by the withdrawal of God's grace? Or was it an inexplicable rebellion despite the presence of divine grace? The question emerged during Augustine's controversy with the Pelagians. The two options: treating evil as a privation of goodness in a person; or treating evil as an active presence in a soul were both developed by Augustine but in time he came to focus on evil as a positive reality and, with that, sin as a self-love that displaces and denies a proper love of God.[3]

Augustine's definitions of sin

Sin as a privation of grace. Augustine first used a negative or privative doctrine of evil—*privatio*—in his rejection of Manichean dualism: a notion that reality is divided into an eternal good-versus-evil polarity. He argued against this, that God's goodness and his role as absolute creator preclude any true existence of evil.[4] Evil, as he wrote in *De Libero Arbitrio*, is only a distortion—a privation or absence of God's goodness.

> When all good is completely taken away, there will remain not even a trace—absolutely nothing. All good is from God; therefore no kind of thing exists which is not from God. Hence that movement of turning away, which we agree to be sin, is a defective movement, and a defect comes from nothing. Notice, then, what is its source and be sure it does not come from God. Yet, since the defect lies in the will, it is under our control.

> If you fear it, you must simply not desire it; if you do not desire it, it will not occur. . . . But, though man fell through his own will, he cannot rise through his own will . . . .[5]

This was the first distinct exposition of *privatio.* It avoided making God the author of evil and dismissed an eternal duality of good-and-evil. Additionally it set up a free-will solution to evil by conceding relative autonomy to humans. Augustine's use of concrete language in viewing the problem led him to visualize, in G. R. Evans' summary, an "evil mass in some way more confined or limited than the good. This evil mass is not God's creation. Indeed, at the point where he confronts evil, God is finite, although he is infinite in every other respect."[6] In his later and revised view, by contrast, he would have affirmed G. C. Berkouwer's position that, "Sin is not 'material' but is parasitic on creaturely reality" and a "deformation" of God's good creation.[7]

Augustine's shift from his early doctrine came with his realization that sin must exist as a positive reality: as an active disposition to abandon God through self-love (*amor sui, cupiditas*).[8] The clarification was a response to Pelagius' use of *privatio* to his own ends. Evans summarizes the issue:

> As it proved, he had put the Manichees behind him only to move to a position which the Pelagians could claim to be close to their own, because in order to clear God of blame, he insisted that the free will of men can return to the good. He has no need of divine assistance. Grace need not come into the picture. Here

lay the source of Augustine's embarrassment in later years. The Pelagians were able to point to the *De Libero Arbitrio* as a step on Augustine's part in their direction.[9]

A point must be made here about the problem sin presents in any Christian effort to explain it. Sin in Adam's fall first occurred in an act of disobedience. In denying dualism and affirming God's goodness Augustine initially held the free-will solution to be the least problematic option for explaining sin. It arose through the moral freedom God allowed in his premier beings in order for true moral agency to exist. Yet this failed to relieve certain logical and moral dilemmas: even if the first sin was birthed spontaneously in Satan, God, as the sovereign ruler of creation and the maker of Satan and Adam, would bear responsibility for the flaw in nature that precipitated that sin.

Pelagian and semi-Pelagian theologies were both aligned with Augustine's early *privatio* theology. In their view, God is best protected from the charge of creating sin by viewing grace as an intermediary quality. It is absent in sin and present in righteousness. Gluttony or adultery, for instance, are un-graced activities: each is displaced from its creation purpose. Pelagius, with this approach, defined grace as God's goodness offered in his law. Since the soul is able to choose or refuse that goodness a person becomes his or her own sustainer of grace.

For Perkins, as will be seen, grace was more hypostatized: an infused energy given the will that enables the soul to make righteous choices. In either example the men defined grace as separate from God himself, thus making it a gift rather than God's Spirit-based presence in the soul as Augustine came to believe. Privative theory also established the privation of grace—*privatio gratiæ*—as the ground for all sins after the fall. Humans are victims of Adam's sin, crippled by a lack of grace despite any desire they might have to be righteous.

Positive sin. When Pelagius cited Augustine's *De Libero Arbitrio* in support of his own position Augustine responded by writing *De Natura et Gratia*. Two important aspects of Augustine's revised perception of sin were introduced in this work. First, he set out his case in favor of participation in Christ's life by the Spirit; and, second, he restated the cooperation of nature and grace in affective rather than volitional terms. This was God's compatibilistic solution to sin.[10]

The doctrine of real participation in Christ's life was a necessary obverse in his solution to the Pelagian claim that nature and sin were qualitatively unrelated. That is, as Pelagius argued from Augustine's early doctrine of *privatio*, sin does not have any substance: it is merely a lack of goodness. Therefore at birth every human is free from any taint of sinfulness. This in effect overturned Augustine's certainty that the Bible teaches that every person is at first dead in Adam's original sin.

This was a dawning moment for Augustine. The Pelagian thesis—and Augustine's own early view of grace—undermined original sin. Augustine then returned to the biblical claim that before faith all humanity is dead in its sins. This in turn led him to conclude that nature and grace are necessarily engaged. Grace, Augustine insisted, is not "in opposition to nature" but is that which "liberates and controls nature".[11]

The question he was forced to answer, however, is how grace "liberates and controls" nature in light of his earlier statements that the will is free and sin is privative rather than positive. Thus, in an effort to clarify—if not to revise—the implications of *privatio*, he adopted an argument that affirmed sin as present within nature as corruption, without denying his earlier point that sin is not to be attributed to God.[12] He did this by affirming God's substance in terms of relations. Pelagius had argued that since sin is merely a set of unrighteous choices, without a substance, then nature, which is substantial, does not contain sin. This, of course, precluded the doctrine of original sin. Augustine answered by explaining the link between sin and human nature by an analogy: if bodily health is broken when starved of food so the loss of God, the very ground of all substance, corrupts the human soul.

> In the same way sin is not a substance; but God is a substance, yea the height of substance and only true sustenance of the reasonable creature. The consequence of departing from Him by disobedience, and of inability through infirmity, to receive what one ought really to rejoice in, you hear from the Psalmist, when he says: "My heart is smitten and withered like grass, since I have forgotten to eat my bread."[13]

The human condition, then, is dead without the "substance" of God to sustain its life. The free will is able to depart from God, but, in doing so, the sinner dies toward God as does his or her ability to return to God: "He has need of a vivifier because he is dead."[14] The sickness-and-cure symmetry of sin and salvation thus required a restoration by the substance of God's life. This, in turn, established a basis for a doctrine of participation in God's life. Augustine's solution was twofold, juridical *and* ontological: God justifies the ungodly *and* offers divine assistance to enable the person to avoid further sin.[15] This divine assistance requires God's presence, a matter reinforced by Augustine's caveat that his solution is not a deification of nature.[16] Yet the creature, while incommensurate to the creator, may be united with him. The Spirit—"poured out" in the believer's life to save and heal—achieves this.

Augustine repeatedly used this pouring imagery from Romans 5:5 to make his point and to establish the framework for an affective solution to sin: "For the love of God has been poured out in our hearts through the Holy Spirit who was given to us."[17] Augustine's exposition of these points often employed the language of divine enablement and human cooperation. This fostered claims that he treated salvation and sanctification as an exercise of human cooperation with God; and if framed by Aristotle's anthropology that conclusion would have merit.

But Augustine's regular references to Romans 5:5 in elevating divine initiative dispels notions that he believed in a libertarian free will. He was, rather, a compatibilist: holding that an elect person is led by God's love to walk freely in God's ways. That is, God's continuing love through the Spirit draws believers to live in response to God. Augustine's conclusion to the treatise serves as a crescendo in making that point:

> "A new commandment," says Christ, "I give unto you: that you love one another." And, "For he that loves his neighbor has fulfilled the Law." And again, "Love is the fullness of the law." In the same sense is this statement also: "If they walk in good paths, they will indeed find the ways of righteousness easy." . . . The

paths are hard for fear, easy for love. Thus the beginning of love is the beginning of righteousness; progress in love is progress in righteousness; great love is great righteousness; perfect love is perfect righteousness . . . . Yet wherever and whenever it becomes complete, in such a way that nothing can be added to it, it is certainly not "poured forth in our hearts" by the powers of nature or the will that are within us, but "by the Holy Spirit who is given to us", who both helps our weakness and cooperates with our strength. For this is the very "grace of God by Jesus Christ our Lord," to whom, with the Father and the Holy Spirit belong eternity and goodness, for ever and ever. Amen.[18]

Definition of grace. Augustine's debate with Pelagius led him to portray Adam's sin as a departure from grace defined as God's bond of relationship, rather than a privation of grace with grace viewed as a feature of the creation. The loss of the "substance" of God is a loss in spiritual terms. Grace is the Spirit whose love brings inward transformation in the believer's heart. By this definition, Augustine displayed his relational model of grace—the expression of God's personal kindness—rather than as an intermediary quality.

Grace, then, is not embedded in nature; instead nature displays grace, just as any gift displays the graciousness of the giver. Similarly nature is good as it operates according to God's good purposes; it is a virtue of relationship rather than quality inherent to nature. Thus, in Augustine's affirmation of an affectionate God he saw that God meant for humanity to share in the divine communion with this communion offered as a gift—and as such it is not imposed. In the Genesis account of creation all of nature was declared good; and only those beings able to commune with God in love—the angels and Adam—were free *not* to fulfill God's good purpose. Augustine, then, by defining grace as God's kindness also portrayed sin as Adam's departure from God's love despite the presence of such grace.

Aquinas on privative sin

The first major proponent of privative sin in the medieval period is Anselm whose pioneering work was followed and developed by Aquinas.[19] In a matter crucial to the development of the nomist tradition, Anselm based his doctrine on Augustine's early doctrine of *privatio* rather than his post-Pelagian view. The implication picked up by Pelagius—that salvation requires a free act of the volition in choosing God—was assimilated roughly a century later by Aquinas.

Aquinas, as a student of Augustine, was apparently alert to Augustine's shift on the issue of *privatio*: he attributed *privatio* to Anselm and a positive definition (sin as *habitus*) to Augustine. Aquinas, in fact, sought to synthesize the views of Augustine and Anselm through an analogy much like Augustine's lost-food solution: "As in a bodily illness there is privation, in that the balance of health is upset, yet also something positive, the disturbed bodily humours, so also in original sin there is privation [*privatione*], the lack of original justice, yet along with this there are the disturbed powers of the soul."[20] In this explanation, however, he failed to adopt Augustine's solution that grace is God's presence in the elect by the Spirit. This followed Aquinas's premise that human nature and divine being are wholly incommensurate—a topic taken up in the next chapter.

Significantly, Aquinas believed that Adam's original state of righteousness was not something natural to his humanity but a gift of supernatural grace (*donum gratiæ*):

> Original righteousness [*justitia originalis*] was a definite gift of grace [*donum gratiæ*] divinely bestowed upon all human nature in the first parent, which, indeed, the first parent lost in the first sin. Hence even as that original righteousness would have been transmitted along with human nature to the offspring of the first parents, so the opposite disorder is in fact transmitted."[21]

Thus, subsequent sin in humanity resulted from an incapacity, the loss of Adam's original righteousness that the *donum gratiæ* had maintained. Adam had squandered humanity's golden opportunity by failing to guard his original righteousness.

Aquinas, in these discussions, located *privatio* within nature, viewing sin as the loss of a created quality. The symmetrical cure for sin, with sin defined as a *privatio gratiæ*, is a resupply of grace. To this end, Aquinas held that grace has dual aspects, one created and the other uncreated.[22] This doublet allowed him to resolve the tension between original sin and actual sin. When Adam fell he lost the *created* grace of original righteousness. The implicit ground for his fall was an absence of *uncreated* grace that was needed because of his human mutability.

This two-stage arrangement assumed that morality is defined by the use of a free will to choose either good or evil. Thus it was God's purpose to generate a vulnerability in Adam in order to test and affirm his morality. His failure was then transmitted to his progeny by the absence of original righteousness. *Privatio*, in this arrangement, was twofold: a lack of uncreated grace that led to, but did not compel, Adam's fall; and a subsequent lack of created grace after the fall due to Adam's loss of original righteousness. Adam was therefore culpable because of his own initiative in the fall. After the fall Adam's progeny now lack the grace, both created and uncreated, necessary for righteousness. We are therefore helpless and God's twin resources of grace are needed for salvation.

Among the Puritans these were points of conversation. Perkins adopted the Thomistic solution with its reliance on a duality of grace. He believed it offered the most coherent solution to the problem of sin when sin is defined as *privatio.* Sibbes, however, came to see sin as self-love even though he first held Perkins' view. And with that he also took up Augustine's view of grace as God's relational bond to the elect.

Perkins' and Sibbes' Doctrines of Sin

Perkins' doctrine of sin

In the *Golden Chain* Perkins explained that "The fall is a revolting of the reasonable creature from obedience", thus describing it in positive rather than privative terms, but he immediately clarified the matter: "Sin is the corruption, or rather deprivation of the first integrity."

> Here a doubt may be moved, whether sin be a thing existing or not. The answer is this: of things which are, some are positive, others privative. Things positive are all substances together with those their properties, powers, inclinations and affections which the Lord hath created and imprinted in their natures. The thing is called privative, which grants or presupposes the absence of some such thing as ought to be in a thing. Such a thing is sin, which properly and of itself is not anything created and existing, but rather the absence of that good which ought to be in the creature: and though it be inherent in things positive as a privation, yet it is always to be distinguished from them.[23]

Thus, even when Perkins spoke of sin in positive terms it was to be understood as an aspect of creation evacuated of its goodness. He also subdivided sin into two categories of the human condition: "a defect, or impotence, and disorder."[24]

In the symmetry of sin and grace, his portrayal of sin as "impotence" carried with it a crucial implication. Sin is thus analogous to the lame man who longs to walk. The discrimination of the elect and the non-elect could therefore be formed on the basis of a victim's desire for, and use of, enabling grace in order to be righteous—a view held by Baro and Jacob Arminius in their belief that election is based on God foreseeing those who would desire and apply grace if it were available to them. Calvin rejected this Thomistic logic in favor of Augustine's theology. It made humans to be helpless victims of sin rather than antagonists toward God.

Perkins followed the lead of continental theologians in accepting the Thomistic model of sin. He was familiar, for instance, with the works of Zacharias Ursinus; he included, for instance, a "Briefe Discourse" by Ursinus in his own *Works*. Ursinus affirmed sin as *privatio* in his *Commentary on the Heidelberg Catechism*, and also identified its medieval source: "the common definition of original sin, which is generally attributed to Anselm, [is that] 'Original sin is a want of original righteousness which ought to be in us.'"[25]

Perkins' understanding of original sin is evident in his presentation of the origin of evil in "men and angels".[26] They shared an original capacity for good that "God hath ingrafted in the nature of his creature". The fall led to the loss of this capacity because, in their mutability, his creatures failed God's test: "[I]n this trial, God doth not assist them with new grace to stand but for just causes forsaketh them. Lastly, after God hath forsaken them and left them to themselves, they fall quite from God". Implicit in this arrangement is Aquinas' assumption that grace is both created and uncreated. The withholding of "new grace" left the creatures to rely on their prior capacity of created grace by itself, which although perfect, was still an aspect of nature. Because mutability is inherent in a creature, Adam's will eventually changed its course in the face of temptation. Thus his fall was inevitable but not necessary.

Perkins' privative definition of sin displayed Adam's role in the fall in a manner suitable to his Federalism by setting up a reciprocity between grace and faith. It also helps to account for the logic of *habitus gratiæ*, developed in the next chapter, in both Aquinas and Perkins: the reasonable solution to the loss of the *donum gratiæ* in Adam would be a supernaturally resupplied *donum gratiæ* in Christ. Created grace, for both

Aquinas and Perkins, offered a device that gives nature a moral task. Both men held that Christ's atoning work is the source of saving merit, but their common views invited a notion of concomitant merit. Perkins, in line with the Protestant doctrine of immediate justification, rejected this in principle. Nevertheless, the obligation to live up to the moral standard lost in Adam is still present even if the duty is not rewarded with saving merit. With the grace of enablement the elect are resupplied with the same capacity Adam lost, and are now adequate to meet the duty of God's moral law.[27] This, however, became a sharp edged issue whenever the practical syllogism was explained: the new enablement in the elect would presumably demonstrate itself through law-keeping which, in turn, assured a person of their election. But, as John Cotton complained, "we must not speak of good works as causes or ways of our first assurance" lest faith come to rest in human actions rather than God's work.[28]

Strengthening the mind and will (both depleted as a result of privation and distracted by wayward affections) became the primary concern for restorative ministry under Perkins' model: with the new capacities of grace saints were to seek a proper knowledge of God and, with a new ability to will the good once known, to keep the moral law. The paradigm for sanctification in Perkins' system thus emphasized catechism and casuistry; education and obedience. Thus he pioneered the Protestant use of casuistry. His two works, as noted already, were *A Discourse of Conscience* and *The Whole Treatise of Cases of Conscience*. They set out directions for godly living. For most Protestants this approach was too closely tied to the Roman Catholic theology of merit. Perkins, however, saw real benefits in it: the clearer the application of law to life, the easier the obedience.

He also took steps in this direction through his catechetical study, *The Foundation of Christian Religion Gathered into Six Principles,* in which he presented humanity's responsibility for sin and the lifelong task of "dying to sin". He explained that God prepares eventual believers by "bruising them" with guilt over moral failures before salvation, and then equips them to keep his laws after conversion.[29] This law keeping was properly directed through the use of casuistic manuals and all the other means of grace.

What role did the affections have in Perkins' theology? More will be said about it in a later chapter. For now it enough to say that he affirmed the affections as one of the triad of faculties in the soul. But he and the nomists were consistent in making the mind and will dominant rather than the affections just as they gave primacy to God's intellect and will while denying divine affections

The nomists, in fact, identified the affections as a cause of sin but not as its cure. "[S]in", Perkins wrote, "is either inward or outward. Inward is of the mind, will and affections."[30] The mind and will, in tandem, are the locus of conversion, while affections oppose righteousness: "That which the affections receive [from the fall] is a disorder by which they therefore are not well affected, because they eschew that which is good and pursue that which is evil."[31] Similarly, Paul Bayne, in describing obstacles to righteousness, commented, "The second kind of general lets are the unmortified affections wherewith believers are oppressed."[32] The affections were therefore to be ruled by newly enabled wills.[33]

Perkins' doctrine of sin, then, established his doctrine of grace. Created grace is to be used to seek after greater resources of uncreated grace. Thus human initiative, newly enabled from its privative past, emerges as the crux of salvation and holiness.

Sibbes' doctrine of sin

The affective tradition. Leaders of the affective tradition were consistent in defining both original and actual sin in positive terms. That is, sin is concupiscence, a distorted self-love; it is also a selfish usurpation of God's prerogatives.[34] The affiliation of this position with the affective tradition was introduced in chapter two: the linkage of affections to sin reflects the symmetry of sin as both caused and cured by love. A love for God was displaced in Adam by his self-love; it is overcome in the elect by God's gracious self-disclosure that elicits a response of love, namely, faith. Thus, it presses beyond the question of free choices and addresses, more fundamentally, the motivation of every choice. Two implications emerge: 1) sin is a pervasive issue because every action is motivated either by a devotion to God, or by indifference, if not hostility; and 2) the enslavement of sin is intrinsic, an extension of self-love.

Sibbes on privatio. Sibbes, on one occasion, affirmed *privatio* as it related to the fall of the angels: "The angels were subject to fall as well as the devils, for every created thing is changeable, and so the angels; only God suspendeth that possibility of sin, and establisheth them in grace, but he withdrew his support from the devils and suffered them to fall."[35] As Sibbes explained the subsequent transmission of evil to Adam, privation was no longer in view; human sin was thus positive, a rebellion rooted in concupiscence. Nevertheless, the origin of sin in the serpent was *privatio.*

On another occasion Sibbes held that the fall is explained because Adam "had not the Spirit to uphold him, nor had he the promise of it to keep him that he should not fall. Therefore the covenant of works was frustrate."[36] Sibbes, by this argument, set up the superiority of the New Testament over the Old, by holding (elsewhere) that the Spirit is given only after Christ's resurrection. His intention was not to suggest that Adam's original righteousness consisted in the Spirit who was then withdrawn; rather, that the coming of the promised Spirit would solve the problem of sin. Implicit in this, of course, was Sibbes' agreement with Perkins that sin came because human nature by itself is unable to resist temptation.

But at some point Sibbes came to reject the key assumption of *privatio* altogether—whether in angels or in Adam. This becomes apparent in his response to the claim that Adam's original righteousness was a supernatural capacity—the *donum gratiæ* of the Thomistic system—rather than a righteousness intrinsic to Adam's human nature. Such an approach, he argued, implies an "inward rebellion" in Adam's nature before his fall. This underlying disposition was only "curbed in by the bridle of original righteousness, which they would have accessory and supernatural".[37] Thus, if the withdrawal of the supernatural gift that sustained Adam's righteousness somehow unleashed sin within Adam's natural capacities, God, the creator of those capacities, must be liable for the inherent sin. This solution is unacceptable since it made Adam's first sin and humanity's subsequent concupiscence "less odious and more excusable in us."[38]

Sibbes' discussion in *Soul's Conflict* lacks a direct argument but certain issues may be inferred. He apparently came to examine a premise in the *privatio* scheme that nature requires a measure of independence from God in order for the will to be free. If *privatio* is a withdrawal of grace so that Adam was forced to resort to an inferior free will—now based on innate or natural goodness—the scheme still fails to account for a choice of evil rather than good because the *direction* of the will is not determined by the *strength* of the will. There must be something in nature that accounts for the redirection of Adam's will once it was weakened. Even if the object of the first *privatio* was Satan rather than Adam, the question still pertains.

Sibbes, it seems, recognized that there must be an ultimate source for the actual sin that *privatio* unleashed. If sin—that grace-deprived nature is said to produce—makes victims of humans then God, as creator, is implicitly at fault and his creatures are "less odious". If this is Sibbes' reasoning it bears resemblance to a similar insight by Aquinas who accepted an argument that rational deliberations in a free will are by themselves liable to the fallacy of infinite regress. That is, the first act of rational deliberation requires an external stimulus. It seems likely that it was on this basis that he abandoned his early semi-Pelagianism.[39]

Sibbes' doctrine of positive sin. The key problem for both Adam and his progeny, in Sibbes' view, is jealous ambition. In one of Sibbes longer discussions of sin he began with a common refrain: "Man's nature doth affect a kind of divinity; he would be a god to himself".[40] God's purposes in salvation, as Sibbes saw it, are to offer a cure appropriate to the disease: "but God will teach him that he is not a God, but a dependent creature." Sin as self-deification grew through human exercises of self-confident rationality: "He affects a divinity. Thus he will set upon things in confidence of his own wisdom, without prayer, and thinks to work things with the strength of his own parts, to compass things with his own wit to bring things to a good issue. O no! it will not be so." Thus, his basic premise about sin was radically different from Perkins' view, namely that any synergistic elevation of nature runs afoul of God's intention to teach individuals that in each moment of life he or she is "but a dependent creature." The solution to sin for Sibbes is overt and continuous dependence on the Spirit.

Sibbes, then, saw Adam's sin as usurpation—trying to be like God—because of self-love; and salvation is, symmetrically, achieved by a restored love for God: "Certain it is, whatsoever we esteem, or affect most, that, whatsoever it be in itself, yet we make it our god—*Amor tuus, Deus Tuus.*"[41] Thus, he portrayed sin in relational rather than behavioral terms: it is a "leaving of God".[42] Why should one leave God? After discarding a privative solution he offered no answer other than to place the responsibility for original sin at Adam's feet and for "actual sins" at the feet of individuals. It is "our own thraldom" in evil desires that causes "this spiritual captivity under sin."[43]

The solution is found in "his glory which we behold in the face of Christ".[44] If sin was a loss of desire for God, salvation is a return to God by a restored desire for him. The original "leaving" found in Adam was described (although not explained) as his succumbing to the temptation to "*become like God*", thus infecting subsequent humanity with a passion to "*do things in our own strength and by our own light*, as if we were gods to ourselves. Man naturally affects a kind of divinity."[45] It is this disposition to displace God by self, Sibbes believed, that causes a "veil of unbelief" to descend which, in turn supports the Pandoric unleashing of particular sins. Sibbes recognized an immoral synergism in sin: the attitude of autonomy in self-deifying human hearts and the particular choices of disobedience are mutually reinforcing. But there is no point, he believed, in addressing particular sins if the underlying problem is not solved first by seeing God "with open face" so as to change the understanding.

> There must be a double veil taken away before we can behold the glory of God: the veil of obscurity, and the veil of slavery; the veil of ignorance and infidelity within, and the veil of the things themselves. These two veils are both taken away before we can with open face behold the glory of the Lord.[46]

Sin within, then, has a mirror relationship to salvation: the "veil of slavery . . . of ignorance and infidelity", is to be "taken away by the Spirit illuminating our understandings, and giving us a spirit of faith."[47]

Sibbes, in holding the positive view of sin, recognized that it forces a continuing humility upon nature through its requirement of direct and continuous dependency. It was, then, by following a path different than that taken by Aquinas, Perkins, or the nomists in their reliance on the will, that Sibbes described the ministry of the Spirit in spiritual life. If love is an affection then the Spirit works through the affections even more than through the other two faculties. Furthermore if the pursuit of virtue is the central concern of faith, even by means of *habitus*, it can also disguise the core evil of positive sin: self-confident autonomy.

The failure of the nomist model to represent conversion as primarily relational—a transformation of the soul's desires stirred by the supernatural unveiling of God's loveliness—was Sibbes' main complaint against it:

> When we are drawn therefore to duties . . . with foreign motives, for fear, or out of custom, with extrinsecal motives, and not from a new nature, this is not from the Spirit. This performance is not from the true liberty of the Spirit. For the liberty of the Spirit is, when actions come off naturally without force of fear or hope, or any extrinsecal motive. A child needs not extrinsecal motives to please his father. When he knows he is the child of a loving father, it is natural.[48]

Sin, then, is a hatred of God that displays itself in lawlessness; but it is not identical to law-breaking. Instead it is a positive antipathy toward God, even when hidden in the moderating guise of religious settings that rely on the extrinsic satisfactions of duty. Salvation—sin's cure—is God's direct and effective self-revelation that opens the eyes of the elect to see him as a loving father who invites them into the fellowship of the Godhead as Christ anticipated in his prayer of John 17. It is by this vision that the believer's desires are changed. This differed in a fundamental way from Perkins' model.

Humphrey Mills, a contemporary layman, shared how he felt a dramatic release from his nomist heritage when he heard Sibbes preach.

> I was for three years together wounded for sins, and under a sense of my corruptions, which were many; and I followed sermons, pursuing the means, and was constant in duties and doing; looking for Heaven that way. And then I was so precise for outward formalities, that I censured all to be reprobates, that wore their hair anything long, and not short above their ears; or that wore great ruffs, and gorgets, or fashions, and follies. But yet I was distracted in my mind, wounded in conscience, and wept often and bitterly, and prayed earnestly, but yet had no comfort, till I heard that sweet saint . . . Doctor Sibbs, by whose means and ministry I was brought to peace and joy in my spirit. His sweet soul-melting Gospel-sermons won my heart and refreshed me much, for by him I saw and had much of God and was confident in Christ, and could overlook the world . . . . my heart held firm and resolved and my desires all heaven-ward.[49]

It was just such a confidence in Christ that Sibbes promoted as the purpose of grace. God's plan in resolving sin is not simply restorative but an exercise of advancement for humanity by union with Christ.

Sin and Regeneration: Adam Restored or Divinity in Christ?

Sibbes and the nomists, together, believed that Christ's death and resurrection ended the domination of Adamic sin in the elect—although short of glory some corruption always lingers. Through redemption, all agreed, believers gain new life in Christ the "second Adam" and by that life a new disposition towards God emerges. The Puritans differed, however, in explaining what union with the second Adam means beyond freedom from the guilt and domination of sin; or, in slightly different terms, what Christ's incarnation continues to accomplish beyond conversion.

Was Christ sent by God in a restorative effort, to bring the elect back to the intimacy experienced by Adam before the fall, or was Christ sent to take man *beyond* Adam's experience into an experience of the son's own Trinitarian intimacy?[50] The motivation and functions of sanctification differ markedly, depending on the perceived goal.

Perkins and the Nomists: Restoring Adam's Image

The nomists represented the restorative model. In holding it, they characterized Adam's role in sustaining fellowship with God to be the exercise of obedience or law-keeping. This was only a temporary arrangement—a probationary period—after which a capacity for ongoing sinlessness would be bestowed.[51] Restoration to fellowship was, therefore, measured by the quality of law-keeping evident in the sanctification of a given believer.[52] This reliance on the law became their defining theological trait.

Paul Bayne, for instance, juxtaposed Christ's work of justification and continued law-keeping as coordinate issues: "[God's] justice is satisfied by suffering the punishment due to sin, and by the present keeping of the law."[53] The incarnation, including Christ's passion, was interpreted as God's design to repair the damaged *imago dei* by providing a juridical solution to Adam's violation, and by providing a second chance to acquire the behaviors of the law that display holiness.

"The fall", Perkins explained with an analogy, "is whereby the soldier through infirmity fainteth, being subdued by the power of the enemy. To this appertaineth the spiritual remedy . . . to restore him which is fallen, to his former estate."[54] Christ's work of justification satisfied any shortcomings, just as his gifts of grace enable the human will to obey God's moral law in this new righteousness.

The doctrine of sanctification, in this view, is a synthesis of these two features. It restores the relationship of Eden in which God is the loving law-giver and the elect are devoted law-keepers. Christ's work now assures moral success by forever canceling any debt for sin and by eternally buttressing the restored human nature by the Spirit's enabling grace. Perkins held, then, that biblical commandments are offered in two forms: legal and evangelical.

The two are discriminated not by a distinct moral hierarchy—as, for instance, in Catholic distinctions of mortal and venial sin—but by their accessibility in practice. Commands "show us our disease, but give us not remedy; and the perfect doing of them according to the intent of the lawgiver, by reason of man's weakness and through man's default, is impossible in this world. As for evangelical commandments, they have this privilege, that they may and can be performed according to the intent of the lawgiver in this life."[55]

In this arrangement Perkins displayed the modified synergism of his Federalism. By assuming the Thomist duality of grace, the human will is restored through created grace—being "in Christ"—to a mitigated capacity for the moral task of doing one's duty on the strength of uncreated grace acquired through the means of grace (sermons, sacraments, Bible reading, etc.). This provided assurance of salvation to all who profess faith and display the moral effort that indicates a Spirit-enabled will at work.

> Because with the commandment is joined the inward operation of the Spirit in the elect, to enable them to effect the duty commanded; and the will of God is not to require absolute perfection at our hands in the Gospel as in the Law, but rather to qualify the rigour of the law by the satisfaction of a mediator in our stead. And of us (we being in Christ) to accept the upright will and endeavour for the deed; as the will to repent, and the will to believe, for repentance and true faith indeed. Now then, if things required in the Gospel be both ordinary and possible, then for a man to have an unfallible certainty of his own salvation is both ordinary and possible.[56]

The goal of salvation, then, is to achieve as much "endeavour for the deed" as possible as part of the ultimate goal of creation as presented in the *Golden Chaine* and later affirmed as the "chief end of man" in the catechisms of Westminster: God's glory.

Sibbes: Surpassing Adam's Image

The alternative view, offered by Sibbes, affirmed the juridical aspect of the incarnation but went well beyond it. God, while addressing the guilt of sin, *also* altered his relationship with redeemed humanity. This was done through union with Christ that elevates those "in him" into a true participation in divinity, thus eclipsing the merely natural capacities of the first Adam. Redemption was accomplished by Christ's death for the elect by satisfying God's wrath against sin: "Now Christ satisfying divine justice redeems us. He buys us again. . . . for mercy must have justice satisfied; the attributes of God must not fight one against another. Christ, therefore, is Lord of us, because by death he gave full content to divine justice."[57] It was, then, a juridical transaction meant to confront the curse of sin; but it was also the means to a greater end: "He had a mind to marry us, but he could not till he had rescued us."[58]

Thus, sanctification, the second aspect of salvation, displays God's underlying purpose for offering the justification, namely, marital communion. As will be seen in chapter four, mystical marriage achieved an indefinable but real union with Christ by which his nature is imparted to the spouse. Through this shared nature the Spirit draws the spouse toward perfection, a process only completed in the eschaton. In a reversal of Augustine's favorite metaphor for original sin (Adam's progeny were seen to be a single corrupted "mass"), Sibbes described his understanding of the incarnation with the same metaphor, and applied it to the question of what defined a true Christian:

> Briefly, a man may know that he is in Christ, if he find the Spirit of Christ in him; for the same Spirit when Christ took our nature, that sanctified that blessed mass whereof he was made, when there was a union between him and the second person, the same Spirit sanctifies our souls and bodies. There is one Spirit in the head and in the members. Therefore if we find the Spirit of Christ in us, we are in Christ and he in us.[59]

It is this elevation into a shared nature with God himself, through the Spirit, that ensures eternal righteousness in the elect: in juridical terms on earth, actual terms in glory, and in a progression from one to the other following conversion. It is a process generated by growing love, accomplished by the Christian's new vision of the Father as seen through his son's eyes. The proof-text—Sibbes' favorite verse on matters of sanctification—was 2 Corinthians 3:18.

> The very beholding of Christ is a transforming sight. The Spirit makes us new creatures, and stirs us up to behold this servant, it is a transforming beholding. If we look upon him with the eye of faith, it will make us like Christ; for the gospel is a mirror . . . that when we . . . see ourselves interested in it, we are changed from glory to glory, 2 Cor 3:18. A man cannot look upon the love of God and of Christ in the gospel, but it will

change him to be like God and Christ. For how can we see Christ, and God in Christ, but we shall see how God hates sin, and this will transform us to hate it as God doth, who hated it so that it could not be expiated but with the blood of Christ, God-man.[60]

The differences between Sibbes' and Perkins' approaches were twofold: first, as noted already, Perkins rejected any form of direct union between God and fallen humanity, while Sibbes viewed the entire gospel in light of such a participatory union. Second, Sibbes called for all the attention of spirituality to be invested in looking "upon the love of God" in Christ, as against Perkins' greater confidence in the practical syllogism of using behavioral change to give evidence of salvation.

The question of human vulnerability to sin helps to account for these differences. In Sibbes' view if Adam's sinless will failed to protect him in Eden it seemed implausible that the power of the will would be the solution to sin through the second Adam. Sin is not active through a weakness of the will. Rather it is the misguided yet still robust will that is ruled by its evil desires. Thus, as noted above, Sibbes' infralapsarian theology was based on his confidence that God's intention in Adam's fall was to create a superior and enduring arrangement for the elect through participation in the divine nature with God's holy desires now in control. It allowed a partnership in which Christ rules through the new desires of the elect.

Herein consists the main happiness of a Christian, that whether he lives or dies he is not his own, but he is his, that can dispose of him better than ever he could of himself; for if we had the disposing of ourselves, as Adam had, what should become of [us]? What became of Adam when he was master of himself? He lost himself and all. The 'second Adam' hath bought us with his blood and life, to rule us for ever. Will he then suffer us to be disposed of by ourselves? No. Whether 'we live or die, we are his,' if we yield ourselves sweetly to his government, in life and death.[61]

The differing goal of salvation, and the point of God's "government", becomes clear once Sibbes' understanding of spiritual motivation is clarified. Sibbes saw the first effect of union to be God's work of transforming desires. It is intrinsic through a shared life in Christ as accomplished by mystical marriage. It was a theme he returned to as a necessary juxtaposition to any discussions of juridical benefits.

Obj. Oh but will a poor soul say, Christ indeed is Lord of the living and of the dead, but I find a great deal of corruption in me, &c., and I am a sinner.

Ans. Why, he is Lord over thee. He hath a sweet lordship over thee, as well as a commanding lordship. He is not only a king, but a husband, as it is Eph. v. 26, 27, "He gave himself to purge his church," and to make his church fit by little and little. Thou hast sin and corruption, but thou hast a merciful husband that will bear with the weaker vessel. . . . Christ purgeth and cleanseth his church; he doth not cast it away.[62]

The mutual love of this marital partnership was, for Sibbes, the "grand relation" against which "all other relations among men are but shadows" and through which Christians "must be directed by his will, not their own." It is in *this* context, of living "to God" that Sibbes affirmed the importance of God's glory: "we must aim *at the glory of Christ in all things*, and not at our own credit." As the first section of this chapter underscored, the affections are the pivotal in making such a determination: self-glory conflicts with God's glory. It is not the outward workings of religious activity that glorifies God, but the intention; or more accurately, the affection that directs them. The corruption of Adamic sin is centered in misdirected love:

> Naturally proud man is led with a spirit of self-love; and he seeks himself in all things, even in his religion. . . . So long as God's will is not contrary to his, he will do God service; but if it cross his will once, then he will give God leave to seek him a servant. Thus man makes himself an idol; he sets up himself in the room of God; he doth all things, as from himself, so for himself; nor indeed can he do otherwise, till he put off himself wholly, and deny himself—a man cannot go beyond himself but by grace, that raiseth a man above himself.[63]

Sibbes thus believed that attempts by people to succeed in religious activities apart from a motivation of love are already unacceptable because by their very nature they are done for personal glory: the love of God is not in view. His point was to deny that any actions achieve righteousness or glorify God if the actor is not moved by love.

> The end hath a main influence into all actions . . . So it differenceth between natural men and Christians; they differ in their aims, not in their actions. Both do the same thing. One doth it for base ends of his own; keeps within the circle of those ends. The other having a light discovering excellencies better than the world can afford, and having another spiritual life above, he is thereby directed to further aims in all; yea, even in his civil actions. Saint Paul gives a rule, that 'whether we eat or drink, or whatever we do, we should do all to the glory of God,' 1 Cor. x. 31.[64]

The polarity between genuine and false spirituality that Sibbes established here is intrinsic rather than extrinsic. It emerges from differing natures (natural or fallen versus Christian) and is intentional, the one serving "base ends" and the other a "life above". Sibbes' exposition of this difference revealed his belief that Adam's fall is the key to understanding the separate dispositions of fallen and redeemed humanity.

Conclusion

Some final observations may be made about the positive and privative views of sin. The two approaches differ fundamentally on the reason for sin. While man is identified as responsible for sin in both views, he tends to be portrayed more as a pliable innocent overcome by the serpent's deceit in the privative model.[65] It is Adam presented as inadequate, not because he was unable to fulfill the law, but, because, in his mutability as a creature, he was vulnerable to moral change. This the serpent exploited while God was willfully away.

In scholastic terms, the formal cause of sin was twofold, given the double causality associated with God's sovereignty. God, as the primary agent for all things, determined the outcome by his withdrawal. In this he was arbitrary but just. The second agent, Adam, failed to apply the grace he had available and thus was culpable for his own fall, albeit as something of a victim. In both considerations the issue of grace is pivotal in its absence. For the privative model, as seen in both Thomistic and Reformed theology, this leads to a greater emphasis on the acquisition and application of grace in hypostatized or commodity-like terms, and a tendency toward Aristotelian moralism—the establishing of one's righteousness through righteous actions based on grace. The more that grace is portrayed as a created quality, the more certain it is that an appetite for human merit is present.

The doctrine of positive sin, on the other hand, rejects any tendency to see man as a victim. Adam is always the culprit in that he willfully replaced the Creator with the creature as his focus of devotion. It also recognizes human mutability as a feature of the fall but rejects it as a useful explanation of why the fall occurred. When viewed within the framework of positive sin the fall is an impenetrable mystery: Adam is not portrayed as deceived and God is not portrayed as withholding grace. In the positive model sin is always a competition. Adam seeks to usurp God's role and God confounds Adam's autonomy.

Thus, the most important difference between the two models is found in the way God is portrayed. In the privative view as Aquinas and Perkins have it he remains an arbitrary supplier of grace—giving what is needed for salvation to the elect while withholding it from others. He is even parsimonious to the elect but is increasingly generous as their efforts prevail.

In the positive view, on the other hand, he is an enemy until conversion comes by the Spirit's direct intervention. He invites the elect to see God as he always was: righteous, strong, and loving. Conversion, in fact, is a litmus for the two views: the privative model generally adopts a catechetical process which culminates in an affirmation of faith. The positive model, while recognizing that the Spirit uses prevenient stirrings, expects a more distinct Paul-like conversion that displays the moment in which selfish autonomy melts before God's self-disclosure. In the one, nature remains very much in view; for the other, God, once unveiled to a heart by his grace, is central.

The importance of the affections for Sibbes and the nomists differed in profound ways. For Sibbes the affections were both the avenue by which sin entered the world and the avenue by which God, by the Spirit, restores the fallen soul. Slavery of a person's will is desire-based—what the person wants most—and that slavery is only broken when God becomes more attractive than anything else in life: thus explaining the transforming power of love. Perkins and the nomists, on the other hand, saw the affections as subordinate to the will. And they embraced a will-centered theology in the Thomist privation-enablement model of sin and grace.

Perkins and the nomists thus established human responsibility as the center-theme of salvation: the moral law became the locus of the soul in the process of sanctification. The belief that the covenant of grace is essentially a legal contract led to a portrayal of spirituality as a restorative exercise. Life is an effort to regain and sustain Adam's original obedience through the Spirit-enabled will. This generated a Christology that emphasized the contractual elements of salvation. And, in turn, pastoral calls to faith became exhortations to greater moral effort.

Sibbes, against this view and in line with Augustine, portrayed Christ as much more than the source of justification. Instead he is a lover to be loved. The promise of the indwelling Spirit, whose ministry in Christ's life is now present in the Christian, gives promise of a greater hope than the nomists offered: full and eternal intimacy of the Godhead through a true, although mystical, union with Christ. The feet of the soul are the affections and the affections are meant for communion with God.

In the next chapter we consider the separate covenantal structures found among the Puritans, comparing differences between the two primary models of sin-and-grace. The motif of mystical marriage provided Sibbes with a version of God's covenant that invited mutuality through the devotion of marital love. Perkins' Federalism, on the other hand, was represented as an exercise of mutual obligation.

150

Chapter Four

Mystical Marriage
"Speak peace unto us in thy Christ . . . and by thy Holy Spirit"

The *unio mystica* of Christ and the church was the existential nerve of Puritan piety.[1] The concept of union, however, also presented difficulties for theologians as they sought to define it in light of the moral and ontological gulf between God and humanity. Two models of union emerged, each aligned with other aspects of the Puritan division over grace. Richard Sibbes, in rejecting William Perkins' cooperative approach to salvation, adopted a model of marital union as the ground for justification.

Marital union was tied to Luther's argument that both the righteousness of the Son and the Father—the *iustitia Christi* and the *iustitia Dei*—belong to believers as their *possessio* through marital union. Sibbes held that salvation is applied to the elect through their participation in the hypostatic unity of Christ. The means needed for humanity's restoration from sin is an equivalency in natures between God and mankind as found in Christ: "[H]e was the image of God. And none but the image of God could restore us to that image."[2]

> Whence is it that we are 'sons of God?' Because he was the "Son of man," "God in our flesh." There are three unions: the union of natures, God to become man; The

> union of grace, that we are one with Christ; and the union of glory. The first is for the second, and the second for the third; God became man that man might be one with God; God was "manifested in the flesh," that we might be united to him; and being brought again to God the Father, we might come again to a glorious union.

Sibbes emphasized the continuity between Christ's hypostatic union and Christ's union with believers, while remaining alert to the different qualities of union. But he believed that to establish a radical discontinuity is to deny the point of the incarnation.

> But there is a more supernatural conjunction of man when all of us, sinners as we are, are knit to Christ our head, and head and members make one Christ. Here is a wondrous conjunction. St Paul calls it a mystery, Eph. 5:32.[3]

Sibbes thus believed that God provides this union of Christ with man from within the unity of the Godhead as expressed by Jesus in John 17. It is a real affiliation with God—a "mystery" revealed by Paul in Ephesians that human marriage is merely a proleptic view of the greater marriage: Christ and the church.[4]

However William Perkins, like Aquinas, held that the incommensurability of creator and creation disallows any form of real union.[5] Therefore Perkins read the biblical language of union through the lens of the western legal tradition: it is a juridical transaction accomplished through adoption. Legal righteousness is imputed to the elect and, in the same moment, the Spirit's superadded quality of grace in the elect enables them to reciprocate God's offer of salvation through a work of faith. This reciprocity fulfills the moral symmetry of Federalism.

In this chapter the two models are examined. Perkins' juridical theology of union is considered first, with special attention given to his twofold definition of grace. Then Sibbes' use of mystical marriage is assessed. Their differences display another aspect of the responsibility versus response split among Puritans over the meaning and functions of grace.

Perkins' Model of Union

Perkins' model of union rested on two primary assumptions. First, because of a radical incommensurability in being, man is incapable of direct contact with God. Thus union is achieved only by the intermediary agency of created grace. Second, he believed that the cooperative model of salvation is a moral necessity. This led to his voluntarist spirituality that treated faith as an act of the enabled will. His full theology required an alignment of these two assumptions. This was achieved by the doctrine of *habitus gratiæ* that Aquinas had earlier developed on similar grounds. It represented a major shift away from the Augustinian doctrine of grace by making the benefits of grace—though not its provision—contingent on human will.

Resolving incommensurability: habits of grace

Habits of grace—*habitus gratiæ*—in Federal theology were a mechanism for divine-human cooperation in salvation as has been noted already. William Stoever summarizes the scheme.

> No one can truly believe from his own power, but only as the Spirit, infusing a supernatural principle, enables him to do so; and the act of faith does not merit justification but is merely an arbitrary condition imposed by God when he set up the system of covenants. Faith is, nonetheless, ontologically prior to union with Christ, as the movement of which union is *terminus ad quem*, and without it there is no union. At the same time, justification (which follows from union) is "by faith" and "by grace" alone, for the Spirit, who works gratuitously, is—in scholastic terminology—the "efficient cause" of union, faith being the "instrumental cause" of it. Crucial to this understanding was the scholastic distinction between "habit" and "act," the habit of faith being defined as the principle or power of faith as the motion put forth from the habit. In receipt of the habit the soul is passive; in virtue of it the soul actively believes in Christ.[6]

Federal theology, Stoever explains, offered a way in which God "accommodated man's created nature" by providing the appearance of mutuality in the saving transaction. The elect person is enabled to gain salvation by offering his or her faith through a prevenient "gracious capacity" given by God.[7]

Thomistic origins. Aquinas, who adapted his *habitus* theology from Aristotle's anthropology, developed it not with a view to support the appearance of mutuality between nature and grace but in order to honor the ontological gap between creation and creator. A. E. McGrath identifies the motives behind this synthesis.

> The starting point for this discussion of [supernatural habits in justification] is generally agreed to be Peter Lombard's identification of the *caritas* infused into the soul in justification with the Holy Spirit. For Thomas Aquinas, this opinion is impossible to sustain, as the union of the uncreated Holy Spirit with the created human soul appeared to him to be inconsistent with the ontological distinction which it was necessary to maintain between them. Thomas therefore located the solution to the problem in a created gift which is itself produced within the soul by God, and yet is essentially indistinguishable from him—the supernatural habit.[8]

Aquinas, however, knew that Augustine was not so troubled by the problem of incommensurability. Augustine, in fact, had affirmed the realist imagery of union—that is, that a real, rather than mediated union is assumed in scriptures—by treating Christ's headship over the church as a defining imagery. Indeed, Augustine wrote of Christ's incarnation which he initiated that "He might truly and properly be called at the same time the Son of God and the Son of man—Son of man on account of the man taken up, and the Son of God on account of the God only-begotten who took him up".[9] God's strategy of grace is to elevate human nature in the manhood of Jesus, and by uniting the elect to Christ through the Spirit: "By the same Spirit also the former is born again of which the latter was born." This made the Spirit's gift of life common to both:

> Let there become manifest to us, then, in our Head, the very source and spring of grace, from which it pours forth through all his members according to the measure of each. From the beginning of his faith each man becomes a Christian by that same grace by which that man from his first beginning became Christ.[10]

It was in weighing this passage that Aquinas, after hesitation, parted from Augustine. He, instead, used the biblical imagery of adoption that could be more readily aligned with his own synthetic understanding of union. Cornelius Ernst, a Thomist scholar, summarizes the matter:

> A single divine initiative of grace, founding a regime of grace, unites Christians and Christ as members to Head. This text, naturally enough, seems both to fascinate and trouble St Thomas, and he returns to it several times in the Christological treatise of the *Summa*. He has finally, with some regret it seems, to distinguish between the grace of union by which Christ is natural Son, and habitual grace by which a Christian becomes adoptive son.[11]

Thus the later use of adoption by Perkins and other as an alternative and defining metaphor of union—rather than as a metaphor that complements a theology of participation—first emerged. It represented a Federal embrace of the Thomistic axiom of divine-human incommensurability. As an aside, this arrangement may have satisfied certain terms of logic but, arguably, it meant that Christ's unity as one who is fully divine and fully human would seem to violate incommensurability.

The division of grace by Aquinas into created and uncreated aspects in order to resolve incommensurability led to issues later theologians would need to address.[12] Created grace gave its recipients a new capacity in their own nature to recognize and choose the Spirit's values—yet this grace existed apart from the Spirit's immediate work. But in Augustine's theology the uncreated graces are God's love, mercy, benevolence, and faithfulness; and, as Augustine saw it, the grace-enabled believer looks *solely* to God's character in his or her faith. For Thomas, however, this uncreated grace was only one element in the equation of faith and salvation.

The Thomistic duality of grace affirmed God's rule over nature while maintaining ontological incommensurability but in practice the result was an increasing commodification of grace.[13] Thomas's synthesis supported the traditional tie of grace to the elements of the Eucharistic in transubstantiation so that worship tended to treat the elements as objects of adoration in themselves.

This, in turn, tended to shift the focus of theology away from God as gracious—a relational emphasis—to seeing grace as some*thing* to be pursued for its benefits: a pragmatic and anthropocentric emphasis. This, in turn, engendered the sacramentalism and sacerdotalism that the first reformers treated as the greatest fault of the church in prior centuries

Perkins' use of habitus. Perkins' doctrine of incommensurability was presented in his response to the larger question of ontology: what does Christ offer in the mystery of union—the *unio mystica*? Is it only his human nature, or his full divinity?

Perkins answered that it is Christ's full divinity. But he hedged his view with a crucial caveat: "[The] whole Christ, God and man is given. . . . for the communication of the Godhead is merely energetical, that is, only in respect to operation in that it doth make the man personally united unto it to be propitiatory for our sins and meritorious of life eternal." Thus the union is twofold: enablement ("merely energetical") and an imputation of juridical benefits ("propitiatory" and "meritorious"), rather than the immediate union assumed in Augustine's theology of participation.

The ontological gap between nature and grace was at issue for Perkins: "And to avouch any communication of the Godhead in respect of essence, were to bring in the heresy of the Manichees, and to maintain a composition and a commixtion of our natures with the nature of God."

He held, instead, that Christ's juridical benefits are distributed through mystical union: that Christ "as redeemer . . . is really communicated to all ordained to salvation . . . that Christ himself with all his benefits is theirs". This work is compared to the inheritance of a family estate: "as truly as any man may say that house and land given him of his ancestors is his own both to possess and to use."[14]

Perkins identified three forms of union. The distinctions were critical to his position and differed from

Sibbes' view by emphasizing discontinuity rather than continuity in the nexus of nature and grace in Christ:

> [I]n what manner is Christ given to us? *Answ.* . . . not in an earthly or bodily manner. . . but the manner is altogether celestial and spiritual, partly because it is brought to pass by the mere divine operation of the holy Ghost, and partly because . . . this gift is received by *an instrument which is supernatural.* . . . In the Scripture we meet with three kind of conjunctions. The first is conjunction in nature [the essential unity of the Trinity] . . . . Now Christ and the believer are not joined in nature . . . . The second . . . is in person, when things in nature different, so concur together that they make but one person [the body and soul make a person]. Now Christ and a Christian are not joined in person, for Christ is one person, Peter a second . . . . A Third conjunction is in spirit and this is the conjunction meant in the place, whereby Christ and his Church are joined together; for the very same spirit of God that dwells in the manhood of Christ, and filleth it with all graces . . . dwells in all true members of the Church . . .[15]

Each of his three options must be taken in turn. First, he denied any essential union of Creator and creation: God's eternal nature precludes any commensurability of being with his creatures. All orthodox Christians would agree here. The second option, a union of persons in Christ, which he also denied, was the point of his departure from Augustine. For

Augustine the incarnation is God's means for bridging the gap of incommensurability. That is, Christ's hypostatic union is the means by which humanity is "taken up" into union with God.[16]

The Chalcedonian definition set the stage for this by affirming the perpetual distinction of Christ's divinity and humanity while still affirming that they exist in one person. This was a basic tenet of Christological orthodoxy. The early reformers also held that Christ's union with the church is like the union of husband and wife: two persons who become one, yet without loss of individuation. Perkins' third option for union and the one he approved—the shared presence of the Spirit in Christ and in the elect—was only superficially Augustinian. It denied the ability of humanity to be taken up into Christ's divinity while remaining fully human and individual. In the highlighted portion of the cited text Perkins displayed just such a belief in a full incommensurability by insisting that even the Spirit avoids immediate contact with humanity by the supernatural "instrument" of *habitus*—God's created grace

Perkins' approach, then, addressed the question of the relationship of the church-Christ union and Christ's hypostatic union by use of radical incommensurability. This helps account for his restricted expressions of personal union, and his emphasis on the legal and adoptionist aspects of union.[17]

Sibbes, by contrast, emphasized the continuity of Christ's double nature and his union with human nature. Thus, while Perkins and Sibbes might appear to have much in common in the language of union, they maintained fundamentally different positions. Sibbes held that union with Christ was equivalent to marital union (sometimes described as a conjugal bond) in which the two persons remain distinct but are nevertheless united as one.[18] And in the same manner that the Spirit directed Christ the Spirit also intends to direct Christ's bride, the church.

Perkins also addressed marital union but he portrayed it as a function of roles: "The like we see in wedlock. The husband saith, This woman is mine . . . so that . . . I may both have her and govern her."[19] In this discussion, from the *Golden Chaine*, Perkins shifted the imagery to his favorite expression for union, "ingrafting". This also carried with it the crucial ontological caveat:

> Hence cometh that admirable union or conjunction which is the ingrafting of such as are to be saved into Christ and their growing up together with him; so that after a peculiar manner Christ is made the head and every repentant sinner a member of his mystical body. This albeit it be a most near and real union, yet *we must not think that it is by touching, mixture or, as it were, by soldering of one soul with another*; neither by a bare agreement of the souls among themselves; but by the communion and operation of the same Spirit which, being by nature infinite, is of sufficient ability to conjoin those things together which are of themselves far distant from each other. The like we see in the soul of man, which conjoineth the head with the foot.[20]

The last sentence displays the conjoining work of the Spirit in functional rather than personal terms; the Spirit is, in modern terms, the invisible but coordinating work of the nervous system of the body of Christ. Perkins rounded off his discussion by reverting to the language of imputation: "This union is made by the Spirit of God applying Christ unto us and on our parts by faith receiving Christ Jesus offered unto us. And for this cause it is termed a spiritual union."[21] Thus, despite his language of union that sometimes suggested a real participation in Christ's life, Perkins held that the gulf between nature and grace is never bridged.

Christ in Perkins' habitus theology. Perkins' emphasis on the nature-grace gulf elevated God's transcendence. It also tended toward an instrumental approach in his Christology and doctrine of salvation. In his systematic works, for instance, Perkins applied the rule of incommensurability to Christ's humanity by making his divinity a gift-based reality: "the putting on of such habitual gifts which, albeit they are created and finite, yet they have so great and marvelous perfection as possibly can befall any creature."[22]

While this emphasis made Christ's works fully accessible to the elect, it also tended to undermine the unity of the hypostatic union, producing a very human Jesus and a distant *Logos*.[23] Perkins also explained the believer's union with Christ in instrumental terms: "The same Spirit descending from Christ the head to all his members, creating also in them the instrument of faith, whereby they apprehend Christ and make him their own."[24]

Thus, the "instrument of faith" was the centerpiece of Perkins' covenantal structure. As has been seen in chapter three, he assumed that God's permissive will is necessary to resolve the question of sin. In this approach Perkins held that God underwrites a secondary indeterminacy of the human will by which a person is enabled to "apprehend Christ". That is, in order to create the moral space in which the human will operates in choosing or refusing Christ, God offers a gift of enablement. Faith, in the *Golden Chaine*, is "a miraculous and supernatural faculty of the heart, apprehending Christ Jesus".[25] Sanctification, as well, is "nothing else but a created quality in every true member" of the church.[26]

Early reformers and habits of grace

Before turning to Sibbes' alternative model of covenantal union it is important to raise the question of theological continuity. Is Perkins' use of a Thomistic synthesis—the heart Federal theology—aligned with the views of the earlier reformers? Not in the cases of Luther, Zwingli and Calvin. They all rejected any suggestion that grace exists as a created quality, disposition or essence. They held, instead, that faith results from the Spirit's continuing grace in a believer's real union with Christ.[27]

Why this was an issue for them is made clear by considering the roles of nature and grace in western theology. The church, Alister McGrath points out, oscillated between two views: "The intrinsicist and ontologically determined theology of justification associated with the earlier period is replaced with the extrinsicist and deontologized theology of the later period."[28] *Habitus* provided the mechanism for the extrinsic system. The reformers, then, consciously returned to the ontological theology of the early church.

Luther's rejection of habitus. Luther's understanding of faith was examined in chapter two and must be recalled, briefly, as it applies to the present question. He was insistent in disallowing any medieval attempts to coordinate nature and grace. Nature is always subordinated to grace.[29] His resistance to habits of grace must be linked to his pessimism about nature that, in turn, was based on his doctrine of sin. As was seen in the *Disputation against Scholastic Theology*, Luther rejected an extrinsic definition of sin and its corollary, behavioral righteousness. Any acceptance of the premise in Aristotle's *Ethics* that righteous character is formed by righteous deeds is disallowed. Brian Gerrish argues: "It is, in short, the doctrine of *habitus* (*hexis*) which is the focal point of Luther's assault on Aristotle, for, as used by the Nominalists, it was diametrically opposed to Luther's own fundamental doctrine that a man . . . must first be righteous before he can do any righteous deeds."[30]

Zwingli's rejection of habitus. Zwingli, like Luther, also sought to explain nature and grace not in terms of balance but as the immediate, although mystical, presence of the Spirit in the hearts of believers, and as the source for all ongoing benefits of sanctification. The debate between Luther and Zwingli over the meaning of the Eucharist illuminates the latter's rejection of *habitus*. His Pneumatology surpassed Luther's in emphasizing unmediated grace, thus accounting for his disagreement with the German reformer. Zwingli insisted that the immediate activity of the Spirit in believers is not shaped, moved, or limited in any manner. Zwingli displayed this difference in a response to Luther's affirmation that "The Word, I say, and the Word alone, is the vehicle of God's grace".[31] Zwingli countered, "Neither guidance nor vehicle is necessary for the Spirit; He himself is the power and vehicle by which everything is carried along."[32] Gottfried W. Locher points to the salient issue in Zwingli's position:

> Even before the Fall, from the moment of his creation onwards, man was dependent upon the Holy Spirit—that is, that God should unceasingly and graciously attend to him, guide him and communicate with him—which could well constitute one of the sharpest reformation rejections of the medieval teaching about *habitus*.[33]

Calvin's rejection of habitus. Calvin also rejected the notion of grace-as-a-created-quality, insisting instead that grace is always relational. He was sharply critical of the scholastic discussions of grace, charging in the *Institutes* (1559) that by it the "schools" have "plunged into a sort of Pelagianism".[34] In book three of the *Institutes*, Calvin developed his own doctrine of grace. His view that faith is relational and a matter of the heart—a personal certainty of God's gracious benevolence—is implicit if not explicit throughout the exposition. The Spirit is the "bond by which Christ effectually unites us to himself". He cited Rom. 5:5, the verse so important to Augustine's affective theology, that the Spirit pours God's love into the believer's heart.[35] He readily associated this with the affective language of moderate mystics: as the Spirit is "persistently boiling away and burning up our vicious and inordinate desires, he enflames our hearts with the love of God and with zealous devotion."[36]

In defining faith Calvin derided the medieval-scholastic notion of formed and unformed faith as an attempt "to invent" a "cold quality of faith."[37] He was similarly critical of the moralistic tendencies inherent in the Thomistic model: "Hence we may judge how dangerous is the scholastic dogma that we can discern the grace of God toward us only by moral conjecture . . ." Against such ideas, faith actually "consists in assurance rather than in comprehension".[38] Even Phil. 2:12-13, with its explicit synergism ("work out your own salvation with fear and trembling, for it is God who is at work in you both to will and to work for his good pleasure"), was seen to portray a believer's appropriate humility as a counterpart to his or her assurance of God's goodness. He attacked "certain half-papists" who represent Christ as "standing afar off" as an object of faith "and not rather dwelling in us".[39] The work of justification is, he insisted, a gaze in which the believers are led "to turn aside from the contemplation of our own works and look solely upon God's mercy and Christ's perfection".[40]

Luther, Zwingli and Calvin, then, understood and rejected the use of *habitus* as an intermediary reality that serves to buffer God from his creation. Grace, instead, is present in the elect through a real union and subsequent communion.

Sibbes' Use of the Song of Songs *and Marital Union*

Mystical marriage shaped Sibbes' covenantal theology. It was developed in—and was probably derived from—his exposition of the Bible book, *Song of Songs.* The sermons also illustrate Sibbes' disinterest in predestination. In his use of a marital model of union Sibbes refused to portray union in terms of a predestinarian first decree of the Father—a transcendent theology—but instead held a Trinitarian emphasis in which the

Father is still fully transcendent but the Son, by the Spirit, is portrayed as relational and immanent.

Earlier uses of marital imagery

Sibbes' approach placed him in company with many of the central figures in the Christian mystical tradition in using marital imagery to describe spirituality. The *Song of Songs* was the most common point of reference. Fascination with the book may be traced to Origen who believed it to be, using Bernard McGinn's description, "the central textbook for 'epoptics,' that is, the place where scripture reveals the heart of its message about the love of the descending Christ for the fallen soul, [and] it is in the interpretation of the erotic language of the *Song* that the deepest inscription of the mystical message takes place."[41]

The Song of Songs among English theologians. General interest in the book flourished during Sibbes' era. The notes of the 1560 Geneva Bible supported the association of the figures in the book to Christ and the church. This Bible, by its wide circulation and acceptance in Puritan circles, was a resource that would have made the marriage-allegory interpretation of the Song a commonplace among Puritans. The marginal notes, for instance, began: "The familiar talk and mystical communication of the spiritual love between Jesus Christ and his church."[42] Further support for this approach was to be found in the explicit New Testament use of the marriage metaphor, particularly with the apocalyptic imagery of Revelation and its culminating vision of Jesus as the "Alpha and Omega" proleptically offering readers eternal bliss with the church, having been wedded at the marriage supper of the Lamb: "And the Spirit and the bride say 'come'!"[43]

Also, in 1587 an English translation of Theodore Beza's commentary on the *Song* was published in Oxford.[44] The nonconformist preacher, George Gifford (d. 1620) of Maldon, Essex, was another promoter of the book. Gifford also displayed an affective theology that anticipated many of Sibbes' subsequent emphases (but no direct connections have been traced between them). Gifford published two sermon collections on the *Song of Songs* as well as a series on the book of Revelation that included discussions of the Song. John Cotton also offered sermon series on the book. Another interesting work represented the more Dionysian mystical tradition among Puritans: Francis Rous, two years junior to Sibbes, published *The Mysticall Marriage* in 1635. It borrowed the language of the *Song* and regularly alluded to it, yet without intending to offer an exposition.[45]

The importance of Bernard of Clairvaux. At least some of Bernard's works were available to Sibbes, including sermons on the *Song of Songs*.[46] Sibbes may well have followed the example of early reformers in this appreciation, but if so, he fails to comment on it. Luther and Calvin regularly noted Bernard, even more than did Sibbes. In the early period of the Reformation Luther either cited or referred to Bernard more than five hundred times, and shared much in common with him including, as will be noted, the motif of marital devotion.[47] Calvin, as well, drew heavily from Bernard's works, including a number of citations from Bernard's *Song of Songs* sermons.[48]

Bernard, as a more cataphatic theologian, identified the church and Christ as the partners of the *Song of Songs*. His views of sin and grace demonstrated the later Augustinian symmetry of sin as driven by self-love and grace as a restoration of God's love to the soul. In accepting a Solomonic authorship of Ecclesiastes, Proverbs, and the *Song of Songs*, Bernard portrayed a triadic structure. Sin is characterized by two chief evils: a vain love of the world and an excessive self-love. Ecclesiastes addressed the former sin and Proverbs engaged the latter. Grace is revealed in the love of God for the person and the *Song of Songs* disclosed God's gracious love in Christ.[49]

Luther's use of marital imagery. Luther used the marital imagery of Ephesians 5:30 to explain how faith functions in realist terms. It served as an alternative to the medieval theology of infused righteousness, including the dual aspects of *habitus* and *actus*. His marital language was explicitly relational and not simply a matter of juridical attribution.

> But faith must be taught correctly, namely, that by it you are so cemented to Christ that He and you are as one person, which cannot be separated but remains attached to Him forever and declares: "I am as Christ." And Christ, in turn, says: "I am as that sinner who is attached to Me, and I to him. For by faith we are joined together into one flesh and one bone." Thus Eph. 5:30 says: "We are members of the body of Christ, of His flesh and of His bones," in such a way that this faith couples Christ and me more intimately than a husband is coupled to his wife. Therefore this faith is no idle

> quality; but it is a thing of such magnitude that it obscures and completely removes those foolish dreams of the sophists' doctrine—the fiction of a "formed faith" and of love, of merits, our worthiness, our quality, etc.[50]

By speaking of a real parallel between the union displayed in human marriage and the union present between Christ with the elect, Luther's marital exposition offered context for God's work of grace by the Spirit. Faith is a direct work of God through the Spirit. From the believer's point of view, faith is a full response to God, touching every aspect of life.

> For this life is in the heart through faith. There the flesh is extinguished; and there Christ rules with His Holy Spirit, who now sees, hears, speaks, works, suffers, and does simply everything in him, even though the flesh is still reluctant. In short, this life is not the life of the flesh, although it is a life in the flesh; but it is the life of Christ, the Son of God, whom the Christian possesses by faith.[51]

Calvin's use of marital imagery. Calvin failed to produce a commentary on the Song of Songs and, apart from three minor citations, ignores it in the *Institutes*.[52] Yet that is not to say that Calvin overlooked the imagery of marriage as a basis for unfolding the doctrine of spiritual union with Christ. It was, in fact, central to his understanding of how God's grace is applied in sanctification. In the *Institutes* Calvin noted that marriage was meant by Christ "to be an image of his sacred union with the church."[53] Calvin's view of spiritual union posited a certainty of Christ's "spiritual presence" through the Spirit in a mystical fashion that corresponded to his presence in the Lord's Supper. That is, Calvin took the promise of spiritual union—modeled by marital union—along with the elements of the supper to represent the reality of God's continuous spiritual activity:

> We explain the nature of this by a familiar example. Water is sometimes drunk from a spring, sometimes drawn, sometimes led by channels to water the fields, yet it does not flow forth from itself for so many uses, but from the very source, which by unceasing flow supplies and serves it. In like manner, the flesh of Christ is like a rich and inexhaustible fountain that pours into us the life springing forth from the Godhead into itself. Now who does not see that communion of Christ's flesh and blood is necessary for all who aspire to heavenly life? This is the purport of the apostle's statements: 'The church . . . is the body of Christ, and the fullness of him' [Eph 1:23]; but he is 'the head' [Eph 4:15] 'from whom the whole body joined and knit together by . . . joints . . . makes bodily growth" [Eph 4:16] 'our bodies are members of Christ' [1 Cor 6:15]. We understand that all these things could not be brought about otherwise than by his cleaving to us wholly in spirit and body. But Paul graced with a still more glorious title that intimate fellowship in which we are joined with his flesh when he said, 'We are members of his body, of his bones and of his flesh' [Eph 5:30].[54]

Like Luther before him Calvin's doctrine of mystical marriage was guided by Paul's linkage of Ephesians 5:30-32 to Genesis 2:23 & 24.

> For when Eve (who he knew was formed from his rib) was brought unto his sight, he said, 'She is bone of my bones, and flesh of my flesh' [Gen 2:23]. Paul testifies that all this was spiritually fulfilled in Christ and in us, when he says that we are members of his body, of his flesh, and of his bones, and thus one flesh with him. Finally he adds this summation: 'This is a great mystery.' And that nobody may be deceived by an ambiguity, he explains that he is not speaking of carnal union of man and woman, but of the spiritual marriage of Christ and the church.[55]

A crucial question is raised by Calvin's exposition. If Paul's point here surpasses analogy and thus represents a reality, in what sense is the believer united with Christ? Is it ontological, covenantal, or mystical; all, any or none of the above?[56] A second Pauline passage used by Calvin, 1 Corinthians 6:17, addresses sexual immorality and draws upon the same inaugural passage of marriage in Genesis 2:24 as did Ephesians 5:22-32. Here Paul turned his argument on the equivalency of conjugal union in creating human oneness with the oneness generated by spiritual union: "But the one who joins himself to the Lord is one spirit with him." It was this commitment, a spiritual and mystical union, rather than covenantal or ontological union (in the sense of God infusing grace) that characterized Calvin's doctrine of sanctification.

Sibbes' use of the Song of Songs

Sibbes sermons on the *Song of Songs* included two separate pieces and a set of twenty sermons. One of the separate sermons was entitled *The Spouse, Her Earnest Desire After Christ,* and addressed verse two of chapter one. The second, *The Church's Blackness*, addressed verses five and six.[57] The large series of twenty was first published as the *Bowels Opened* in 1639 and later as *Union Between Christ and the Church* in 1641.[58] This collection surveyed chapters 4:16 to 6:3 of the *Song.*

Sibbes' personal study drew explicitly from Bernard whom he cited throughout his own exposition in *Bowels Opened.* Their specific expositions, however, did not overlap since Sibbes began his major set of sermons in chapter four and thus beyond the point where Bernard's work ended in chapter three.[59] Sibbes was, in fact, more arbitrary in his overall approach to the book than other expositors.[60] While all others began at the beginning of the book and continued without interruption, Sibbes explored only three verses in chapter one and, separately, just over a chapter-length section in the middle of the book for his extended series, *Bowels Opened.*

Sibbes' covenantal use of the Song of Songs. The key to understanding Sibbes' use of the book is found in *The Spouse.* It was here that he presented both the covenantal foundation for his understanding of spiritual union and introduced the importance of the *Song* to his overall theology. Unlike most other commentators, Sibbes began with a literal explanation of the introductory clause, "Let him kiss me with the kisses of his mouth": it sets out the mutual love of the key figures in the story as the context for all that follows. This introduced Sibbes' chief concern, namely, the mutuality of marriage. The marriage he finds in the *Song* is, he observed, "*a spiritual contract between Christ and his church.*" He argued, from the lesser to the greater, that the nature of civil contracts which establish human marriage "holds firm resemblance" to the spiritual contract of Christ and the church. His emphasis on the mutuality of marital commitment developed this point:

> That this civil contract may hold, *both parties must consent.* So it is between Christ and his spouse. He was so in love with mankind, that he hath taken our nature upon him; and this his incarnation is the ground of all our union with Christ. First, his incarnation is the ground of all our union in glory. Now, that we may be a spouse to him, he gives us his Spirit to testify his love to us, that we might give our consent to him again, as also that we might be made a fit spouse for him.[61]

He restated the point, "the duty on our part is to love him again with a mutual love, and obedient love".[62] Sibbes thus identified spiritual marriage as the key to the nature-grace nexus.

Bernard had earlier noted the same principle in his sermons on the *Song*: the reciprocity of love is the one point where believers could offer unrestricted effort without that effort being construed in terms of the cooperative model of enabled independence. McGinn offers a summary of Bernard's view: [He] "insists that the only power by which humans can deal reciprocally with God is love, and that marital love is the highest form, the love that best expresses union."[63] In this Sibbes was appropriating a means by which humans can grasp

God, not in terms of Perkins' predestinarianism, but by the elevation of the contractual commitment in marriage.

It was in reversing the status of marriage from metaphor to a mystical reality that the elect were to be understood as actually participating in a union with Christ and God with genuine reciprocity. The critical factor in this understanding is that marriage represents real union, yet without forming an ontological identity. The Pauline use of the term "mystery" to reverse the assumed priority of Christ-church and husband-wife relationships in Ephesians 5:32, when buttressed by the language of 1 Corinthians 6:17 ("the one who joins himself to the Lord is one spirit with him"), represented this inexplicable union of the church and Christ: the *unio mystica*. This characterized a moderate mysticism rather than the Dionysian mysticism, represented by stages of spiritual ascent, or other mystic forms such as asceticism or quietism. Sibbes, instead, held that God's self-disclosure centers in the bridegroom, Christ, in whom mutual love is discovered.

This approach displaced marriage from its presumed creation status as an end in itself—with procreative, social and societal functions. Instead it gained a new status by illuminating, proleptically, the divine-human relationship which begins at conversion and continues into eternity. Thus, mystical marriage surpasses human marriage in the same way that an eternal reality is greater than a temporal reality. This model also emphasized the gracious initiative of Christ in first coming to the bride. The bride, once approached, is free to reciprocate the ardor of her lover. It is this reciprocity that establishes the ground for a person's pursuit of God. For Sibbes it was this matter that needed to be established before he could explore the meaning of the "kisses" in the text at hand. In continuing his exposition, he displayed the implications of this affective and spiritual covenant:

> This is the desire of the church, and of every Christian soul, that Christ would thus kiss her; that he would reveal himself every day more and more unto her, in his word, in his sacraments, by his Spirit, by his graces, by increasing of them. This is the desire of the church and of every Christian soul, that Christ would thus 'kiss her with the kisses of his mouth.'[64]

Sibbes' application of marital theology. Sibbes' discussions of the movement from initial salvation into sanctification show how deeply his reading of the *Song of Songs* influenced his broader theology. Believers are invited to "see" Christ in biblical promises, which is the ground for the formation of a love relationship.[65]

> We must be wholly moulded anew. Where there is a condition so opposite as the frame of our hearts is to God, he being holiness and we a mass and lump of sin, of necessity there must be a change. . . . "Flesh and blood, as it is, cannot enter into heaven," 1 Cor 15:50; that is, the nature of man, as it is corrupted; we must have new judgments of things, and new desires, and new esteem, new affections, new joys, new delights, new conversation, new company. All the frame of the soul must be new. There must be a new bent of the

soul. It must be turned another way. The face of the soul must look clean another way.[66]

At the very beginning of the process of transformation, the question of how one who is steeped in sin and disaffection toward God can be brought to "look clean another way" must be raised. Any decisions therefore belong to the person but must be accounted for by God's grace.

Encountering God. Sibbes' theology was theocentric and favored the use of visual metaphors. Vision was given a transformative force in accounting for the first step into faith, much like the Eastern Orthodox doctrine of *theosis*.[67] Christ is the focus of spiritual vision, displacing the viewer's self-awareness: "By looking to the glory of God in Christ we see Christ as our husband, and that breeds a disposition in us to have the affections of a spouse. We see Christ as our head, and that breeds a disposition in us to be members like him."[68]

The cause of change is in the one perceived rather than in the will of the perceiver. This comes, in turn, through a new capacity to see: "God created a new eye in the soul, a new sight which they had not by nature; for even as the natural eye cannot see things that are invisible, so the natural man cannot see the things of God, which are seen not by a natural, but by a supernatural eye."[69] Thus, as lost trust, through rebellious unbelief, had caused the fall of Adam, so a restored vision or encounter with Christ's trustworthiness is the evidence of conversion and the first step of sanctification—the frame of faith:

> By faith we are set in a right frame and condition again, as by want of faith we fell. The same grace [that is, faith] must set us right, for want of which we fell. How came we to fall at the first? You know Adam hearkened to his wife Eve, she hearkened to the serpent. They trusted not in God, they began to stagger at the promises, to stagger at the word of God. Satan robbed them of the word. He observes, and continues the same art still, to take the word from us, and to cause us to stagger and doubt whether it be true or no. . . . So Adam fell. Now we must be restored by the contrary to that we fell. We fell by unbelief and distrust, by calling God's truth in question; we must learn to stand again by the contrary grace, by faith.[70]

With the supernaturally restored "eye of faith" a restoration begins because the soul encounters God as he really exists.

God's Persuasion. With this capacity of spiritual sight, the drama of salvation and sanctification centers on the Spirit's work in overcoming Satan's distortion of God's character. One of the primary issues of pastoral ministry, Sibbes believed, is to face "the wicked, poisonful disposition that the devil stirs up" against Christ and his elect.[71] By elevating the affective faculty above all others, Sibbes had engaged the crucial Bible premise for spiritual growth, that God is relational: "I will be thy God" and "You shall love the Lord your God with all your heart . . ." Sibbes simply assumed God's goodness, believing that he must be committed "to bring us to happiness . . . to be our portion, to be all in all." This assumption was borne out in the incarnation.

God's election is therefore an expression of favor: "To be a God, then, is the fundamental and principal favor. From thence cometh our election; his choosing of us to eternal salvation . . ." God's new covenant is an offer of marital mutuality made in love and the Spirit's work is one of persuasion:

> [Y]ou must know that to be a God is a relation. Whosoever God is a God to, he persuadeth them by his Spirit that he is a God to. The same Spirit that persuadeth them that there is a God, that Spirit telleth them that God is their God, and works a qualification and disposition in them, as that they may know that they are in covenant with such a gracious God. The Spirit as it revealeth to them the love of God, and that he is theirs, so the Spirit enableth them to claim him for their God, to give up themselves to him as to their God. . . . Though God's grace do all, yet we must give our consent; and therefore the covenant is expressed under the title of marriage.[72]

The first work of persuasion is conversion that opens the door to ongoing persuasion. It begins, Sibbes held, with an enlightenment of the understanding, followed by a dialogic "minding" of the truth, a will to "choose the better part", and finally, "loving him as the chief good." Sibbes regularly called for ministers to re-present God's character in accurate terms, as Christ had done: "And what is our Saviour Christ's whole course, but to free men from suspicion of want of love?"[73] The test of real faith, then, is a desire for God in himself: "Love is the first-born affection. That breeds desire of communion with God."[74]

Using the analogy of a lodestone's ability to overcome gravity, Sibbes argued that regeneration draws the believer to God through newfound trust: "for it is confidence and trust that draws us near to God . . ." The first battle in persuasion, then, is a battle over who is most to be trusted: Satan or God. "Even as at the first we fell from God by distrusting of his word; saith the Devil, 'Ye shall not die at all,' Gen. 3:4, we believed a liar more than God himself. Now we are recovered by a way contrary to that we fell; we must recover and draw near to God again by trusting and relying upon God."[75] The re-establishment of trust comes through reframed affections.

> When the understanding was enlightened to see the truth, and to be persuaded of the truth of the promises, then the will and affections, they join and embrace those things. The will makes choice of them, and cleaves to them, the affection of desire extends itself to them, the affection of love embraceth them, the affection of joy delights in them. Spiritual conviction always draws affection. For God hath framed the soul so, that upon discovery of a good out of itself, it doth stretch out itself to embrace that object, the good thing presented. It cannot be otherwise.[76]

What is the good to be considered? The will is not reliable unless it embraces a reliable object. "The soul is as that which it relies upon", Sibbes argued. "God hath prescribed trust as the way to carry our souls to himself, in whom we should only rely, and not in our imperfect trust, which hath its ebbing and flowing."[77] This ebb and flow of will comes from the equivocations of desire that can be stirred by the infamous triad of the world, the flesh (self-love) and the devil. Sibbes warned, "we see God alone must be the object of our trust." Sibbes thus linked trust to the affections by assuming that a person's affections direct the will by selecting the *most* desired "good": "Man hath a nature capable of excellency and desirous of it, and the Spirit of God in and by the word reveals where true excellency is to be had . . . ."[78]

Persuasion, then, is the process by which the soul is redirected from false desires to the one proper desire by a supernatural enlightenment of the soul. As the "Spirit of God in and by the word" achieves this persuasion the soul is able to take the next step of embracing the truths it now accepts, a step also accomplished in the affections.[79]

Embracing God. In conversion and sanctification the mind and will are active as the informing and guiding faculties but the affections actually embrace the truth: "The heart embraceth what we are persuaded of."[80] God, of course, is the one to be embraced above all others. All persuasion is to be directed to that end, and is supported in the elect by God who is "framing us every way to be such as thou mayest take pleasure and delight in". Just as the believer finds delight in God, God finds delight in the believer: "This embracing of Christ and heaven, it is a mutual embracing; and it is a second, reflexive embracing. We embrace God and Christ, because we find God in Christ embracing our souls first in the arms of his love; therefore we embrace him again in the arms of our affections, because we find Christ embracing us in the arms of his affections."[81] This mutual embracing—the bond of union with Christ—explained God's creation purpose for Sibbes and set out God's goal in salvation and sanctification as well.

Sibbes displayed a perspectival shift away from a human point of view by his emphasizing mutuality—in a person looking to discover what God demands and offers. Instead he invited listeners to consider a divine stance by taking up God's motivation in creation. God's loving kindness, not his law, is given theological primacy. From the stance of believers, then, sanctification is the fruit of this distributed goodness coming to them.[82] And by this sharing God both motivates and transforms the elect. The believer is drawn to God by God's self-disclosures, revealing one "so loving, and so gracious" that if unbelievers or inattentive believers were to pause to consider him, "their hearts would melt . . ."[83]

Sibbes used the divine description in 1 John 4:8 that "God is love" to support this: therefore, "his course to man is love." Sibbes—with the contrary values of the nomists in view—pressed the point: "He doth not say, he is justice, or rigour, but he is love." As a result, "we are saved by a manner of love."[84] Furthermore the experience of God's love results in "a sweet kind of tyranny in the affection of love, that will carry a man through thick and thin . . ."[85] Sanctification not only displays the energy of love but also takes its form from the one who is beloved. "Is not love a glorious grace, that melts one into the likeness of Christ?" Thus, having been awakened by God's love in Christ, the believer is called to a voluntarism, not of the self-moved will, but of the will shaped by love: "Beloved, get love" Sibbes urged, because, "It melts us into the likeness of

Christ. . . . Nothing can quench that holy fire that is kindled from heaven. It is a glorious grace."[86]

Perkin's Federal model of covenant was at odds, then, with Sibbes' portrayal of life in Christ. Perkins began with the incommensurability of nature and grace and with that ended with a spirituality of distance and duty. Sibbes' model of mystical marriage, by contrast, saw Christ in his humanity as commensurate with elect humanity so that marital union expressed a real participation of human life in the divine life of Christ, yet without suggesting a fusion of being. The ultimate basis for the union of finite human nature and the eternal life of God came about in the hypostatic union of Christ—in the God-man who is wholly one—and whose human life is the point of access to his eternal life for all who are united to him through the Spirit by marriage.

Conclusion

The distinction between Perkins' model of Federal mutuality based on the use of *habitus* theology and radical incommensurability, and Sibbes' model of the Spirit's union of Christ and his bride, helps resolve the confusion in Puritan historiography. That is, it differentiates separate forms of voluntarism as found in the separate traditions. While Perkins' nomism elevated the function of human initiative—the *actus* of the restored will—Sibbes was also free in exhorting his listeners to spiritual exertion. Norman Pettit's suggestion in *The Heart Prepared*, that Sibbes attributed more to nature than any of his colleagues, must be corrected by the caveat that Sibbes viewed such initiatives as those of a lover pursuing her beloved spouse:

"This is the desire of the church, and of every Christian soul, that Christ would thus kiss her".[87] The marital paradigm also established the ongoing quality of this desire, "that he would reveal himself every day more and more unto her".[88]

The "second doctrine" in *The Spouse* was a review of the anticipated elements of such a pursuit: "That the church (and so every Christian) after this contract and taste of Christ's love, hath evermore springing up in them an insatiable desire for a further taste and assurance of his love." Such "true love" would never be satisfied nor would the "infinite riches" of Christ's person be exhausted. Union, by its very nature, ensured "an infinite desire to have a further taste of his love and a nearer communion with him."[89]

This contrast in Puritan models of covenant must be placed in a larger context. To that end a final question must be asked: how was it that Perkins' Federalism returned to the very extrinsicist model that the reformers rejected? Some preliminary suggestions must suffice. The reappearance of Thomistic values may be explained, in part, by the heavy Aristotelian training Protestant ministers continued to receive at universities as was noted in the first chapter. The uncritical use of definitions and assumptions from Aristotle's *Metaphysics* and *Nicomachean Ethics* engendered an atmosphere for the acceptance of Aquinas' model of Aristotelian-informed theology. Younger university students were, no doubt, readily carried back to the arms of Aristotle when the relatively unsophisticated and imprecise biblical language of the reformers was made to compete with the philosophically-driven synthesis of Thomas.[90]

Indeed, not all the early Protestants were prepared to distance themselves from Aristotelian-Thomistic views in the first place. This created an impression that the opposition to Aristotle found in Luther and others was only a minor issue. Key figures such as Girolamo Zanchi and Peter Martyr Vermigli, unlike Luther, Zwingli and Calvin, continued to view the core theology of the Roman Catholic church as essentially sound. Thus, Muller views them as "Calvinist Thomists". Otto Gründler also argues: "Zanchi's doctrine of God and of predestination will reveal his Thomistic heritage and the extent to which it influenced and determined his thinking and gave structure to the emerging Reformed orthodox dogmatics."[91]

It seems that Sibbes' acceptance of mystical marriage from a Bernardian reading of the *Song of Songs* drew him away from the cooperative theology of his initial training and led him to a unilateral view of the covenant. He came to hold that the affections are crucial in the function of mystical marriage and that mystical marriage is the ground of saving union. In his emphasis he was well aligned with the view of the early reformers who held that the marriage of Christ and the church explains and requires a theology of participation—of real union.

The competing Puritan views of salvation and spirituality were not simply based on their differing definitions of grace. They also required separate understandings of the human soul as the receptacle of grace. The question of the relation of the mind and will to the affections was pivotal to the Puritans, as has been evident already. They called these psychological functions as the "faculties" of the soul.

Next we turn to the question of how these faculties were treated among the Puritans as competing versions of sanctification—the application of God's grace—were explained by different versions of spiritual anthropology.

Chapter Five

Sibbes' Anthropology

"Opening our understandings and clearing our judgments"

The importance of anthropology in theology can hardly be overstated. In Genesis Adam is set above the rest of creation as the *imago dei*: he was made for an intelligent and engaged communion with God. The balance of the Bible then looks back to that relationship as its context. Biblical anthropology explores how humans can commune with God; how to account for human sin; and how the pathway to restored communion is paved.

In Richard Sibbes' final public prayer he held that it is by God "opening our understandings and clearing our judgments" that salvation and sanctification come about in the face of sin. How then, we might ask him, does God's grace engage the soul? And what role do the faculties of the soul—identified by the Puritans as a triad of understanding, will, and affections—function as a whole?

In pursuing these questions we find Sibbes' anthropology to have been eclectic: a blend of philosophy and theology. Like other Reformed theologians of his era, including William Perkins, he began with an Aristotelian synthesis of physical and cognitive mechanisms to describe human functions in what is now referred to as faculty psychology.

Aristotle's anthropological categories, for instance, helped Sibbes—like other Puritans—to chart inward operations of human conduct: Adam, as one example, was "created in an absolute temper of all the humours".[1] Yet at other time Sibbes drew from Bible content as when he described the Spirit's role in moving the human heart: "The spirit of a man is the chief seat of God's good Spirit, wherein he frames all holy devices and good desires."[2] And, at times, he blended his sources:

> the Spirit . . . must move upon the waters of our souls, for we have not the command of our own hearts. Every natural man is carried away with his flesh and humours, upon which the devil rides, and carries him whither he list . . . .[3]

All the Puritans spoke with confidence of humours, heart, soul and mind as if describing tangible features. Yet even with their common language about the soul—language that blended Bible terms with Aristotle's faculty psychology in *De anima* and *Parva naturalia*—the theologians had two problems.[4] First, their versions of the soul could differ widely because—under a facade of shared terminology—their varied efforts were hugely speculative.[5] Second, the preachers treated two conflicted tasks as if they were one. That is, they spoke of conversion as if addressing a natural cause and effect system of psychology; yet they also spoke of the mystery of conversion in terms of biblical supernaturalism that dismissed purely natural causes.

Perry Miller summarized the issue: The Puritans were "faced, even though refusing to admit it, with a problem of reconciling their new doctrines of regeneration and conversion with old doctrines of human nature. Because they held fast to medieval theory in psychology, Puritans were forced to describe regeneration in the terms of a psychological mechanism as well as in the language of theology."[6]

The challenges of setting out a coherent anthropology within arguably conflicted assumptions have already shown up in our study: in Perkins' use of Aristotle's *habitus-actus* linkage to define grace; in his moral assumptions used to describe cooperative salvation; and in his premise of a necessary divine-human incommensurability in order to align both Christology and sanctification with Aristotelian ontological assumptions.

In each of these cases Aristotle's views were used to guide the task of theology at a fundamental levels. The Puritan use of Aristotle's naturalistic cause-effect anthropology invites a closer examination of the ways in which anthropology was applied by Perkins, Sibbes, and most Puritans. Yet it is apparent that over time Sibbes, for one, moved away from his early ties to the primacy of the mind and the will and came to focus on the affections.

To be specific Sibbes held that participation in Christ's life and love is the entry point for communion with God: "God hath made the soul for a communion with himself, which communion is especially placed in the affections, which are the springs of all spiritual worship." But his discussion of the crucial role of the affections contained a caveat, that "our affections are never well-ordered without judgment".[7]

Sibbes, in fact, treated human affections and judgment—when brought under the Spirit's leadership—as centers of God's spiritual direction. This chapter considers features of Puritan anthropology while looking more closely at Sibbes' unique position: what he called God's "spiritual government" of souls.

Elements of Sibbes' Anthropology

Differences between Sibbes and Perkins are most evident in their views of how the affections play a role in faith. Perkins, for instance, separated faith from the affections in conversion:

> Now as the property of apprehending and applying of Christ belongs to faith, so it agrees not to hope, love, confidence, or any other gift or grace of God. But first by faith we must apprehend Christ and apply him to ourselves before we can have any hope or confidence in him. And this applying seems not to be done by any affection of the will, but by a supernatural act of the mind . . .[8]

Sibbes' view was the opposite. Mark Dever, for one, notes the force of Sibbes' affective theology. "Sibbes" he wrote, "radically interiorized Christianity."[9] This underscores a critical feature: Sibbes' theology was heart-based. While Perkins saw the will as more reliable—in modern terms: more objective—than a love-based ("interiorized") faith, Sibbes was not daunted by such skepticism towards his affective spirituality.

He framed his position with a confidence that only a relational theology—through God's spiritual government—begins with a proper view of God. And, as such, it differs from the extrinsic—law-keeping—spirituality of the nomists. Sibbes saw God's government as an objective reality—as objective as the nomist model with its reliance on the informed mind and disciplined will. In his view the measure of such things begins with God's existence—the bedrock of reality by any measure—and this existence consisted for Sibbes in God's inherent Triune love.

The Spirit's ministry of revealing that love to the elect soul served to ground Sibbes' confidence. Conversely, Sibbes' doctrine of sin viewed the will as defined by personal desires and, therefore, as wholly subjective and unreliable.

Faculty psychology

Puritans views of the soul relied on faculty psychology. Sibbes used the language of faculty psychology, for instance, when he spoke of depression as "a suffusion of the eye by reason of distemper of humours . . . so whatsoever is presented to a melancholy person, comes in a dark way to the soul." He also described sleep as "the obstruction and binding up of the senses by vapours which arise out of the stomach."[10] The question must be asked, however, whether his comparative resistance to speculative philosophy, noticed in chapter one, was also present in his anthropology.

The answer is yes, but his resistance was not expressed at the level of terminology. That is, Sibbes did not hesitate to describe aspects of the soul's operations in contemporary terms. It was the period equivalent to a modern theologian's use of medical descriptions. But Sibbes—unlike many of his Puritan colleagues—presented a picture that he felt was more consonant with Scripture and orthodox tradition, especially in describing relations between the key psychological elements in Puritan anthropology: the understanding, the will and the affections. As noted already, he refused to treat reason and volition as operative apart from the rule of the affections.

How, then, did Sibbes portray the particular functions of the faculties? Reflecting the conventional cause-effect connections of organic fluids and gases in a person's health, Sibbes expressed spirituality in tangible terms: a "soul" is a nearly tangible object with varied facets. Key doctrines were expressed by compounded metaphors: God by his Spirit "sets up his chair in the very heart, and alters [its] frame"; and the Spirit is conveyed by the promises of the word "as the veins and arteries that convey the blood and spirits".[11] He regularly returned to the Pauline metaphor of the soul as having eyes, and of conversion as a lifted veil. Salvation, then, is a restored vision of God: the disclosure of the spiritual presence of Christ to the soul.

Faculties and moral conduct

Yet the analogies of fluids and vision were just that: analogies. The practical question for Sibbes and his colleagues was one of applied ethics: how in light of the faculties does a believer grow in applied righteousness? Separate presuppositions led to separate conclusions.

Two main traditions were available to English Reformed theologians. The intellectualist tradition, associated with Aquinas, identified ethics with efforts of the soul directed by the conscience. Aquinas elevated the intellect by positing that *synteresis*—the knowledge of moral principles—is a natural property of the mind. Aquinas was confident, then, that truth could be reached by using syllogistic reasoning as guided by *synteresis* to supply the conscience with correct judgments.[12]

The second tradition, voluntarism, was associated with Augustine. It reversed the relationship of mind and will, holding that the will is self-determined by "rational appetites". Norman Fiering argues that Perkins' protégé, William Ames, was the most prominent advocate of Augustine's volitional scheme among the Puritans in Sibbes' era. His suggestion that Perkins and Ames were Augustinian voluntarists—when until now I have linked them to Aquinas and not to Augustine—invites an excursus on Fiering's *Moral Philosophy at Seventeenth-Century Harvard.*

Fiering's examination of the moral philosophy points to the emergence of a third tradition in moral theory, namely, the "sentimentalist school" of the eighteenth century. Fiering identifies this alternative to the intellectualist and voluntarist views, with the Scottish moral philosopher Francis Hutchinson whose work held much in common with that of Jonathan Edwards in America. Fiering seeks to identify sources of "inchoate sentimentalism" in the seventeenth century that accounts for "the most significant development in the history of ethics between 1675 and 1725."[13]

It is in this context that Fiering links the voluntarism of Perkins and Ames to Alexander Richardson's *The Logician's School-master; or a Comment upon Ramus' Logicke*, a manuscript in circulation at Cambridge University during the Perkins-Ames era. In this work the "extraordinary emphasis on, and expansion of, the Aristotelian ethical concept of *eupraxia*, meaning 'well-acting'" was promoted.[14] Fiering's investigations, in identifying the first resistance to the prevailing voluntarism of the Perkins'-Ames' school, or the intellectualism of Beza, Zanchius and others on the continent, led him to William Fenner's little-known *Treatise of the Affections* (1640) as "possibly the most significant work on the passions" to be found among English Puritans to that date. Fiering summarizes Fenner's contribution:

> In Fenner the unity of will and higher passion is already accomplished. The passions or affections are only "the motions of the will, by which it goes forth" to the embracing of its object as good or the avoidance of it as evil.[15]

Fenner "thoroughly depreciated 'understanding' as a factor in the religious life and warned ministers against preaching to it, and held, as would Jonathan Edwards in the next century, that the affections are 'the maine matter of grace . . . *the material of grace*'".[16]

What of Fiering's thesis? For one, he gives Fenner an undue place of honor that then skews his historical review. As we have seen already Melanchthon's treatment of affective theology in the 1521*Loci Communes* reflected Luther's thesis that the will is bound by its greatest affection. Fiering also overlooks Sibbes as an earlier proponent of affective theology among Puritans. Sibbes (b. 1577) was Fenner's (1600-40) senior by twenty-three years and was far more prominent than Fenner in Puritan circles.

Still, Fiering's work demonstrates a broader reaction against both the voluntarism and intellectualism that flowered in the Bezan and Perkinsonian period. His study is a "recounting of the steps by which the Scholastic-Aristotelian approach to ethics was abandoned in favor of newer modes of thought" so that "the moral philosophy texts in use at Harvard in 1650 were vastly different from those in use in 1710."[17] It would seem, then, that Sibbes' affective emphasis was not at all an oddity but represented at least one strand of a movement away from the anthropocentric morality of Federal theology.

Finally, in returning to the question about an affinity to Augustinian voluntarism in the Perkins-Ames' position, it is important to recall that Augustine's position shifted on the function of the will when he was faced with Pelagianism.[18] His early position assumed a self-determining capacity in the will, while in his later position he held that the will is directed by love, whether for good or for ill. The position of Aquinas, Perkins, and Ames all affirmed the early version of Augustine's doctrine of the will. For them the Aristotelian notion of an "appetitive" function of the will served as the foundation for moral conduct. Fiering's summary serves to conclude the excursus.

> Rational guidance is not what is needed. Only the renewed heart, with its godly love, is required. If the term "will" is still used, it no longer means anything like rational appetite but is simply another term for heart or love and is not strictly an intellectual faculty at all. In the Peripatetic and Thomist systems the passions were morally indifferent because the good or evil of an act

> depended not upon the impulse of passion but upon the consent of the will to the impulse. . . . Everything of moral concern hinges upon grace or the Spirit—that divine grace that infuses the will (or the heart), with the will understood not as rational appetite but as the seat of the passions.[19]

The understanding. Sibbes, in fact, denied the intellectualist and voluntarist traditions in favor of Augustine's affective portrayal of the will. But before considering his view of the understanding something must be said about Protestant views on the viability of reason. Gerrish traces the separation of faith and reason in the church first from Anselm's confidence in reason alone; then through Albert the Great's belief that some truth is only known by faith; and finally to Aquinas' idea of a gap between faith and reason in his "twofold way to truth".[20]

In Luther a fundamental gulf between theology and philosophy was assumed, with philosophy being competent to serve *das irdische Reich*—the kingdom of earth—but not the kingdom of heaven: "As long as reason is exercised within these limits, Luther has nothing but praise to heap upon it." The world, however, can know "nothing of Christ's doctrine."[21]

Calvin affirmed Luther's rejection of the capacity to know God through autonomous reason. Sin creates an insurmountable moral barrier, with sin understood as the ambition to be like God, such that,

> in seeking God, miserable men do not rise above themselves as they should, but measure him by the

yardstick of their own carnal stupidity, and neglect sound investigation; thus out of curiosity they fly off into empty speculations. They do not therefore apprehend God as he offers himself, but imagine him as they have fashioned him in their own presumption.[22]

Sibbes held the same view. Sin blocks any understanding of spiritual truth among unbelievers. While there might be an apparent knowledge of God, it is inferior, even among scholars, to the knowledge of God attained by the simplest believer: "As a blind man can talk of colours, if he be a scholar, and describe them better than he that hath his eyes, he being not a scholar. But he that hath his eyes can judge of colours a great deal better." True knowledge is thus grounded in an experience of God.[23]

In one sense, then, every sin is an act of ignorance. Sibbes argued that "If a man by nature believed the truths he says he knows, he would not go directly against them." Indeed, if such a person "knew what he were about, and apprehended that God saw him, and the danger of it, he would never sin. There is no sin without an error in judgment, there is a veil of ignorance and unbelief. What creature will run into a pit when he seeth it open? . . . All sin supposeth error."[24] Intellect, then, is not disabled in its operational functions—in processing data. Instead its assessments fail because the person has a caricature of God in view. How so? Because God is too forbidding to embrace when he is seen through the morally distorted lenses of human autonomy.

Sibbes held that this myopia is resolved by a faith that corrects distorted understanding: "Faith is an understanding grace; it knows whom it trusts, and for what, and upon what grounds it trusts." Faith, as a supernatural work of the Spirit, uses reason as its instrument not as its guide. Reason, in fact, has no inherent capacity to generate faith: "Reason of itself cannot find what we should believe, yet when God hath discovered [disclosed] the same, faith tells us there is great reason to believe it. Faith uses reason, though not as a ground, yet as a sanctified instrument to find out God's grounds, that it may rely upon them." In this arrangement all volitions and affections are tended by reason: "The soul guides the will and affection . . . . by ministering reasons to them".[25] In Sibbes' spiritual morphology, then, the Spirit guides every function of the believer's soul, and the understanding, corrected by faith, is one of the Spirit's chief instruments.

In its instrumental capacity the understanding operates by receiving external experiences or "phantasms" that are gathered by the heart. Sibbes located the practical center for sorting these understandings in the brain, but he saw the brain as inferior to the greater entity of the heart: "Christ . . . by his Spirit subdues the heart to obedience of what is taught. This is that teaching which is promised of God, when not only the brain but the heart itself is taught."[26]

Thus Sibbes denied the intellectualist tradition, not only in his belief that the understanding is spiritually blind, but also by its status as the least dynamic faculty of the soul. The understanding receives information, analyzes it by values received from the heart, and delivers its judgments to the will for possible actions. It was, in moral terms, the quietest voice of the inward triad of faculties. The relationship of understanding or reason to the will and affections, then, is simply one of providing information.

The will. Sibbes affirmed the standard view that the will functions as the elective capacity of the soul: it makes choices.[27] His exhortation-laden sermons, calling for his auditors to apply their wills to spiritual advancement, leads Stephen Beck to represent Sibbes as a voluntarist: "In Sibbes' soteriology [the] free grace of God calls for labor. The command to "labour" saturates Sibbes' sermons". Beck then offers a litany of such imperatives and concludes: "Preparation, while a divine work, is not God's work on a passive soul, but a cooperative responsibility that belongs to the spiritually dead."[28]

Beck's conclusion—that Sibbes held that the "spiritually dead" people can bear a responsibility to cooperate with God in salvation—reveals something of the modern confusion in reading Sibbes' view of the will. Suffice it to say that not even Perkins, who *did* promote a cooperative model of salvation, argued that efforts to reach God are possible when a person is spiritually dead: that view, Perkins believed, is a Roman Catholic fallacy.[29]

Sibbes viewed the will as an instrument of the heart. It is moved by the influence of the Spirit who "moves according to our principles" in that he "opens our understandings to see that it is best to trust in God." So the will is drawn by desires rather than coerced, compelled, or frightened as it makes its free choices. The failure of scholars to capture this belief reflects, no doubt, their shared assumption that Sibbes affirmed the volitional mutuality of the Federal covenant.

Rather Sibbes' use of moral imperatives must be read in light of a marital covenant: calls to "labour" were part of his affective rhetoric in the context of a mutual ardor of marital love. Even with nonbelievers present Sibbes' infralapsarian doctrine allowed him to call an audience to God's attractiveness, knowing that only the elect would recognize the applicability of God's free mercies to themselves and respond. His was the task of displaying God's love; God's task is to open the unbelieving heart to hear what is an accurate portrayal of God rather than the caricature that sin generates:

> Let us labour, then, to see where to have all the supply in all our wants. We have a full treasury to go to. All treasure is hid in Christ for us. What a comfort is this in anything we want! If we want the favour of God, go to his beloved Christ, desire God to love us in his beloved, and to accept us in his gracious Son, in him whom he hath made his servant, and anointed with his Spirit for that purpose. . . . Why are we so weak and comfortless? Why are we so dejected as if we had not such a rich husband?[30]

The key question about Sibbes' view of the will is whether he accepted the cooperative premise of Perkins and others that a self-moved will (albeit, aided by enabling grace) must be present in faith in order for the secondary agent—the believer—to be morally validated. Sibbes denied this premise on Augustinian grounds: "If we should hold our will to move itself, and not to be moved by the Spirit, we should make a god of it, whose property it is to move other things, and not to be moved by any."[31] Instead, God "first makes our will good, and then works by it."

Sibbes again alluded to Augustine in attributing a continued dependence of the human will on God's will:

> Indeed, the understanding is ours whereby we know what to do, and the will is ours whereby we make choice of what is best to be done; but the light whereby we know, and the guidance whereby we choose, that is from a higher agent, which is ready to flow into us with present fresh supply, when by virtue of former strength we put ourselves forward in obedience to God. . . . Therefore, we must both depend upon God as the first mover, and withal set all the inferior wheels of our souls agoing, according as the Spirit of God ministers motion unto us.[32]

The affections. In Sibbes' model of anthropology, then, the way in which "the Spirit of God ministers motion unto us" is found in God's prior motions and not in the human will. How is this motion transmitted? Through the affections as they respond to God's love.

Sibbes saw the affections as preeminent in the soul because they reveal a person's defining desires: "As we are in our affections," he taught, "we are in religion."[33] "Love", Sibbes argued, "is the first-born affection." This love "breeds desire of communion with God" and stirs up "dependence, confidence, and trust in God."[34] "If God be thy God", Sibbes asserted, "you have grace given you to love him above all things. . . . He loves us, and we love him again . . . . This is a sure sign that God is our God, if we love him above all." Knight captures this motive function in Sibbes' theology, noting that he defined "a God who was a lord, but more importantly, a lover; one who melted the heart instead of hammering it".[35] In this model, then, grace is seen to be God's effectual affections.

Other Puritans saw the affections—and their connection to mind and will—differently.[36] There was a common point of reference, however. Puritan pietism, when broadly construed to include both the nomist and affective strands, was bound together by a fundamental commitment to intentionalism: God's judgment of human conduct always looked at the intent behind an action when considering the action itself. This was even true of Perkins as his casuistic writings pressed readers to focus on behavioral righteousness.

At points in his writing Perkins went so far as to affirm the place of the affections in decision-making: "In the work of our regeneration, three graces be required: the preventing [prevenient] grace, the working grace, and the co-working grace. The preventing grace is, when God of his mercy sets and imprints in the mind a new light, in the will a new quality or inclination, in the heart new affections."[37] Thus, Perkins held elsewhere, "God measures the obedience due to him rather by the affection and desire to obey, than by the act and performance of it."[38]

The crucial point, however, is that Perkins believed that the affections are directed by the will, rather than vice versa. Thus, the new enablement of the will, or "the setting or imprinting of the new qualities and inclinations in the mind, will, affections of the heart" is God's work in which "we in it are *merely passive not active*." This, of course, describes the granting of *habitus* in the *habitus-actus* duality of the Thomistic doctrine of cooperation.

Perkins acknowledged as much: "And thus the will is not merely passive, but *passive* and *active* both: first passive, and then active. For we being acted and moved by God, who works the will and the deed, it also acts and moves. And we do not utterly deny the cooperation of man's will and God's grace."[39] With this notable affirmation of his cooperative doctrine, the question addressed to Sibbes above, must also be asked of Perkins: how, then, does God's motion move the will if God also requires an aspect of human cooperation?

In a key discussion of the matter, Perkins compared his view with two alternative views of the motive ("effectual") power in grace. He rejected a view that grace cooperates with a person's fully independent free will, the so-called Pelagian position. He also rejected a view, which he attributed to the Roman Catholic, Robert Bellarmine, that effectual grace is a response: "Others place the efficacy of grace in the congruity of the object, that is, in moral persuasions, which God knows to be apt and fit to move and allure the will according to the condition thereof, even as a beast is moved by the sight of hay." Perkins' answer is that grace, once granted, is effective by its own nature, functioning as an intermediary quality created by God: "We . . . place the efficacy of grace in grace itself."[40] Sibbes' position, then, was closer to Bellarmine's than to Perkins'. If external objects that "allure" a soul include even God himself, then the affective theology of Sibbes, with Augustine, Luther, and Calvin before him, is denied.

The heart. Sibbes held that there was an even higher capacity than the triad of faculties, namely the "heart" or "soul". His discussions of this capacity are less distinct but critical to understanding all the inward functions of the believer. As it guides or adjudicates the functions of the understanding, will and affections, the heart produces either "peace" or "turbulence".

Only the presence of the Spirit offers clear direction to the heart that would otherwise be drawn after faulty affections. His presence generates a gradual transformation. Sibbes' drew this model from the Pauline discussion in 2 Corinthians 3 that presents the superiority of the new covenant of the Spirit to the old covenant of Moses. The lifting of the veil of unbelief and the entrance of the Spirit generates the change: "The same Spirit that enlighteneth the mind, inspireth gracious inclinations into the will and affections, and infuseth strength into the whole man."[41] Sibbes compared the different operations of a believer and a nonbeliever:

> Judgment should have a throne in the heart of every Christian. Not that judgment alone will work a change, there must be grace to alter the bent and sway of the will, before it will yield to be wrought upon by the understanding. But God has so joined these together, as that whenever he does savingly shine upon the understanding, he gives a soft and pliable heart by the Spirit of God; it will follow its own inclination to that which it affecteth, whatsoever the judgment shall say to the contrary. There is no connatural proportion betwixt an unsanctified heart and a sanctified judgment. For the heart unaltered will not give leave to the judgment coldly and soberly to conclude what is best . . . . Judgment has not power itself where the will is unsubdued, for the will and affections bribe it to give sentence for them . . .[42]

The key issue is thus one of the heart's desires. The question left to be answered is what the heart consists of if it is higher in order to the other faculties—in that it directs them—while still being part of nature. Perkins had seen man's "spirit" to be a composite of the "mind, the conscience and the affections of the heart. For in these is the first and principal seat of divine and spiritual worship."[43]

Sibbes, however, generally spoke of the heart as separate from the faculties but on one occasion he adopted two of the three as a composite definition: "Where Christ is comfortably, he takes his throne and lodging in the heart, he dwells in it by faith. By heart, I mean, especially, the will and affections."[44] Sibbes, then—although somewhat unsettled on the subject—usually viewed the heart or soul as the unified quality of the personality that serves as the Spirit's center of operations. The affections are the Spirit's primary instrument.

Sibbes' Applied Anthropology: "Spiritual Government"

Some modern historians treat Sibbes as a founder of Federal theology despite his dismissal of Perkins' main themes.[45] Statements that seem to support the Federal notion of divine-human cooperation would explain this. Stoever, for instance, cites Sibbes in apparent favor of his thesis: "God frames his manner of dealing suitable to the nature he hath created us in."[46] Similarly Dever, in concluding his discussion of Sibbes' orthodoxy as a Reformed theologian in alignment with later Westminster standards, cites Sibbes: "we carry about us a double principle, nature and grace."[47] Kendall even goes so far as to see Sibbes as surpassing Perkins in his Federalism: "While Perkins might not be happy with Sibbes's statement, 'Labour to be such as God may love us', . . . such a remark reveals how far one can go towards an anthropocentric doctrine of faith when assurance is regarded as a reward for 'exact walking'."[48]

Indeed, in one strong statement Sibbes sounded like a Federal theologian: "This order of Christ's government by judgment is agreeable unto the soul, and God delighteth to preserve the manner of working peculiar unto man, that is, to do what he doth out of judgment: as grace supposeth nature as founded upon it, so the frame of grace preserveth the frame of nature in man."[49]

The key here, however, is to notice Sibbes' emphasis on "judgment" as touching nature and grace: the believer's judgment is the point of contact between man and God by the Spirit's indwelling presence. As that judgment is responsive to the Spirit it produces the fruit of sanctification. This alternative to nomist duties was Sibbes' belief in "spiritual government". This government comes about through God's immediate communion.

Participation in Divinity

The idea that the elect somehow "participate in the divine nature", as promised in 2 Peter 1:3-4, commanded the attention of all Puritan expositors.[50] Sibbes looked to this verse as the foundation for all of regeneration and a concomitant to his theology of marital union. It was a regeneration of love for God rather than an effort of the will in becoming more religious:

> Our disposition must be changed, we must be new creatures; they seek for heaven in hell that seek for spiritual love in an unchanged heart. When a child obeys his father, it is so from reasons persuading him, as likewise from a child-like nature which giveth strength to these reasons. It is natural for a child of God to love Christ so far as he is renewed, not only from inducement of reason so to do, but likewise from an inward principle and work of grace, whence those reasons have their chief forces; first, we are made partakers of the divine nature, and then we are easily induced and led by Christ's Spirit to spiritual duties.[51]

This "inward principle" was seen by Sibbes to be offered as part of a coherent exposition by Peter. But the same section was seen through different lens by the nomists. Verses five through seven of 2 Peter 1 lists a set of Christian virtues that were linked to divine participation. The set includes goodness, knowledge, self-control, perseverance, godliness, brotherly kindness, and love; and together they summarize the accouterments of faith. Verse eight exhorts, "For if you possess these qualities in increasing measure, they will keep you from being ineffective and unproductive . . ." Verse ten informs the earlier verses in that it seemed to connect personal initiative in seeking these qualities with an increased assurance of salvation: "Therefore . . . be all the more eager to make your calling and election sure."

This section, then, offered Puritans a litmus for the varied perceptions of faith and assurance—an assurance needed because of continued sin in their lives. Perkins, for instance, viewed it as the anchor for his use of the practical syllogism: "They [the elect] have not this knowledge from the first causes of Election, but rather from the last effects thereof, and they are especially two: the testimony of God's Spirit, and the works of sanctification, 2 Pet 1:10, Rom 8:16."[52]

Perkins' subsequent caveat was crucial: "If the testimony of God's Spirit be not so powerful in the elect, then they may judge of their election by the other effect of the Holy Ghost, namely sanctification"; thus, the door was open to use moral behavior as the touchstone of election.[53] This understanding of assurance, linked by the nomists to the priority of the will over the other faculties, seemed to affirm the moralistic tendencies of their synthesis. All who hoped to be among the elect and who lacked the direct witness of the Spirit—their number seems to have been legion—were to apply themselves to escape the corruption of sin in order to gain assurance.

Thomas Taylor reflected this anthropocentric thrust of nomism in his reading of 2 Peter 1; believers were to "stir up ourselves to grow up in holiness". He saw holiness as a future, possibly even eschatological, reality: "we shall be daily partakers of the divine nature, 2 Pet 1:3, which is not in respect of the nature and essence of God which is incommunicable, but in respect of the most excellent . . . qualities and gifts bestowed by the Spirit of God".[54] Taylor, then, followed Perkins' approach in his use of the verse as a ground for moral exhortation that emphasized the enabled will—now restored to Adam's original moral capacity—as the foundation of sanctification.

Sibbes compared Adam to Christ in an illuminating discussion of this text—especially in light of this nomist understanding. Sibbes turned to Genesis three: Adam's fall. While Adam once enjoyed the presence of the Spirit but then lost him, Christ's human life has a greater relation to the Spirit: he was fully reliant on the Spirit's life. The believer's union with Christ's life then shared in this greater reality, thus providing "a way far more near and sure than we had in Adam; for in him God was in man, but now man subsisteth in God, so as our nature is now strengthened by him, who also hath enriched it and advanced it; and what he hath wrought in his own human nature, he by little and little will work in all his mystical members."[55]

The pace of this transition—as a benefit of union with Christ—reflected the limited transformation that the elect could expect in their life on earth. Short of glory the believer's life is lived in the overlap of two natures: in the person's own human nature; and in Christ's nature through the Spirit who takes residency in the Christian's heart at regeneration.

> He hath put into us his own Spirit, so as wc are one spirit with Christ; and by that Spirit he worketh in us and by us by that Spirit. We hear, read, pray, and as by the soul in us our bodies do live, breathe, and move, and the like, so he maketh his Spirit to move in us to a holy conversation and a heavenly life, being thus made 'partakers of the divine nature,' 2 Peter 1:4; and this sanctifies us to a holy communion with God.[56]

The promise of 2 Peter 1, Sibbes assumed, was based on a real participation of the Spirit in Christ's human nature. By emphasizing continuity rather than discontinuity in the divine-human relationship Sibbes pushed beyond the ontological restrictions in Perkins' version of incommensurability. Christ, by the Spirit, rules as a "King" who "alters the nature of his subjects."

> He makes them subject . . . [including] the changing of our natures . . . For, beloved, . . . in the second covenant we are not left, as Adam was, in the hands of our own free will to stand or fall, but now in the second covenant that is founded upon Christ's death and satisfaction for us, Christ gives grace. He gives his Holy Spirit to bring us within the compass, and performs both our part and his too. He makes good his own . . . and he performs our part too, or else the second covenant, the covenant of grace, should be frustrate as the first was, if it were left to our freedom. . . . He gives us the very doing, the affections and loving.[57]

But unlike Christ's sinless human nature that responded to the Spirit without any failure, the believer's humanity is corrupted by both original and actual sin: "Christians have two sides, one to heaven-ward and God-ward; and that is full of glory, certain and immovable. Another towards the world; and that is oftentimes full of abasement, full of disgrace, and dejection."[58] So on the one hand the Christian continues to struggle with sin but on the other he or she is equipped by the Spirit to live the spiritual life successfully.

> Thus we have 'grace for grace,' both favour and grace in us, and privileges issuing from grace, we have all as they are in Christ. Even as in the first Adam we receive of his emptiness, curse for curse, ill for ill; for his blindness and rebellion we are answerable; we are born as he was after his fall: so in the second Adam, by his Spirit, we receive grace for grace. Hence issues this, that our state now in Christ is far more excellent than our state in Adam was.[59]

In this new state Christ, after the analogy of the sun, which by its elevation "doth convey his light and heat and influence . . . so Christ [after his ascension to heaven] being so highly advanced, is fitter to infuse his Spirit and grace here below." Thus, with "God being fully appeased" and the Son exalted, "the Spirit should be poured upon all flesh more abundantly than before. And that is the reason that the apostles so differed from themselves, before and after Christ's ascension."[60] This belief that the New Testament-era work of God through the Spirit was superior to that of Old Testament was the foundation for Sibbes' antinomism.

For the nomists, then, 2 Peter 1:4 promised the Spirit's work of enablement in believers who were then restored to their capacity as keepers of the moral regimen that followed; success in this was evidence of election. For Sibbes the passage represented the immediate presence of the Spirit within the believer's soul, shaping his or her affections and behavior by a continuing and direct work of grace.

Grace suffusing nature

In describing the government of the Spirit as an alternative to the nomist elevation of cooperative duties, Sibbes was also describing communion. He offered his closest exposition of the subject in *The Bruised Reed and Smoking Flax*. The Spirit governs believers by informing their intellect; this, in turn, leads to godly judgments. The arrangement implied a full suffusion of nature by grace. In Sibbes' version of faculty psychology the mind is the receptor of the Spirit's immediate communications.

Transformed nature. Thus, without reverting to a newly created faculty of grace as a pure intermediary, nature is transformed into a fitting instrument to receive grace: "Grace likewise maketh a gracious use even of natural and civil things, and doth spiritualise them. What another man doth only civilly, a gracious man will do holily. Whether he eateth or drinketh, or whatsoever he doth, he doth all to the glory of God".[61] Sibbes was careful to reiterate the Spirit's direct work in achieving this: "But there are no seeds of supernatural goodness at all in us. God findeth nothing in us but enmity; only he hath engraven this in our nature to incline in general to that which we judge to be good."[62] The Spirit is working to bring "victory" through judgment; a judgment based on "God's word". As promised in Jeremiah 31:31, the law in the believer's heart affirms the written law:

> By judgment here is meant the kingdom of grace in us, that government whereby Christ sets up a throne in our hearts. . . . Our spirit being under the Spirit of Christ,

> is governed by him, and so far as it is governed by Christ, it governs us graciously. Christ and we are of one judgment, and of one will. He hath his will in us; and his judgments are so invested into us, as that they are turned into our judgment, we carrying 'his law in our hearts written by his Spirit,' Jer. 31:33. The law in the inner man and the law written, answer as counterpanes each other.[63]

Faith, then, is a person's ongoing reliance on God's word. Entrance into this state of continuing reliance comes through repentance, that is, a fundamental shift in the "taste of the soul" which is generated by the Spirit's presence.

> The whole work of grace in us is set out under the name of judgment, and sometimes wisdom, because judgment is the chief and leading part in grace; whereupon that gracious work of repentance is called a change of mind, and an after-wisdom. . . . [As] taste is the most necessary sense, and requireth the nearest application of the object of all other senses. So in spiritual life, it is most necessary that the Spirit should alter the taste of the soul, so as that it might savour the things of the Spirit so deeply, that all other things should be out of relish. . . . [J]udgment . . . includeth the government of both mind, will, and affections . . .[64]

The question of how this transformation is accomplished without the coercion or compulsion was answered by ascribing a formational power to love. While love was often portrayed as an undefined quality of the heart in his works, Sibbes spoke as if he and his audience shared a clear definition. He located love in the affections although in his spiritual morphology it could readily be expressed as a product of the will (or judgments). He held the affections to be the inwardly sensitive faculty that forms or identifies values for the soul; and the devotion of the affections informs the will that, now regenerated, follows those desires.

Thus, both the intellect and will, no longer morally dissonant, act as instruments in fulfilling the desires of godly affections. They transmit information to and from the external world: the mind receives and transmits data from the senses to the soul; the will in gaining knowledge, applies values derived from the affections and makes judgments that lead to actual conduct. Thus the affections are the guiding faculty of the soul by establishing the soul's values and priorities. Love was the inclusive term used for the quality of desiring. It encompasses and describes any positive values whether or not they are objectively good.

It is God's love, as his desire for the elect, that informs every event of the order of salvation—the *ordo salutis.* The motive force of God's love, beginning in the Father and presented to the believer through Christ's works and by the indwelling Spirit, simply needs to be recognized by the elect who are irresistibly attracted to the source of such kindness. The believer, saved and governed by love, is, in turn, a subordinate governor of his or her own soul, growing to enjoy the same desires that God enjoys.

> He [Christ] so pardons as he will be obeyed as a king; he so taketh us to be his spouse, as he will be obeyed as a husband. The same Spirit that convinceth us of the necessity of his righteousness to cover us, convinceth us also of the necessity of his government to rule us. His love to us moveth him to frame us to be like himself, and our love to him stirreth us up to be such as he may take delight in . . . [H]e maketh us subordinate governors . . . to subdue in some measure our base affections. . . . Again, remember this, that Christ, as he ruleth us, so it is by a spirit of love from a sense of his love, whereby his commandments are easy to us. He leadeth us by his free Spirit, a Spirit of liberty: his subjects are voluntaries. The constraint that he layeth upon his subjects is that of love: he draweth us with the cords of love sweetly.[65]

Sibbes, then, saw nature as honored rather than violated by the presence and governance of the Spirit. It was a rule of love rather than a rule of extrinsic compulsion or duty. It rejected any need for the relative autonomy presupposed in the alternative system of nomism.

The hypostatic union and saving union. Sibbes' theology of the Christ-church union drew its covenantal structure from mystical marriage, as examined in the last chapter. He also developed the head and body imagery. The Spirit, representing Christ, is poured into the soul of the believer, thus bringing life: "So that Spirit which is in him, a full running-over fountain, dropping down and being also infused in us, unites us unto him."[66] The individual believer and the collective church are, together, "the temple of God, and . . . the habitation of God by the Spirit" so that "we are inseparably knit and united unto him."

This union, Sibbes argued, is based on "the same quickening spirit and life which is in both, and which causeth a like motion . . . so that it is the same spirit and life which is in the things conjoined that unites." Sibbes regularly pointed to this organic unity of the body, using the Bible imagery, as representing the reality of spiritual ontology.

> Yet to explain this more—as I have often in the like case spoken—imagine a man were high as heaven, the same life and spirit being in all parts, what is that now that can cause his toe to stir, there being such a huge distance betwixt the head and it? Even that self-same life which is in the head being in it; no sooner doth the head will the toe to stir but it move. So is it with us; that very Spirit which is in him being in us, and he in us, thereby we are united to him, grow in him, and live in him, rejoice in him, and so are kept and preserved to be glorified with him. He is the 'second Adam,' from whom we received the influence of all good things, showering down and distilling the graces of his Spirit upon all his members . . .[67]

A question arises. Is the work of the Spirit in distributing the life of Christ offered through his capacities as a human or as the God-man? The humanity of the elect is compatible with the humanity of Christ but falls radically short of his divinity. Sibbes believed that the very point of the incarnation would have been to offer the full personhood of Christ to the elect—both natural and divine—yet without affirming any ontological confusion of Creator and creature. Sibbes' Christology displayed his distinctive form of Spirit-Christicism: Christ's ministry modeled the Spirit's guidance to believers; and the Spirit worked in Jesus' humanity to shape all his choices and enabled him to respond to his own deity. That is, Christ in his deity, directed the Spirit to guide himself in his humanity.[68]

This view either assumed that Christ's divine nature is eternally divisible, displaying both sending and receiving capacities in the same moment; or that Christ's hypostatic union is explained in adoptionistic terms, with the Spirit coming on an otherwise human (albeit perfect) nature. Sibbes, however, was satisfied that his synthesis unlocked the secret of regeneration and sanctification. In practical terms it combined Christology and Pneumatology: "Whatever Christ did as man, he did by the Spirit."[69] By this arrangement the full presence of the godhead enters humanity through Christ's human nature; and through union with Christ the believer receives the same benefits that were available to Christ in his humanity.

Sibbes' theme was expressed most explicitly in his sermons, *A Description of Christ.* This series introduced the subsequent *Bruised Reed and Smoking Flax* series. There is a clear relationship between the two—they form an extended exposition of Christ's servant role found in Matthew 12:18-20. If God changes a person's nature by giving them all the qualities of Christ's own nature through spiritual union as presented in *A Description*, then the task of the minister is to elicit the desires and actions of holiness which reside in that nature. He then exhorts a full rejection of Adam's old nature that still survives.

This assumption was a guiding theme in Sibbes' exposition of God's work throughout *The Bruised Reed.*

It will be helpful, then, to notice Sibbes' argument in *A Description* as it resolves the problem of sin for him through human participation in Christ's double nature. Sibbes represented salvation as God's "great master-piece of service" to "bring God and man together again".[70] This was accomplished through "four notable conjunctions" which characterized an ontological continuum between God and humanity. The continuum is divided by the ontological gulf between deity and nature, so that, of the conjunctions, there are "two in us and two above us." The first is the union of body and soul; the second, of Christ and the church ("head and members make one Christ"); the third is the hypostatic union; and the fourth, the union of the godhead.[71]

It is in the second conjunction that the ontological gulf between God and man is bridged. Sibbes' doctrines of sin and union intersected at that point. There is, he believed, an ironic reversal of pride and humility apparent in Christ's incarnation. Through it Christ, the creator and one to whom humility was inappropriate, came as a servant to his rebellious creatures, in whom humility is appropriate and pride is vile. It was an arrangement motivated by love:

> Whence comes it that Christ is a servant? It is from the wondrous love of God, and the wondrous love of Christ. To be so abased, it was wondrous love in God to give him to us to be so abased, and the wondrous misery we were in, that we could not otherwise be freed from; for such was the pride of man, that he, being

> man, would exalt himself to be like God. God became man, he became a servant to expiate our pride in Adam, so that it is wondrous in the spring of it.[72]

In developing his view, Sibbes emphasized continuity rather than discontinuity in the incarnation and defined sin as a prideful self-exaltation so consuming as to be inescapable. Christ's purpose in the incarnation, then, was to redress sin by becoming a complete opposite to the first Adam. Love motivated God to send his son in a humbling intervention; humility expiated pride; and power came through service.

This logic displays Sibbes' infralapsarianism in that it defined the purpose of the incarnation on the basis of human need consequent to the fall. Yet Sibbes portrayed this arrangement not in terms of God's contingency—reacting to the fall—but as satisfying a greater purpose. When viewed from the human point of view, he argued, the hypostatic union displayed God's willingness to form a real and enduring bond between creator and creation: "If we regard his human nature, it was an advancement for man's nature to be grafted into God by conception and incarnation; but if we regard his Godhead, for him to conceal himself, and lay aside the beams and rays of majesty, and clothe himself with man's flesh, this was the first degree of humiliation."

Having demonstrated twin perspectives—God's and humanity's—in the incarnation, Sibbes extended this principle of the divine-human reciprocity to the atonement.[73] He argued: "Our sins must be imputed to him, and then his righteousness and whatsoever is good is ours; . . ." It was a service "perfectly done", achieved by "Christ, God-man."[74] Election, Sibbes argued, is to be seen in the context of God calling Christ to this role of servant. The inaugural sermon text for the *Description of Christ*—Matthew 12:18—captured that intention: "Behold my servant whom I have chosen." Thus, election is *into* the Son, and, through union with the Son, to salvation through his benefits.[75]

Perkins addressed the question of the relationship of the church-Christ union and Christ's hypostatic union differently. While Sibbes emphasized the continuity of Christ's double nature in its application to his union with the elect, Perkins' doctrine of radical incommensurability restricted any expression of personal union. This in turn led him to represent a believer's union with Christ in legal and adoptionist terms.[76] Thus while Perkins and Sibbes might appear to have much in common in the language of union they actually held fundamentally different positions. Sibbes held that union with Christ was equivalent to marital union—or a conjugal bond—in which the two persons remain distinct while truly united.[77] In the same manner that the Spirit directed Christ as the God-man, the Spirit is also available to direct his bride, the church.

Sibbes, through his assumption that Christ's humanity is fully operative while still fully responsive to the Spirit's leadership, was satisfied to offer Christ's life as a model to his listeners in light of this real union. The fallen man, however, is unlike Christ since he lacks an immaculate human nature. It is through the reciprocal nature of the marital love that the blemished bride can, despite her moral faults, pursue the bridegroom as the *Song of Song* imagery called for.

In Sibbes' view of the spiritual life, then, there can be full continuity between the power of God as manifested in

Christ's earthly ministry and that available to the Christian. "Our lives", he taught on the basis of Galatians 2:2, "should be nothing but an acting of Christ living in our souls." He insisted on the Spirit's immediate, versus mediate, presence in believers:

> This is not a mere analogical truth, but it floweth naturally. Whosoever are to have the benefit of his birth and conception, Christ sendeth into their heart the same Spirit that sanctified the mass wherof he was made, and so frameth a disposition suitable to himself. He sets his own stamp upon the heart. As union of his human nature, so the Spirit of God, uniting us to Christ, is the cause of all grace in us. If we have not the Spirit of Christ, we are none of his.[78]

It was in the context of this Spirit-Christology that Sibbes definitively rejected any use of *habitus* theology as a basis for secondary indeterminacy. Sibbes insisted in opposition to the "philosophers" that "all habitual graces in us" must be seen "not as they are streams derived to us, and resting in us, but as they are knit to a spring which is never drawn dry".[79] Thus, Sibbes was explicit in calling for a full dependence of nature on grace by the Spirit's immediate and active presence in the elect.

Conclusion

This chapter examined Sibbes' anthropology, with special attention given to his belief that God establishes a real union of participation with the elect through Christ for the purpose of communion. In his description of the standard Puritan triad of human faculties, Sibbes pointed to the affections rather than the intellect or will as the point where "communion is especially placed".[80] Sibbes spoke of human affections and judgment, once they are under the Spirit's leadership, as centers of God's spiritual government.

We first considered the general elements of Puritan anthropology where it was shown that beneath the common terminology of faculty psychology and biblical imagery there existed at least two, if not three, anthropological models to describe God's saving work. Separate but similar traditions treated the mind and will as paired features of the soul: the intellectualists and the voluntarists. Fiering's examination of the "sentimentalist" tradition, while flawed by its failure to identify Augustine's early and later versions of voluntarism, still helps to clarify underlying tensions in the division in English Reformed theology. He shows that the voluntarism of Perkins and Ames was actually a short-lived system. The first real resistance to that approach is linked to the counterposition of affective theology. Fiering, however, fails to identify its major forerunners in the early Lutheran theology of Melanchthon; and in Sibbes' theology among the Puritans.

Sibbes, as we saw, applied his anthropology under the rubric of spiritual government. This was based on the affective emphasis in his anthropology and a theology of participation. This set up his antinomist spirituality that featured "spiritual judgments" as guided by the active work of the Spirit. Sibbes treated this divine government as a product of the formative power of love. His assumptions stood in sharp contrast to Perkins' nomism in which the efficacy of grace is self-inherent and, therefore, not a feature of a person's relations with Christ. This supported the mitigated autonomy of the human will, which was required in Perkins' Aristotelian model of morality. It also reinforced the conspicuous anthropocentricism of his spirituality.

In the next chapter we come to the relationship between biblical promises, both conditional and unconditional, and the implications of conditional promises to saving faith. Sibbes, against Calvin and despite his own consistent emphasis on God's unilateral initiative in salvation and sanctification, is shown to share with Perkins an openness to the use of conditional promises as a ground for salvation. The position, crucial to Perkins' more anthropocentric spirituality, produced confusion in Sibbes' doctrine of grace, a confusion that reveals Sibbes' incomplete departure from his Perkinsonian heritage.

Chapter Six

God's Work in Forming Faith

"Framing us every way to be such as thou mayest take pleasure and delight in"

God is the ultimate free agent, Richard Sibbes reminded one of his audiences: "If we esteem not the Spirit as we should, the Spirit may withdraw and suspend the sweet exercise of faith, though not wholly take it away, because it is a grace that proceeds from a free agent, the Holy Ghost."[1] Sibbes thus reversed an anthropocentric emphasis of nomism—that human free agency in the context of secondary indeterminacy—is God's mechanism not only for conversion but also for sanctification.

Sibbes accepted two free agents in the nature-grace nexus through the Augustinian linkage of the will and the affections. Yet he could be inconsistent in his applied ministry. For instance he *also* affirmed a crucial aspect of William Perkins' bilateral theology: that saving faith may result from a response to the conditional promises—"if you . . . then I"—of the Bible. This countered Calvin's insistence that true faith will arise only through God's unconditional promises.

Sibbes' apparent departure from the kind of consistent unilateralism that he shared with Calvin was significant. Indeed, Perkins' Federal bilateralism found its greatest support in just such promises. Given Sibbes' broader theology what accounts for his acceptance of this premise? The question is the main interest of this chapter as we consider Sibbes' incomplete disengagement from Perkins' theology.

Conditional Promises and Saving Faith

Sibbes, with his contemporaries, held the Bible to be the word of God.[2] As such, it served as the objective ground for faith. The divisive question in Reformed circles concerning the scriptures was whether all scriptures are equally suitable to be used by the Spirit in the work of saving faith. The question focused on whether the promises that seem to offer salvation as a reward for human activity can ever be grounds for saving faith, and if not, what those promises actually signified.[3]

God's Promises

The Bible offers conditional and unconditional promises related to salvation.[4] Do both serve as grounds for saving faith? Or is a reliance on conditional promises the source of 'works-righteousness'? These questions were near the heart of the debate over grace in Sibbes' era. A concomitant question addressed the work of the Spirit in applying these promises. Is the ministry of the Spirit overt; or is it covert, a work hidden in the "means of grace"? And, of the means of grace—that is, the word, sacraments, fellowship, prayer and preaching—how does the Spirit relate to the Bible? Does the Spirit offer an immediate work of revelation as the Quakers later asserted? Or is revelation always mediated through the Bible? If so, does the more immediate revelation open a potential for conflict between the Bible and inward motions? Since Sibbes' view of revelation offers a context for the question of the Spirit's use of biblical promises, it will be useful to respond to the latter issues before addressing his view of conditional promises.

The Spirit and the Word. Sibbes sometimes discussed grace in the hypostatic terms of Perkins' created grace.[5] While such occasions may have been remnant features in the course of a transition away from Perkins' position, they may also suggest a certain indifference about the terminology of grace. Sibbes' doctrine of faith—construed as an absolute reliance on God's immediate presence—was, in fact, located in the Spirit's effective application of scripture to the soul rather than in the duality of grace that Perkins presumed. This is seen in his discussions of the Spirit and the Word.

In *A Description of Christ* Sibbes explained the parallel between the indwelling of the Spirit in Christ and his work in the believer: "The Holy Ghost . . . makes Christ the pattern of all; for whatsoever is in Christ, the Holy Ghost, which is the Spirit of Christ, works in us as it is in Christ." For Sibbes the main purpose of union with Christ is to "make us one with him, and thereupon to quicken us, to lead us, and guide us, and to dwell in us continually, to stir up prayers and supplications in us, to make us cry familiarly to God as to a Father . . ."[6] Thus, just as the Bible presents the Spirit as directing Christ in the gospels; and the apostles in the book of Acts; so believers can also expect the same work of guidance in their own lives. Sibbes even pointed to the Spirit's essence as "pure act" to suggest that the Spirit's active nature is readily discerned once he indwells the believer.[7]

Sibbes' purpose in elevating the Spirit's activities was to affirm the benefits offered to Christians in the New Testament era: "In a word, if Christ be that Spirit, and have infused the Spirit into us, *it will make us like him*; it will transform us into his likeness, it will make us holy and humble and obedient as he was, even to the death."[8] But Sibbes was also obliged to describe the manner of the Spirit's guidance in daily life. While the main elements of that description have been noticed already in his doctrine of spiritual government a further question must be asked in this context. How are the Spirit's directions—his motions—to be discriminated from emotional excesses, or, among the immature, from careless pretenses?

Most other ministers in Puritan circles were happy enough to leave any immediate or dramatic works of the Spirit to the primitive church. Sibbes was certainly aware of the dangers in opening a door to spiritual enthusiasm, but his position was a logical concomitant to his Spirit-Christicism. In *A Fountain Sealed* Sibbes addressed the functions and limits of spiritual motions. He warned against placing limits on the Spirit, citing Paul's example in being directed by the Spirit: "We must take especial heed of slighting any motion, as being the Spirit's messenger. They are God's ambassadors, sent to make way for God into our hearts . . ."[9] They are the tools of sanctification.[10]

Just how central, then, were these motions to Sibbes' model in actual practice? The answer is ambiguous. On the one hand Christ's dependence on the Spirit's guidance was his paradigm for all spirituality; but on the other Christ, unlike his followers, was sinless. Thus, some motions in believers, even those which seem intrinsically good, might well be stirred by Satan: "But seeing Satan will oft interrupt good motions by good motions, that he may hinder both, *Quest.* How shall we know from whence the motions come?"[11] Sibbes answered with a set of criteria that were ultimately based on biblical content.

Yet he also suggested that the direction, persistence, and quality of the motions indicate their origin. Despite such rules, Sibbes still recognized the potential for deception inherent in motions. This led him back to the scriptures as a basic criterion that supervises motions: "The Breath of the Spirit in us is suitable to the Spirit's breathing in the Scriptures; the same Spirit doth not breathe contrary motions."[12] Thus the Word of God and the words of God were of the same Spirit and can never be at odds with each other.[13]

Sibbes' confidence in the Spirit's use of the Scriptures that characterized his moderate mysticism stood in contrast to the muted acquiescence of Perkins.[14] Perkins preferred to see the Bible as the source of God's will, epitomized in the Decalogue, that is applied by the Spirit-enabled mind and will.

The Promises and Faith. The premises of Aristotle's *Ethics* that morality must be placed in the free will; and of the Pelagian movement—that God will not apply culpability for sin if there is no human capacity to avoid sin—continued to be promoted in nomist circles. These views, when combined with the conditional promises in the Bible, were the foundation of the cooperative model of salvation.

The affective tradition, on the other hand, rejected the Pelagian premise by insisting that the problem of sin is not a disabled or uninformed will, but a will captivated by self-love. Thus the culpability remains. The conditional promises in the Bible, however, drew many theologians to the cooperative solution of the grace-enabled will. The question, then, of the function of conditional promises in the Bible was pivotal to those who held the unilateral model of salvation.

Sibbes on God's promises

It is at this point that Sibbes displays his inconsistency by attempting to represent faith as a unilateral work of the Spirit while, at the same time, affirming the conditional nature of the promises through which the Spirit works. In order to display the issues involved, an extended comparison will be offered, beginning with Calvin's view of the question, then Perkins' alternative position; an assessment of Sibbes' position is made on the basis of the features found in Calvin and Perkins.

Calvin on promises. We need to consider Calvin's view of promises in salvation, sanctification, and assurance because of Cotton's claim, cited already, that Calvin was on his side in the Antinomian Controversy: "[L]et us hold it forth in the language of Calvin . . . who speak of purity of life and growth in grace and all the works of sanctification as the effects and consequents of our assurance of faith . . . ."[15] Cotton, in taking Calvin's view, held that any use of the practical syllogism for assurance only encourages uncertainty or hypocrisy. For the same reason it is necessary to deny any linkage between conditional promises and saving faith:

> Now this faith thus wrought in our effectual calling is not built upon any conditional promise of grace preexistent in us, nor can it be built upon any but upon

> some absolute free promise of God unto our soul . . . . But if the promise be conditional, it is a condition subsequent to faith, not antecedent before it. Our faith closeth with Christ upon a promise of free-grace, otherwise (as saith Calvin) my faith would always be trembling and wavering, as my works be.[16]

Calvin, indeed, believed that the object of faith determines the nature of faith: "We make the freely given promise of God the foundation of faith because upon it faith properly rests." Saving promises represented God's character and were necessarily theocentric, relational, and unconditional rather than those based on fulfilled commandments: "Faith is certain that God is true in all things . . . . faith properly begins with the promise, rests in it, and ends in it. For in God faith seeks life: a life that is not found in commandments or declarations of penalties, but in the promise of mercy, and only in a freely given promise."[17]

So Cotton's complaint against the practical syllogism was indeed supported by Calvin's antipathy towards any form of assurance based on human conduct:

> For a conditional promise that sends us back to our own works does not promise life unless we discern its presence in ourselves. Therefore, if we would not have our faith tremble and waver, we must buttress it with the promise of salvation, which is willingly and freely offered to us by the Lord in consideration of our misery rather than in our deserts.[18]

The logical sequence of the *ordo salutis*, that differed depending on the definition of faith being used, readily distinguished the nomists from the antinomists. The dispute over the place of saving promises in the Antinomian Controversy had to do with the perception of faith in the elect as either active or passive. A passive faith—as in Cotton's view—was a recognition of God's initiative: the filling of an empty vessel. Peter Bulkeley, who represented the nomists of New England with prophetic confidence, held the cooperative position: the core of faith is an act of the will that grasps a promise for oneself. This produces union.[19] Bulkeley criticized Cotton's position accordingly: "For this [Cotton's] union is made before faith worketh, and the work of this faith is but an effect of the union, and not any cause of it."[20] Cotton responded by accusing Bulkeley of holding a position more dependent on Aristotle than on the Bible.[21]

Cotton was on solid ground in his confidence that Calvin's theology supported him.[22] The question being debated by Bulkeley and Cotton had to do with their separate perceptions of God's stance toward the elect at the moment of conversion. Bulkeley, in line with Perkins, described faith as the enabled will of the elect person reaching out to take hold of God. In this portrayal God is standing apart, waiting for the person to reach out after him.[23] The affective model held, instead, that faith occurs in the moment at which the heart recognizes God's mercy and love as its own. God is the one who acts, approaching the person while speaking words of love.[24] The nomist model characterizes the motivation of faith as coming from *within* the enabled heart; while the affective model represents the motive element of faith as residing *outside* the person, namely, in God's self-disclosed love.

Calvin's solution conspicuously rejected the nomistic model.[25] His definition of faith made sin a problem of misplaced affections, following Augustine's mature definition of sin as positive, rather than the product of a disabled will.[26] In the *Institutes*, having made the point that faith rests on God's word, Calvin pointed to the weakness, under sin, of the mind and will: "But since man's heart is not aroused to faith at every word of God, we must find out at this point what, strictly speaking, faith looks to in the Word. . . . But we ask . . . what faith finds in the Word of the Lord upon which to lean and rest." Will not biblical warnings of God's wrath only cause the soul "to shun the God whom it dreads?" From this, Calvin concluded, "merely to know something of God's will is not to be accounted faith. But what if we were to substitute his benevolence or his mercy in place of his will . . . . for it is after we have learned that our salvation rests with God that we are attracted to seek him." He enlarged the ground of this attraction:

> This fact is confirmed for us when he declares that our salvation rests with God that we are attracted to seek him. This fact is confirmed for us when he declares that our salvation is his care and concern. Accordingly, we need the promise of grace, which can testify to us that the Father is merciful; since we can approach him in no other way, and upon grace alone the heart of man can rest.[27]

Calvin held that the will "was so bound to wicked desires that it cannot strive after the right." [28] The guiding desire of the fallen man, he held, is "self-love and ambition", a product of the decision of "our first parent to want to become 'like gods, knowing good and evil'".[29] Calvin's affirmation of sin as self-love set up his belief that a solution is provided by a new and greater affection. That affection is awakened in the elect by the sight of God's benevolence offered in an unconditional ("free") promise. It was in such a context that his definition faith was offered:

> Now, the knowledge of God's goodness will not be held very important unless it makes us rely on that goodness. Consequently, understanding mixed with doubt is to be excluded, as it is not in firm agreement, but in conflict, with itself. Yet far indeed is the mind of man, blind and darkened as it is, from penetrating and attaining even to perception of the will of God! And the heart, too, wavering as it is in perpetual hesitation, is far from resting secure in that conviction! Therefore our mind must be otherwise illumined and our heart strengthened, that the Word of God may obtain full faith among us. Now we shall possess a right definition of faith if we call it a firm and certain knowledge of God's benevolence toward us, founded upon the truth of the freely given promise in Christ, both revealed to our minds and sealed upon our hearts through the Holy Spirit.[30]

Calvin was adamant about the non-conditional nature of saving promises. In positive terms, he described faith both in rational and relational terms: "first, that faith does not stand firm until a man attains to the freely given promise; second, that it does not reconcile us to God at all unless it joins us to Christ."[31] The first of these two, the "freely given promise", excludes any element of contingency as a ground for faith because human contingency (if a promise has conditions) implies a capacity for righteous deeds as well as some claim on merit. The second criterion—that it "joins us to Christ"—points to relationality established apart from any merit. By linking faith to union with Christ, Calvin held that faith is in Christ himself rather than in any creedal affirmations:

> If someone believes that God both justly commands all that he commands and truly threatens, shall he therefore be called a believer? By no means! Therefore, there can be no firm condition of faith unless it rests upon God's mercy. Now, what is our purpose in discussing faith? Is it not that we may grasp the way of salvation? But how can there be saving faith except in so far as it engrafts us in the body of Christ?[32]

Thus the focus of all promises, "the whole gospel", is on Christ.[33] A Bible promise only leads to faith when "God illumines it by the testimony of his grace." Promises, then, express God's love to the world, but only the elect respond. The unbeliever spurns them:

> For they neither think nor recognize that these benefits come to them from the Lord's hand; or if they do recognize it, they do not within themselves ponder his

> goodness. Hence, they cannot be apprised of his mercy any more than brute animals can . . . . Nothing prevents them, in habitually rejecting the promises intended for them, from thereby bringing upon themselves a greater vengeance. For although the effectiveness of the promises only appears when they have aroused faith in us, yet the force and peculiar nature of the promises are never extinguished by our unfaithfulness and ingratitude. Therefore, since the Lord, by his promises, invites man not only to receive the fruits of his kindness but also to think about them, he at the same time declares his love to man. Hence we must return to the point: that any promise whatsoever is a testimony of God's love toward us.[34]

In Calvin's view, then, the elect are displayed by their positive and affective response to the unconditional promises of the gospel.[35] For those who fail to see God's love in his promises, the problem is located in their own character, not in God's. The source of this blindness is found in their insistence that God's character must be like their own fallen character. Calvin used Paul's remarks in 1 Corinthians 2:6-16 about self-knowledge to make the point:

> But if, as Paul preaches, no one "except the spirit of man which is in him" witnesses the human will, what man would be sure of God's will? And if the truth of God be untrustworthy among us also in those things which we at present behold with our eyes, how could it be firm and steadfast when the Lord promises such

> things as neither eye can see nor understanding can grasp? But here man's discernment is so overwhelmed and so fails that the first degree of advancement in the school of the Lord is to renounce it. For, like a veil cast over us, it hinders us from attaining the mysteries of God, "revealed to babes alone".[36]

Self-love, then, veils God's pristine character. This blindness is only overcome, in the elect, by the Spirit's active application of unconditional promises in individual hearts. Illumination, saving faith and engrafting into Christ are all one and the same event: "Christ, when he illumines us into faith by the power of his Spirit, at the same time so engrafts us into his body that we become partakers of every good."[37]

The Nomists on Promises. Like Calvin, William Perkins also referred to God's promises found in Christ's mediatorial work: "The foundation and groundwork of the covenant is Christ Jesus the mediator in whom all the promises of God are yea and amen, and therefore he is called the angel of the covenant, and the covenant of the people to be made with the nations in the last age."[38] However, Perkins' linkage of Christ, the promises, and covenant, is instructive in that it displays Perkins' departure from Calvin's distinct unilateralism.

Subsuming all biblical promises did this, whether conditional or unconditional, under the first covenant with Adam, that was conditional. Knight comments on the particular disposition that this Federalism produced among Perkins' followers in New England: "It is not God as he is in himself, but as he deals with the sinner that engages them—God as exacting lord, implacable judge, or demanding covenanter."[39] Perkins displays this in *A Golden Chaine* where he used the biblical language of promises but sets promises into contractual opposition, as two sides of a bilateral agreement. His presentation has two stages: first the Adamic covenant of works, then the covenant of grace. Both are parallel, thus making Perkins' preliminary statement, with its emphasis on conditions, equally applicable to both:

> God's covenant is his contract with man concerning the obtaining of life eternal upon a certain condition. This covenant consists of two parts—God's promise to man, man's promise to God. God's promise to man is that whereby he bindeth himself to man to be his God if he perform the condition. Man's promise to God is that whereby he voweth his allegiance unto his Lord and to perform the condition between them. Again, there are two kinds of covenant—the covenant of works and the covenant of grace.[40]

The second stage of presentation discriminated between the two covenants: first, "The covenant of works is God's covenant made with condition of perfect obedience and is expressed in the moral law" and epitomized in the Decalogue; and second, "The covenant of grace is that whereby God, freely promising Christ and of his benefits, exacts again of man that he would by faith receive Christ and repent of his sins."[41] Thus both covenants are explicitly conditional, with perfect obedience as the condition of the first, and faith as that of the second.[42]

This, of course, expresses the cooperative model of salvation. As such it differed from Calvin's position. Calvin understood and accepted aspects of mutuality between God and humanity in Adam's original state, yet without making God's promises of mercy subordinate to, or coterminous with covenant as Perkins did.[43] Perkins' Federalism portrayed God's prohibition in Eden as the defining structure for all subsequent relations between God and humanity. That is, the covenant of works is *never* dismissed in the period of human history. For the elect its conditions are satisfied by Christ's human righteousness, with the benefits of his success judicially distributed through adoption.

This distribution is defined by the subsequent and subsidiary covenants of grace (including the Mosaic covenant before Christ and New Covenant in the Christian era). Thus it remains perpetually in effect, a fact that continues to condemn all reprobates. Because all subsequent covenants are merely extensions of that primary covenant, any subsequent promises of grace from God are modified by the presumption of this prior conditionality. When describing the covenant of grace, for instance, Perkins spoke of God as "freely promising Christ and his benefits", a usage which sounds like Calvin's; but, as Perkins went on to point out, the promise actually contains a condition, that "exacts again of man that he would by faith receive Christ and repent of his sins."[44] God's "freely promising", it would seem, referred to God's lack of obligation in offering Christ's atoning ministry.

By exacting faith and repentance from man, Perkins departed from Calvin's version of God's free promises. Even if it is argued that promise and covenant are interchangeable for Perkins, it would still need to be shown that the word covenant meant something other than a commercial (bilateral) transaction to the sixteenth-century listener, or that promise or testament did not, on the other hand, connote a unilateral commitment. Perkins recognized the tension created by his conflation of different theological concepts but failed to address it seriously: "This covenant is also named a testament, for it hath partly the nature and properties of a testament or will."[45] It was only by such blending of unilateral promises and bilateral covenant that allowed the key biblical promises, whether conditional or unconditional, to be absorbed indiscriminately into the contractual mutuality of Federalism.

By subsuming all promises under the covenantal structure, chronological aspects of salvation history were also viewed differently. A crucial modification in this respect is evident in the exposition of the Abraham narrative in Genesis among Reformed theologians. Peter A. Lillback has shown that Genesis 17 came to be the foundation for covenantal thought in continental Reformed circles from which Perkins' similar emphasis would have been drawn. This chapter in Genesis was important to Zwingli but gained distinctive prominence through Bullinger for whom "God's covenant with Abraham in Genesis 17 is the central theme of the entire scriptures."[46]

This prominence is difficult to explain unless the promise and covenant concepts are conflated for others as they were for Perkins. In the chronology of the biblical narrative God's unilateral promise to Abraham is located in Genesis 12:1-3, before the establishment of the covenant in chapter 17. The prominence of the former text, not just in time but in order of importance, is also evident in Pauline exposition (Galatians 3:8) for whom Genesis12:3 served as the "gospel" in the Old Testament. More importantly Abraham's conversion (that Paul used as a paradigm for all subsequent faith in Romans 4) occurs in Genesis 15:6. In the chronology of the text this takes place decades before the covenant of chapter 17 is established.

There can be little doubt that this order of events, as supported by the Pauline exposition, stood behind Luther's argument that the covenant of Genesis 17 is particularistic, offered just to the Jews. Luther further protested that misapplication of the text generated "such powerful arguments in favor of circumcision that St. Paul had to resist with all his might."[47] Thus, only by ignoring Luther's insistence that the biblical chronology is crucial and that Genesis 17 does not serve as the paradigm for faith can the covenant be construed in cooperative terms.

Sibbes on Promises. Sibbes believed, as Luther and Calvin had, that God fulfills his promises of salvation through Christ alone. The sermon series, *Yea and Amen: or Precious Promises*, featured many points in common with Calvin, and one significant difference.[48] While Calvin believed that only the unconditional promises were suitable for saving faith, Sibbes held that *both* conditional and unconditional promises are effective. Two reasons for Sibbes' variation help to mitigate the difference. First, he located all aspects of promise-fulfillment in Christ, as satisfying the legal charges against sin and as offering the bonds of union; and, second, he characterized the promise as God's ultimate expression of love. Both points bear some notice, after which Sibbes' view of promises and their conditions will be examined.

Christ and the Promise. The function of Christ as the second Adam, as discussed already, was shaped by Sibbes' theology of union. God's purpose in sending Christ was to elevate saved humanity so that all the benefits of the Spirit are fully available to Christ's body.[49] The promises of the Bible are thus channeled through Christ: "there can be no intercourse betwixt God and man without some promise in his Christ, so that now God deals all by promises with us."[50]

In *this* context Sibbes was satisfied to emphasize, rather than diminish, the ontological gulf between creator and creation. Any awareness in the elect of their spiritual and moral limitations, even after regeneration, provides an impulse towards greater dependence on God: "he will try his graces in us, by arming us against all difficulties and discouragements, till the thing promised be performed to us. Promises are, as it were, the stay in an imperfect condition; and so is faith in them, until our hopes shall end in full possession." It was the gaze of the soul towards God's promises in Christ that characterized faith.

Thus, Sibbes, like Calvin, linked faith and promises without attempting to emphasize the place of promises as subordinate to the covenant of grace. Furthermore, Sibbes pointed to faith, not the covenant, as the unifying element of the Bible: "*There is one faith from the beginning of the world.* As there is one Christ, one salvation, so there is one uniform faith for the saving of our souls."[51] Sibbes, referred to believers as "children of the promise" as found in Galatians 4:28.[52]

Sibbes divided God's work into the objective and subjective aspects; the legal and the relational. Unlike Perkins, however, Sibbes made justification subordinate to relational union in his summary of the work Christ accomplished in his death. While justification is first in the *ordo salutis*, the underlying motivation is the purpose to achieve marital union: "He had a mind to marry us, but he could not till he had rescued us."[53] Furthermore, Sibbes conflated the benefits of mystical union and adoption: "[It is] As if the Lord had said, I am pleased in him, and in all his; in his whole mystical body. Christ is the Son of God by nature, we by adoption. Whatever good is in us is first and principally in him. God conveys all by the natural Son to the adopted sons. Therefore, all the promises are made to us in Christ. He takes them from God for us."[54]

At an applied level the believer is free to take advantage of Christ's mediatorial role: "This should direct us in our dealing with God, not to go directly to him but by a promise. And when we have a promise, look to Christ, in whom it is performed."[55] The access to God is viewed, in this arrangement, with the same bilateralism that Sibbes described through mystical marriage. In this case, God as promissor, binds himself, "for God and his word are all one", and, "For the promises are as so many obligations, whereby God is bound to his poor creature."[56]

Christ as God's expression of love. This access to God is based on his love for the elect, a point offered in the second and complementary emphasis of Sibbes' sermon. "But what is a promise?" he asked. "A promise is nothing but a manifestation of love; an intendment of bestowing some good, and removing some evil from us." As in Calvin's understanding, the role of promise is rooted in God's affections and provides the ground for a response from the affections of the beloved: "It always comes from love in the party promising, and conveys goodness to the believing soul."[57] Sibbes also affirmed a sentiment similar to Calvin's about the frailty of the fallen person in relation to the promises: "Now what love can there be in God to us since the fall, which must not be grounded on a better foundation than ourselves?" The answer to human instability is Christ's stability. "If God love us, it must be in one that is first beloved. Hereupon comes the ground of the promises to be in Jesus Christ."[58]

The ground of faith, then, is in the character of God as one who loves with absolute loyalty: "If we get fast hold on Christ, and cleave there, God can as soon alter his love to him as alter his love to us; his live is every whit as unchangeable to a believing member, as to Christ the head of the body."[59] Sibbes returned to the passage of 2 Peter as an expression of God's work of love in the believer: "That love which engaged the Almighty to bind himself to us in 'precious promises,' 2 Pet. 1:4, will furnish us likewise with grace needful till we be possessed of them."[60]

Promises and their conditions. With these two issues set, that Christ is the channel of promise and love is the motive in promise, Sibbes addressed the two forms of promise:

> All the promises of God are made to us either,
>
> (1.) *Absolutely*, without any condition. So was the promise of sending Christ into the world, and his glorious coming again to judgment. . . .

> Or (2.) *Conditional*; as the promise of grace and glory to God's children, that he will forgive their sins, if they repent, &c.[61]

In explaining these conditional promises Sibbes accepted the commercial and bilateral functions described by Federal theology, but only after pressing home the prior relational issues: "God deals with men (as we do by way of commerce one with another), propounding mercy by covenant and condition; yet his covenant of grace is always a 'gracious covenant.'" In explaining this covenant Sibbes addressed the tension between monergism and synergism as in the Pauline paradox of Philippians 2:12-13. "For he not only gives the good things, but helps us in performing the condition by his Spirit; he works our hearts to believe and to repent."[62]

The ambiguity of the Spirit's role as one who "helps us" suggests a subscription to Perkins' doctrine of synergistic enablement. Yet elsewhere Sibbes hesitated to make the synergism explicit, arguing that such promises as, "God will forgive their sins if they believe, if they repent . . . are propounded conditionally, but in the performance they are absolute, because God performs the covenant himself; he performs our part and his own too."[63]

It is at this point, however, that Sibbes' theology becomes awkward. Sibbes, in his willingness to accept conditional promises as a ground for salvation, was attempting to synthesize two approaches to sanctification that were fundamentally opposed. One, represented by Calvin's exposition of God's unconditional promises, operates on the basis of the Spirit's direct illumination of the heart. The other,

Perkins' exposition of the covenant of grace, operates on the basis of the Spirit's enablement of the will and is buttressed by the practical syllogism. Sibbes agreed with Calvin's view of sin as disaffection through self-love, but also agreed with Perkins' affirmation of conditional promises as a basis for salvation. In doing this, the problem anticipated by Calvin was given birth: self-concerned introspection tended to displace a Christological focus in both sanctification and assurance. Sibbes' efforts to build a synthesis of the two views in his doctrine of assurance are the subject of the next section.[64]

The Assurance of Faith

If the law was the stick of Puritan theology, assurance of salvation was its carrot. Nomist theology held both elements in tension by relying on the practical syllogism: the justifying work of Christ is the ground of salvation for the elect; the moral law is the guide to sanctification; the elect are enabled to fulfill the moral law; thus, sanctification is the chief indicator of election and, by extension, the source of assurance. Assurance, then, was a precarious quality for those who were unsteady in their application of the law. A brief review of the nomist doctrine as offered by Perkins, and a look at modern assessments of Calvin's position will provide context for an examination of Sibbes' view.

Perkins on assurance

Perkins held that the Spirit "wrought faith" by two actions. "First, the enlightening of the mind: the second, the moving of the will. This done, then comes the second work of the Holy Ghost, which is the inflaming of the will, that a man having considered his fearful estate by reason of sin and the benefits of Christ's death, might hunger after Christ". The will, stirred by fear (seen here as a subsidiary element of the will), then acts to take Christ for itself. This produces assurance: "After which he sends his Spirit into the same heart, that desireth reconciliation with God, and remission of sinnes in Christ: and doth seal up the same in his heart by a lively and plentiful assurance thereof."

This assuring work of the Spirit would seem to be close to Calvin's belief that faith *is* assurance, but Perkins actually held the Spirit's work to be separate from faith and something of an option. Therefore, as discussed already, Perkins also held that assurance may come by "works of sanctification." Indeed, for many people the Spirit's testimony was either absent or so faint as to be uncertain. Therefore the practical syllogism offers assurance just as heat indicates "a fire when we cannot see the flame itself."[65]

The practice of Perkins' position was illustrated in New England when the nomist, Peter Bulkeley, reacted to Cotton's charge that nomist theology is grounded in human works. Bulkeley answered that "real" sanctification "is a blessing of the covenant of grace only. And being so, therefore to prove our justification by our sanctification, is not to go to a covenant of works."[66] From that premise Bulkeley then went on to list eight indicators of *true* sanctification in order to assist uncertain listeners. One of these was a commitment to keep the law.[67] What failed to register with Bulkeley is Cotton's complaint that in using such indicators the focus of the soul is on human conduct and not on Christ himself. Cotton held that assurance is only as strong as the object of faith. If changed behaviors are the object of one's gaze, faith rises no higher than that; and the behavior is then the true object of faith.

Calvin on Assurance

Calvin rejected the practical syllogism in light of his belief that faith is an apprehension of God's love as offered in free promises. This precludes any use of sanctification as grounds for assurance. "Nowhere," Wilhelm Niesel concludes, "does Calvin teach the *Syllogismus practicus*." In fact, Niesel goes on,

> It becomes clear that Calvin is strictly concerned with the theology of revelation . . . For this reason he warns us against the *Syllogismus practicus*; for the latter implies that our view is deflected from God, who is to be found in Christ alone, and is turned towards man. By such a proceeding the hope of salvation is not increased but rather imperiled.[68]

Niesel's view, though, is disputed.[69] Lynn B. Tipson, for instance, argues that Calvin's theology included an element of introspection. He follows Karl Barth in acknowledging the importance for Calvin of "*the* moment when God's purpose for a man was first definitively revealed to him."[70] Tipson also identifies the duality present in Calvin's view of conversion, with the preached word as one aspect and the illumination of the heart by the Spirit as the other.

He argues, though, that this is not to be construed as a strictly private and arbitrary experience that it seems to be; the very setting in which conversion occurs, the church, points to its function within community. Furthermore, "Calvin recognized that the sinner did not always consciously know exactly when God had called him . . ." Calvin seems to assume this when he acknowledges that some will only experience a "weak faith".[71] Tipson sees an affirmation of the practical syllogism in Calvin's view that by means of fellowship in the church (through the nurturing work of the Spirit in the Word and sacraments), "we are fully convinced that we are members of it. In this way our salvation rests upon sure and firm supports."[72]

Tipson's case, however, pivots on a pair of faulty assumptions. First, a recognition of the corporate nature of the church—including the means of grace within it—does not exclude a personal and private experience of God within it. On the contrary, Calvin once argued, that if in a congregation of one hundred members, twenty respond in faith, "while the rest hold it valueless, or laugh, or hiss, or loathe it", the positive response must be attributed "not by their own virtue but by God's grace alone."[73]

Second, Calvin's use of "weak faith" does not express uncertainty, as Tipson assumes, but a faith that fails to generate significant fruitfulness. The context of Tipson's citation is related to the varied responses to God's "divine love" found in society. Calvin's point is that while there may even be a temporary response in the reprobate, the response of the true believer is absolutely distinct, the product of a "secret revelation which Scripture vouchsafes only to the elect." Thus, while there is an undeniable spectrum of responses among those who are saved, conversion is still a distinct work of the Spirit:

> Nor does anything prevent him from lightly touching some with a knowledge of his gospel, while deeply imbuing others. In the meantime we ought to grasp this: however deficient or *weak faith* may be in the elect, still, because the Spirit of God is for them the sure guarantee and seal of their adoption, the mark he has engraved can never be erased from their hearts. . .[74]

The point seems clear here that the work of God is represented as overt and enduring, if not always as fruitful in some as it is in others. Tipson's summary of Calvin's view of conversion is instructive. Calvin, he concludes, *does* emphasize a distinct moment of conversion, despite Tipson's attempts to show it could be "tempered". Tipson then turns to Theodore Beza, who is presented as emphasizing personal experience as Calvin did, but without a "psychologically intense" conversion. Instead, Tipson concludes, Beza "developed the same emphasis on the fruits of faith that Calvin had avoided."[75]

Tipson seems unaware of the virtual reversal of Calvin's theocentric concerns that such a shift to an anthropocentric focus represents. While both views address human experience, Calvin held that an experience of God's love causes the soul to become riveted on God as the object of love, replacing the sinful self-love that preceded God's self-disclosure. Beza's view, displayed later in Perkins' volitional model of sanctification, addressed experience as the inward impulses towards obedient living, a behavioral focus.

Mark E. Dever also questions Niesel's interpretation of Calvin, although his criticism is not against Niesel directly but R.

T. Kendall who supports Niesel's conclusion.[76] He argues that "Kendall's main fault . . . is the presentation of Calvin's views exclusively in dialogue with those of his Reformed followers, without taking sufficient cognizance of their original context . . . [that is,] there is no significant mention of the Roman Catholic doctrine against which Calvin's presentation of the gospel is made."[77] Dever's argument assumes that Calvin needed to emphasize, even to the point of overstatement, the illegitimacy of merit-theology when writing to an audience not far removed from a Roman Catholic heritage. At certain points in Calvin's work, Dever argues, a more balanced perspective may be discovered. For instance, after warning against any reliance on merit in the *Institutes* Calvin offered a caveat: "we do not forbid him from undergirding and strengthening this faith by signs of the divine benevolence toward him."[78]

Perhaps the strongest example in demonstrating that Calvin believed, in Dever's words, "that subjective assurance was distinct from saving faith . . ." is to be found in his *Commentary on Deuteronomy*. Calvin wrote:

> [E]very one of us must have an eye to himself, so as the gospel be not preached in vain nor we bear the bare name of Christians, without showing the effect of it in our deeds. For until our adoption be sealed by the holy Ghost, let us not think that it availeth us any whit to have heard the word of God. . . . But when we have once a warrant in our hearts, that his promises belong unto us, and are behighted unto us by reason that we receive them with true obedience, and stick to our Lord Jesus Christ, suffering him to govern us; that is a sure

seal of God's choosing of us, so as we not only have the outward appearance of it before men, but also the truth of it before our God.[79]

But Dever's case is tenuous. His suggestion may be true that the Puritans faced less pressure, whether theological or political, from Roman Catholics than did Calvin, but this is a point from hindsight rather than by any perceptions of the day. Sibbes' works are littered with polemical blasts against popery, many of which reflect a general concern that the population was still prone to the Roman theology of merit. There was also fear of a second Marian upheaval still might be possible.[80]

Furthermore Dever's use of Calvin's citations may also be questioned. For instance, Calvin's suggestion that believers may "undergird" and "strengthen" their faith by signs is hardly a clear-cut statement of the practical syllogism. Calvin began his paragraph by warning against "any trust in works". For him the "signs of divine benevolence" will include "good works" which are a "grace" given by God: "For if, when all the gifts God has bestowed upon us are called to mind, they are like rays of the divine countenance by which we are illumined to contemplate that supreme light of goodness". In this context, good works are just another sign of God's benevolence; assurance of salvation, however, is prior to this blessing, being based on the *earlier* benevolence of God's unconditional promises. Similarly, the exposition in Deuteronomy contains a clause that suggests assurance as direct apprehension—"when we have a warrant in our hearts, that his promises belong to us"—placed prior to his comment on obedience.

Calvin was explicit, as has been seen already, in representing God's promises (those applicable to salvation) as unconditional rather than conditional. It is *that* issue which Dever must challenge in order to make his point. Calvin's intention, displayed throughout his works, is to emphasize the place of unconditional promises at the beginning of the continuum between conversion and sanctification: it begins with a changed heart—caused by God's loving self-disclosure—and *then* produces changed behaviors.

Thus he could express his confidence that spiritual benefits would *certainly* follow a conversion, thus displaying the integrity of the work "before men"; but he was insistent in holding that assurance itself is a product of being "sealed" by the Spirit.[81] The mere hearing of the word or professing of faith had no benefit unless there was a "truth of it before our God." Thus Calvin, in Deuteronomy, was warning that mere church attendance and listening to sermons fails to represent genuine faith. So, also, good works are not to be used for assurance; they could even be detrimental to salvation by giving false grounds for faith. The crux of the matter is the sealing of the Spirit.[82]

Sibbes on Assurance

Sibbes' theology of assurance was also linked to his Pneumatology. It must be seen within the context of his doctrine of mystical marriage, which allowed both human and divine initiative. It differed from the models offered by both Calvin and the nomists while sharing elements taken from each. To those who lacked assurance Sibbes blended voluntaristic exhortations with teaching about God's absolute initiative in

Calvin's terms. He could, on the one hand, define faith (as Calvin would) as an embracing of God's love: "Faith is nothing but the act whereby we apprehend this effectual love of God to us in Christ."[83]

On the other hand, he stated in the same sermon: "We ought to labor for the assurance of the love of God in Christ."[84] The basis of this assurance is confused. If "labor" achieves assurance, then God's self-disclosure is either indistinct or has not occurred. Thus the person's attention is drawn to something they contribute, not unlike the nomist assumption. How, then, were these views held together? Only with some difficulty, especially in light of his doctrine of positive sin.

Sibbes held, with Calvin, that the unconverted heart is actually hostile to God and is *unwilling* to seek him with any real integrity. Thus, conversion is a turning away from disaffected hostility back to God in a joyful acknowledgement of God's love in Christ. It should, reasonably, reflect a more distinct transition than was expected in the nomist model. But while Sibbes held, with Calvin, that the salvation comes through the Spirit's work of drawing the elect through the mind, will and affections, to encounter the "melting" quality of Christ's love, Sibbes realized that many of his listeners lacked this experience. Thus he affirmed Perkins' position, in part, by setting out a twofold ground for assurance, one by direct illumination and the other by syllogistic reasoning.[85]

Discernment of the Spirit. From the human perspective faith is a "double act". The first is the "direct act", that is, an act of reliance upon the promise of God's work of justification in Christ. The second is the "reflect act", or the moment of fruitfulness from the first act, and in which the soul embraces the certainty that the first act is effective. "Now a man", Sibbes explained, "may perform the one act and not the other."[86] The Spirit accomplishes his work in stages, Sibbes explained. He moves a person through steps of "stablishing", anointing, and sealing; finally, as the work of assurance, he provides an "earnest" or preliminary and partial expression of heaven: "God doth not keep all our happiness till another world, but gives us somewhat to comfort us in our absence from our husband."[87]

Given some uncertainty about the Spirit's illumination, Sibbes felt a pastoral responsibility to treat all his auditors as if they had the inclination and capacity to love God even without their having a clear conversion experience or any personal assurance of salvation. This accorded with Perkins' view.

However, unlike Perkins, Sibbes made the discernment of the Spirit's active presence the *primary* ground for assurance rather than a secondary and largely unexpected experience. He spoke, for instance, of God's "honouring of faith with a superadded confirmation"; the "secret whispering and intimation to the soul" by the Spirit of the forgiveness of sins. The Spirit would be perceived in the believer's experience, particularly through affective assurances of love felt by the soul which, in turn, result in "*heavenly ejaculations to God*" and "fervent supplications to cry, 'Abba, Father."[88] In fact, his confidence in the direct witness of the Spirit was an almost mirror reversal of Perkins' view. But, even with this caveat, Sibbes was closer to Perkins than to Calvin on the matter. Unlike Calvin he held that this "sealing of the Spirit after we believe *is known by the work of sanctification which it effecteth in us.*"[89]

Sibbes, despite this acquiescence, in practice avoided Perkins' form of the syllogism and used, instead, a proof based on transformed affections:

> There can be no holy life proceed but from faith; from the first act of it. There must be that; but sometimes we know not our faith, because the reflect act is hindered; we know not we believe when we believe. There may holy duties proceed from a man when he knows not his grace and estate: in which time let him but examine himself, why doth he duties, whether out of love to God or no? Yes. Can he endure God to be evil spoken of? No. Will he allow himself in any known sin? No. In this case, though he dares not say he is assured, yet the things he doth are from some love and desire of glorifying God.[90]

It is notable that this approach cohered with Sibbes' positive doctrine of sin; and grace is a response to God's love in Christ. Thus, although Sibbes allowed the use of some syllogistic introspection, the assessment is actually based on a transformation of a person's affections rather than his or her behaviors. Nevertheless, if faith is portrayed as a gaze of the soul on Christ (as Sibbes would have it on most occasions), the person lacking assurance is left to an exercise of spiritual oscillation, looking back and forth between Christ's promises and the state of their own affections. Calvin, in contrast, avoided this by his insistence that faith is disclosed only in the recognition of God's love in Christ that makes conversion self-evident.[91]

Why, then, did Sibbes accept this bi-directional tension between nature and grace in matters of assurance, even though he generally avoided the nomist version of the practical syllogism in practice? The greatest likelihood is that his personal exegesis of the Puritan *locus classicus* for assurance, 2 Peter 1, caused him to accept a doctrine which he otherwise might have dismissed in light of his broader theology. In a final sermon before he died Sibbes continued to cling to his Christological emphasis for assurance: "look to him for all perfections and for thy title to heaven, and not to faith".

But he also affirmed the usefulness of sanctification as a secondary witness: While the "very cleaving to Christ is indeed a sufficient ground of comfort", and, indeed, there "may be adherence without evidence", nevertheless, one should "labour 'to make our calling and election sure,' 2 Pet. 1:10; that is, in ourselves, and in our own apprehension."[92] His exegesis of this text in particular, it seems, forced him to accept the linkage that he might otherwise have dismissed.[93] John Cotton, with a different understanding of the same passage, *did* dismiss the connection only a year later in the Antinomian Controversy. In his reading of 2 Peter 1, as he displayed in his debate with his nomist adversaries, he concluded that Peter's list were offered as goads to growth rather than as a foundation for assurance. Both John Piscator and Calvin whom he cited supported him in that conclusion.[94]

Assurance as a stage of grace. The sealing work of the Spirit, as was also true of Calvin, held a primary role in Sibbes' theology of assurance. The biblical use of seals, Sibbes believed, displayed God's initiative and expressed direct dependence of nature on grace: "It pleaseth God thus to keep every degree and act of sealing in his own hand, to keep us in perpetual dependence upon him . . ."[95] In the sermon series, *Yea and Amen*, he concluded a discussion of sanctification, (as represented by the image of anointing oil), and began an exposition of assurance: "Anointing and sealing go together. The same God anoints us doth also seal us. Both are to secure us of our happy condition. Now Christ is the first sealed: John 6:27. . ."[96]

The seals thus represented Sibbes' realistic notion of union: "The same Spirit that seals the Redeemer seals the redeemed."[97] This imagery described the relationship of assurance to sanctification: the Spirit is the source of both.

> The Spirit goes always with his own mark and impression. Other seals, when they are removed from the stamp, the stamp remains still. But the Spirit of God dwells and keeps a perpetual residence in the heart of a Christian, guiding him, moving him, enlightening him, governing him, comforting him to heaven. The Holy Ghost never leaves us. . . . Though he seem sometimes to be in a corner of the heart, and is not easily discerned, yet he always dwells in his sealed ones.[98]

Why did Sibbes portray the Spirit in such a limited fashion here, after such robust portrayals as found elsewhere? He attributed the problem to a variety of causes: spiritual infancy, spiritual "desertions" by God meant to stimulate greater desire, dispositions ("some are of a melancholy constitution"), personal diligence, Satanic temptations, and the like.[99]

The reason, however, may be best answered in Knight's commentary on the Puritans of New England. She points out the tendency of ministers to offer pastoral comfort to distraught listeners, even at the expense of theological purity. Specifically, she notices in the New England setting that nomist ministers displayed a "pastoral pragmatism" in calling for behavioral reform (to make one's salvation sure) that sometimes slipped into legalistic "moralism", presumably of a Pelagian character.[100] Such precipices of heterodoxy were to be found on both sides of the question of assurance.

While the nomists toyed with Pelagian error in their zeal to offer firm spiritual guidance, the antinomists were troubled by their need to explain the lack of a distinct experience of God's presence among many in their congregations who were conspicuously faithful and godly. Searches for such an experience opened the way to excessive introspection, as well as to various peculiar claims of the Spirit's leading among some of the later Spirit-radicals. The problem ministers from both Reformed camps, nomist and antinomist, were faced with was the possibility, raised by their belief in God's sole initiative in election, that only some of their auditors were actually elect. Thus, no matter how strongly they exhorted the flock to search, respectively, their works or their affections, some in the congregation who seemed to want salvation might not receive it.

Conclusion

By setting Sibbes' doctrine against Calvin's and Perkins' views of God's promises the distinctions are striking. All of them looked to God's promises as the sole object of spiritual attention: Sibbes and Calvin recognized the unilateral nature of God's grace, while Perkins represented the promises in light of the obligations of the primary Adamic covenant. Sibbes' entire system of theology operated on a separate assumption, namely, that Adam's original relationship with God was meant for communion. Nevertheless Sibbes accepted the legitimacy of conditional promises as a ground for faith. In doing so he was forced to share, in at least some measure, expressions of human contingency with the nomists.

Thus, after emphasizing the power of the Spirit's presence on the one hand, Sibbes reverted to a rather indistinct understanding of the Spirit's role in assurance. His personal exegesis of the 2 Peter 1 may well have forced the issue for him, but a second issue is more likely. Sibbes' pastoral motivation certainly left him with a dilemma when he faced those under his preaching who lacked a distinct sense of God's presence. These people, if Sibbes were consistent with his broader theology, might lose heart in spiritual matters. If they lacked confidence that God was wooing them with his love, Sibbes felt pressure not to cut them off from the fount of God's goodness as it was offered through his preaching.

Soon after Sibbes' death, John Cotton displayed a doctrinal synthesis much like Sibbes', but he adopted Calvin's doctrine of assurance rather than his mentor's. In doing so Cotton's doctrine of salvation made the theological distance between the nomist and antinomist positions far more distinct. The result was to be seen in the Antinomian Controversy.

Conclusion

Augustine's and Sibbes' Affective Faith

Richard Sibbes' affective theology, when set against the moralistic Federal theology of William Perkins, reflected the unsettled state of English Reformed theology. Their separate positions, despite sharing superficial similarities, revealed very different understandings of God. At the level of basic professions both men believed in God's Trinitarian nature, his absolute authority, his wisdom, and his predestinarian work by which he shows mercy to some and gives others over to sin.

Perkins' God, however, is transcendent: characterized by his determinative will and motivated by his self-glorification. Human concerns then tend to be viewed in utilitarian terms in fulfilling their predetermined roles to bring about God's glory.

Sibbes' view of God, on the other hand, was characterized by the immanent self-love of the Godhead who out of his communion as Father, Son, and Spirit extends "a spreading goodness" to the creation. In fountain-like imagery God's eternal love overflows to his creation—a vision Sibbes found in Jesus' prayer of John 17. Thus God's essential motivation is, paradoxically, a selfless self-love that spreads ever outward. These separate views of God generated competing definitions of grace and faith for seventeenth century Puritans.

The study began by offering an enlarged framework in which the division of Puritan theology must be evaluated. Figures such as Sibbes and Cotton may be easily marginalized if assessed by the values that emerged in later Reformed theology, particularly those of the Westminster Assembly; but they reemerge as significant figures if measured by the broader framework of the Augustinian-Pelagian dispute and the first impulses of the Protestant Reformation. The study thus points to an ongoing historical opposition of 'response' versus 'responsibility' in the application of grace in salvation. With that framework, Sibbes represented one side of a polarity, reacting to the promotion of the alternative position.

Using Augustine as a standard, the moralistic theology of Thomas Aquinas and, later, that of Perkins, are viewed in a different light: as a theological setback rather than a benefit. That is, they both adopted Aristotle's assumption that morality is defined by the self-moved and disaffected will. This precluded, by definition, the possibility that faith is a response to God. This self-moved version of salvation shared, unwittingly, the Pelagian portrayal of faith as a human initiative.

The question of interpretive frameworks is also important in light of the revisionist Reformed historiography led by Richard Muller whose reading of events elevates the rational and dialectical methodology of medieval scholasticism. Yet in his framework Luther and Calvin tend to be marginalized for their "relatively negative relationship" to scholastic methods and theological assumptions, while figures such as Vermigli, Musculus, and Zanchi (among others) are elevated for their greater continuity with the Aristotelian-Thomistic baseline that Muller prefers as the measure of productive theology.[1] This study has not attempted to address Muller's position as a main interest, but the findings of this research help to illuminate a remarkable implication in his proposals (given his Protestant affiliation), namely that Luther's opposition to Aristotle which helped launch the Reformation, was misguided.

In a second historiographical consideration, this study, in identifying and exploring the Perkins-Sibbes polarity, parallels some arguments in modern theology which have not been addressed here, including those of Karl Barth, Thomas and James Torrance, among others, who insist that the emergence of Reformed Orthodoxy in the early post-Reformation era, did much to betray the main impulses of the Augustinian-Calvinist tradition.

This research has not relied on their paradigms for its development but its conclusions show that a contemporary resistance emerged among Puritans to the reacquisition of Thomist theology. This resistance formed on grounds similar to those raised by the modern theologians.[2]

The Antinomian Controversy of Boston first exposed the Puritan division most clearly, and subsequent upheavals during the Civil War underscored its intensity. Ministers, in the heat of the debate, suggested that their opposites were drifting into the errors of the familists, on the one hand, and toward a renewed Roman Catholicism on the other. Such notions were overstated, but both sides had identified divergent trajectories in the theology of their opponents.

The antinomists were oriented toward an elevated Pneumatology and an intrinsic piety; the nomists were oriented toward a moralistic system that was more anthropocentric and its piety more extrinsic. That is not to say, however, that either group would have seen themselves to be dependent on Sibbes and Perkins who anticipated their respective positions.

This fact points to the antecedent nature of the division, which the two men simply reflected in their respective ministries. Questions about nature and grace had divided the primitive church, separated Augustine from Pelagius, and stood at the heart of the Protestant Reformation. The unresolved tensions over grace in England and New England show, as Janice Knight points out, the myth of a monological Reformed theology.

Perkins' and Sibbes' Theologies: A Summary

Perkins' nomistic theology. Perkins' theology, in summary, relied on the bilateralism of Federal theology taken from Reformed sources on the continent. Perkins' model of Federalism, in turn, expressed the ethical framework of Aquinas. Aquinas held, by way of Anselm, that original sin is a privation of goodness through Adam's fall that stripped humanity of original righteousness (the *donum gratiæ*). Thus, all of humanity lacks the power of will necessary to choose the good; individuals, in turn, are unable to gain the real righteousness that the *iustitia dei* requires. The symmetrical corollary of this view is that grace is God's reenablement of the will through a supernatural restoration of Adam's lost moral capacity.

In this view, Aquinas relied on Aristotle's foundational moral premise in the *Nicomachean Ethics* that the will, rather than the passions, is the ground of morality because it is inherent to the person's being; the passions, on the other hand, are "neither praised nor blamed" in that they are responses to extrinsic causes. Aquinas' direct citation of Aristotle is pivotal: "the free man is one who is his own cause".[3] With this *a priori*, Aquinas emphasized the *self-moving* function of the will. Because God's grace must operate within the parameters of this assumption, Aquinas conceived of grace as both created and uncreated. This allowed him to construe grace in intermediary terms, as a part of nature untainted by sin. Human autonomy is thus preserved, and salvation is still dependent on God's grace, defined as a quality distributed by him.

Perkins' Federalism affirmed Luther's fundamental assertion that in faith the *iustitia Christi* and the *iustitia Dei* are the believer's *possessio.* However, Perkins' theology failed to grasp (or accept?—it remains unclear) Luther's rejection of Aristotle's moral assumptions in the *Nicomachean Ethics.* Perkins accepted the bilateral structure of Federal theology as a solution to the conflicted requirements that the primary initiative in salvation must be both God's *and* the elect person's. The main options used to resolve this tension, from Augustine onward, were either an affective compatibilism or a volitional cooperationism.

Both precluded compulsive force, of grace dominating nature by overpowering it. Perkins' acceptance of Aristotelian assumptions supported his use of the two-stage cooperative model of Aquinas: first, God is the sole initiator of salvation, which is accomplished by his provision of *habitus gratiæ* to the elect. Second, the enabled human will is exercised in faith—the *actus* of superadded *habitus.* This satisfied the biblical emphases on God's unilateral initiative in offering salvation; it also met the obedience stipulations found in conditional promises of the Bible, an arrangement that cohered with Aristotelian ethical theory.

Perkins used the Thomistic definition of grace as a created quality infused in the soul. This use of grace as an intermediary between God and the elect person supported Perkins supralapsarian assumptions. God either supplies or withholds grace as determined by his decree of creation. God's will is thus arbitrary and controlling in respect to the creation decree and in accomplishing goodness; but is self-limited in matters of sin.

Just as God permitted the fall of Adam, so he permits every individual the moral space needed to be either culpable or righteous through secondary indeterminacy: "For in that God's will is the first cause of all good things, man's will depends on it . . ." But in respect to evil, God "only ceaseth to confer unto it help and direction, which he is not bound to confer."

That is, God's freedom defines human freedom by privation, an ironic reversal of the definition of sin that may well have caught Sibbes' attention. Thus, God's will is to make the human will free, but inadequate by itself. Sin emerges within that freedom, which glorifies God by displaying his twin characteristics of mercy and justice as he deals with sin.

This approach portrayed human autonomy as the source of sin but it also made the free will the source of salvation. This entire model contained some conspicuous difficulties. In Perkins' view of the Trinity, the Father is transcendent and self-concerned; the Son functions instrumentally, offering justification and adoption to the elect; and the Spirit is controlled by the free human will—able to be dismissed by sins, or to have his powers drawn upon through the use of means. In may be argued, in fact, that Perkins theology was more teleological than Trinitarian, in that the question of the decree of election dominated his applied theology. The task of those who counted themselves to be elect, or those who were striving to discover their election, was to demonstrate their election through obedience.

The use of the practical syllogism, while not assigning merit to works, still made works a virtual necessity because without works it would be certain that the person was *not* elect. God is desired, in this model, but he often remains elusive. Human responsibility, then, protects God's reputation, on the one hand, but actually demeans it on the other, by portraying God as the arbitrary keeper of grace, and the non-elect person as a disabled victim. By trying to synthesize Aristotle and Augustine in this fashion, Perkins actually made Aristotle's absolute freedom of the will appear more just than the freedom described in his supralapsarian Federalism. It was this weakness that drove Sibbes away in one direction, and Peter Baro (and Jacob Arminius) in another.

Sibbes' affective theology. Sibbes' studies at Cambridge exposed him to Perkins' Federalism. While he seems to have initially accepted most aspects of that model, his resistance to it became evident in his shift to an affective theology. This included his rejection of a privative definition of sin in favor of a positive definition of sin as self-love. In the symmetrical concomitant, the doctrine of grace, he held that the will is defined by its affections.

As such it is not self-moving, but is moved by God's self-disclosure as a benevolent saviour. This view shared the theology of illumination used in Augustinian, Lutheran, and Calvinian models of conversion. Grace, in this view, is not an intermediary quality distributed by God, but the ongoing work of the Spirit's illuminating presence. Sibbes' emphasis, then, is theocentric rather than anthropocentric: Christ offers communion through his Spirit, using the scriptures and sacraments. His teleology thus emphasized direct human communion with God through means of a real union with Christ.

The absence of any chronology for most of Sibbes' works blocks efforts to trace the shifts in his position. It may be suggested, however, that his exposition of the Song of Songs played a significant, perhaps primary, role in his transition. Sibbes, as reflected by his attributions, was clearly influenced by early figures such as Gregory of Nazianzus and Augustine, as well as the later Bernard of Clairvaux. Their moderate mysticism, which Bernard McGinn links to an affective reading of the *Song of Songs*—with the church being captivated by the Christic groom—offered an alternative solution to the dilemma of ontological incommensurability that shaped Perkins' theology of union. It provided grounds for a doctrine of real union with Christ.

This was not an ontological fusion, as promoted by radical mystics, but a union analogous to human marriage. Perkins' model, lacking Sibbes' confidence in the effectiveness of the Spirit's immediate communion, emphasized the juridical nature of salvation. Sibbes also accepted the juridical reality of justification and adoption, but he placed them within a context of God's motivations. That is, in his infralapsarian theology he portrayed God's free love and mercy as the motivation for the incarnation. He retained his predestinarian framework in this, acknowledging that only the elect are drawn by the disclosure of God's free love. His preaching, then, was characterized by a free and full exposition of God's love in Christ—it is through the disclosure of God's love that the Spirit elicits a response in the elect. Sibbes, therefore, dismissed the use of the law.

Sibbes' theology also reflects the continued tensions found in early seventeenth-century discussions of grace. He clearly affirmed the sole initiative of God in salvation and avoided the need for human autonomy in ethics by his use of an affectively-defined model of the will: sin is self-love, and conversion is a *response* of the heart (consisting of mind, will, and affections) to the illumination of the God's love by the Spirit. Thus it is not a *responsibility* as Perkins' Federalism would have it. Nevertheless, Sibbes accepted the possibility that the Spirit discloses his saving love through conditional as well as unconditional promises. Thus Sibbes opened the door to the very self-assessing uncertainty that Calvin sought to preclude. Despite Sibbes' inconsistencies his theology demonstrates that some very prominent Puritans were critical of Perkins' Federalism and the version of grace set out by the Westminster Assembly.

Final Issues

This study raises a number of issues that invite further attention among historical theologians and historians. These include a reevaluation of the definitions and functions of mysticism in Christian theology. By accepting only the more radical forms of mysticism, characterized either by Dionysian ecstaticism or quietism, there has been a loss of adequate recognition that the affective theology of Augustine, Bernard, Luther, and Sibbes all represented a Pauline theology of spiritual immediacy—the "Abba, Father" cry of the soul in its encounters with God affirmed in Romans 8 and Galatians 3. It was this moderate mysticism that was affiliated with the bridegroom imagery of the Old and New Testaments that drove an entire wing of theology. This tends to be too quickly overlooked in modern historiography.

Another important function of this study has been the identification of additional tools that must be applied in the examination of the nature-grace nexus in modern and historical theology. The different doctrines of sin, the impact of separate teleologies, and the use of opposed models of the will—one precluding the function of the affections as an *a priori*—all came together to shape the opposed positions in seventeenth century Puritanism. The failure to identify and unravel these complex issues has reduced the effectiveness of recent research in matters of English ecclesiology and politics, as was examined in chapter one.

In concluding, it seems fitting to return to William Erbery's view of a happy progression toward his own radical antinomianism, as noticed in the introduction of this study. He was basically correct in his assessment. "Mr. Perkins, Bolton, Byfield and Dod and Dike" were indeed "low and legal" in their teachings when measured by Erbery's doctrine of free grace. The counter-doctrine to Perkins' nomism had "came forth, but with less success or fruit of conversion by Doctor Preston, Sibs, [and] Crisp" and was followed up by others, including Thomas Goodwin. Erbery's optimism was, of course, misplaced.

This theology was largely marginalized after the Civil War. Nevertheless, it was still propagated in later generations through its more radical expressions such as Quakerism, and in more moderate versions as found in the Wesleyan holiness movement. The extreme expression of the nomistic trajectory, when linked to the laws of nature, was expressed in Deism. The doctrine of grace remained unsettled and unsettling.

Endnotes

Preface and Introduction—What is Grace?

[pages 9-23]

[1] E.g. William K. B. Stoever, *'A Faire and Easie Way to Heaven': Covenant Theology and Antinomianism in Early Massachusetts* (Middletown, CT: Wesleyan, 1978).

[2] See David Weir, *The Origins of the Federal Theology in Sixteenth-Century Reformation Thought* (Oxford: Oxford University Press, 1990). Federalism is examined at length in the body of the study.

[3] R. N. Frost, "Aristotle's *Ethics*: The *Real* Reason for Luther's Reformation?" *Trinity Journal* (18 NS, 1997): 223-241; Richard A. Muller, "Scholasticism, Reformation, Orthodoxy, and the Persistence of Christian Aristotelianism," *Trinity Journal* 19 NS (1998): 81-96; Frost, "A Brief Rejoinder" *Trinity Journal* 19 NS (1998): 97-101. Ronald N. Frost, "*The Bruised Reed* by Richard Sibbes (1577-1635)" in Kelly M. Kapic and Randall C. Gleason, eds., *The Devoted Life: An Invitation to the Puritan Classics* (Downers Grove: InterVarsity Press, 2004).

[4] See, for instance, Amy Plantinga Pauw, *The Supreme Harmony of All: The Trinitarian Theology of Jonathan Edwards* (Grand Rapids: Eerdmans, 2002), in which she notices Edwards' broad appreciation for Sibbes' works.

[5]The pejorative label 'Puritan'—not used of a self-identified group with formal features—will refer in this study to a party in English Reformed circles known as the "godly" for their experiential spirituality. They elevated Bible study, were less formal in worship, and pressed for doctrinal and political reforms. See Patrick Collinson, "A Comment: Concerning the Name Puritan", *JEH* 31 (1980): 483-488.

[6]William Erbery, *The Testimony of William Erbery* (London, 1658), pp. 67-69; cited in Stanley P. Fienberg, "Thomas Goodwin's Scriptural Hermeneutics and the Dissolution of Puritan Unity", *JRH* 10 (June 1978): 36. Here and in subsequent quotations of period literature the punctuation and spelling is modernized except in book titles or if the style is not intrusive; dates which reflect the old style calendar are silently modified to a January new year.

[7]Michael Schuldiner, *Gifts and Works: The Post-Conversion Paradigm and Spiritual Controversy in Seventeenth-Century Massachusetts* (Macon, Georgia: Mercer University, 1991); Janice Knight, *Orthodoxies in Massachusetts: Rereading American Puritanism* (Cambridge: Harvard University, 1994). They will be engaged in chapter one.

[8] A contemporary memoir by Zachary Catlin is available in Sibbes' *Works*, 1.cxxxiii-cxli, appended to the editor A. B. Grosart's nineteenth-century biographical summary, xix f.

[9]See the extended biographical discussion in Mark E. Dever, *Richard Sibbes: Puritanism and Calvinism in Late Elizabethan and Early Stuart England* (Macon: Mercer University Press, 2000): 11-95. This is the published version of Dever's "Richard Sibbes and the 'Truly Evangelicall Church of England': A Study in Reformed Divinity and Early Stuart Conformity" (Ph.D. dissertation, Cambridge University, 1992).

[10] Mark E. Dever, "Moderation and Deprivation: A Reappraisal of Richard Sibbes," *Journal of Ecclesiastical History* 43 (1992): 396-413.

[11] A. B. Grosart attributed this to the political shelter provided by Sibbes' powerful friends at court. See Grosart, "Memoir," Sibbes' *Works*, 1.lx-lxxv.

[12] Grosart notes that a variance would have been necessary for Sibbes' to retain both posts. This arrangement points to Sibbes' high standing at both the University and Grays Inn. Grosart, "Memoir," *Works*, 1.xlviii-xlix.

[13]*The Work of William Perkins*, ed., Ian Breward (Appleford: Sutton Courtenay, 1970).

[14]Sibbes, *Sibbes's Last Two Sermons; From Christ's Last Sermon*, 7.337. All citations of Sibbes' works are from the *Works of Richard Sibbes*, 7 vols., edited by Alexander B. Grosart (Edinburgh: Banner of Truth, 1979; first publ., 1862-5

[15]These two examples are examined in chapters one and three.

[16]He offered a modest and affirming illustration from Perkins' *Cases of Conscience*; in Sibbes, *The Knot of Prayer Loosed*, 7.242.

[17]Beck, "The Doctrine of *gratia praeparans* in the Soteriology of Richard Sibbes" (Ph.D. diss., Westminster Theological Seminary, 1994).

Chapter One—Divided by Grace

[pages 25-70]

[1]David D. Hall, *The Antinomian Controversy, 1636-1638: A Documentary History* (Middletown: Wesleyan, 1968), 61 ("The Elders Reply").

[2]Hall, *Antinomian*, 133-34 (Cotton's "Rejoynder").

[3]Hall, *Antinomian*, e.g. 93, 105-106, 185, 197; re: Augustine, 144-145. Cotton refers to "A Treatise Against Two Letters of the Pelagians", *NPNF*, 5.374-434.

[4]Hall, *Antinomian*, 197; Sibbes is cited as one who (along with Calvin, Ursinus, Ames, Hooker, and Davenport) identified faith as passive rather than active; from *The Saints Cordials* (n. p.).

[5]John Norton, *Abel Being Dead Yet Speaketh* (London, 1658), 12. Norton reported that Cotton's conversion "begat in him a singular and constant love of Doctor Sibbs . . . " (13).

[6]Knight, *Orthodoxies in Massachusetts*, 4.

[7]Knight, *Orthodoxies*, 3. Cotton is a primary figure in Knight's thesis. He must be seen as a companion to Sibbes and not as a solitary figure as some have presented him (*Orthodoxies*, 9). Cf. C. L. Cohen, *God's Caress: The Psychology of Puritan Religious Experience* (Oxford: Oxford University Press, 1986), 126.

[8]Schuldiner, *Gifts*, 5.

[9]Schuldiner, *Gifts*, 6. Cf. Judith Rossall, "God's Activity and the Believer's Experience in the Theology of John Calvin" (Ph.D. diss., University of Durham, 1991) who affirms this view.

[10]Knight, "Introduction", *Orthodoxies*, 1-12. She cites Miller, *The New England Mind: The Seventeenth Century* (New York: Macmillan, 1939); Haller, *The Rise of Puritanism* (New York: Columbia University, 1938).

[11]Stoever's study of the Antinomian Controversy, *'A Faire and Easie Way to Heaven': Covenant Theology and Antinomianism in Early Massachusetts* (Middletown: Wesleyan University, 1978), displays a biased reading of the debate. He presumes that a consensus existed among seventeenth century Puritans about the double nature of grace, a position attributable to Thomas Aquinas (p. 41). Stoever fails to assess Cotton's claims that he relied on Sibbes, Calvin and Augustine for his opposition to such a view. Stoever sees the Antinomian Controversy as a localized dispute in which Cotton was a "crypto-sectarian" who upset the Reformed *status quo*. Cf. Schuldiner, *Gifts and Works*, 3, n. 5; Knight, 95 (see, also, n. 31), 97.

[12]Richard A. Muller, *Christ and the Decree: Christology and Predestination in Reformed Theology from Calvin to Perkins* (Durham: Labyrinth, 1986); Strehle, *Calvinism, Federalism, and Scholasticism: A Study of the Reformed Doctrine of Covenant* (Bern: Peter Lang, 1988), 333-34.

[13]Strehle, *The Catholic Roots of the Protestant Gospel: Encounter Between the Middle Ages and the Reformation* (Leiden: E. J. Brill, 1995), 61.

[14]Kenneth Fincham surveys this historiography in his "Introduction", *The Early Stuart Church, 1603-1642* (London: Macmillan, 1993; ed. by Fincham), 1-22.

[15]Tyacke, *Anti-Calvinists: The Rise of English Arminianism, c. 1590-1640* (Oxford: Oxford University Press, 1987). In much of his discussion Tyacke differentiates matters of grace and churchmanship but the two become inseparably linked in his examination of Bishop Richard Neile's visitation articles of 1624 where he notes the desirability of private confessions by parishioners before their receiving communion, along with Neile's insistence on a Roman Catholic placement of the altar, all of which "connects with the English Arminian emphasis on sacramental grace . . ." (116). From that point onward Tyacke builds a case for "ceremonial aspects" of Arminianism as imposed by the monarchial episcopacy (e.g., 194, 216, 223). Cf. Peter Lake, "The Laudian Style: Order, Uniformity and the Pursuit of the Beauty of Holiness in the 1630s", in Fincham, ed., *Early Stuart Church*, 161-185.

[16]Paul S. Seaver, *Wallington's World: A Puritan Artisan in Seventeenth-Century London* (Stanford: Stanford University Press, 1985). Wallington's suicidal introspection is an extreme example of the broadly-based concern among Puritans over matters of grace.

[17]See Ellen S. More's articles, "Congregationalism and the Social Order: John Goodwin's Gathered Church, 1640-60", *JEH* 38 (1987): 210-30; and "John Goodwin and the Origins of the New Arminianism", *JBS* 22 (1982): 50-70.

[18]J. R. De Witt, *Jus Divinum: The Westminster Assembly and the Divine Right of Church Government* (Kampen: J. H. Kok, 1969), 22.

[19]Stephen Brachlow, *The Communion of Saints: Radical Puritan and Separatist Ecclesiology, 1570-1625* (Oxford: Oxford University Press, 1988), e.g. 17-18.

[20]Perkins, *Workes*, "Introduction", 20.

[21]David Weir, *The Origins of the Federal Theology in Sixteenth-Century Reformation Thought* (Oxford: Oxford University Press, 1990), effectively traces Federalism to Zacharias Ursinus at Heidelberg in 1562. Early English exponents were Thomas Cartwright, Dudley Fenner and Perkins.

[22]*Aerius Redivivus*, p. 341; cited in *DNB*, s.v. "Perkins, William".

[23]Tyacke, *Anti-Calvinists*, p. 30; see Tyacke's summary of this episode, 29-36. These basic elements are affirmed by Peter White, despite his sharp disagreement with Tyacke over their significance, in *Predestination, policy and polemic: Conflict and consensus in the English Church from the Reformation to the Civil War* (Cambridge: Cambridge University Press, 1992), 101-17.

[24]This is Peter Heylyn's assertion, *Aerius Redivivus*, 341; cited in *DNB*, s. v. "Perkins, William (1558-1602). Barrett's sermon is lost but, as noted in White, *Predestination*, 102, n. 3, its main elements are available from his retraction, held

by Trinity College Cambridge, MS B 14/9, 39-41, and reprinted in J. Strype, *The Life and Acts of John Whitgift*, 3 vols. (Oxford, 1821), 3.317-19.

[25]R. T. Kendall, *Calvin and English Calvinism to 1649* (Oxford: Oxford University Press, 1979), summarizes the remarkable extent and breadth of distribution: seventy-six editions and/or reprints within his lifetime, and translation and/or publication of his works in six other countries. His three-volume *Workes* achieved eight printings by the time of Sibbes' death in 1635 (52-3; 53, n. 1).

[26]Zanchius is cited at length in *A Case in Conscience* [*Workes*, 1.429-38], and Beza's discussion of assurance (from his dialogue with Jacob Andreae at Montebéliard in 1586) is offered as an appendix to *A Golden Chaine* [*Workes*, 1.114-117].

[27] Supralapsarianism will be considered below. It was an assertion by Federal theologians, including Perkins, that before creation God determined that sin must exist so that good and evil people—the elect and the reprobate—would display, respectively, God's mercy and justice. The underlying axiom is that God's sovereignty precludes any form of contingency including the Fall—so God preordained it. Infralapsarianism, on the other hand, treats the Fall as an event God anticipated and allowed in order to achieve a good end, but he did not impose sin on the creation.

[28]*Workes*, 1.403; cited in Breward's "Introduction", 4.

[29]Perkins, *Works*; Breward's "Introduction", 3-4; cf. John Twigg, *A History of Queen's College, Cambridge, 1448-1986* (Woodbridge: Boydell, 1987), 98-99; William T. Costello, *The Scholastic Curriculum at Early Seventeenth-Century Cambridge* (Cambridge: Harvard University Press, 1958).

[30]Cited in Twigg, *History*, 99.

[31]Calvin warned, for instance, against speculation about predestination: "For we shall know that the moment we exceed the bounds of the Word, our course is outside the pathway and in darkness, and that there we must repeatedly wander, slip, and stumble. Let this, therefore, first of all be before our eyes: to seek any other knowledge of predestination than what the Word of God discloses is not less insane than if one should purpose to walk in a pathless waste, or to see in darkness." *The Institutes of Christian Religion*, 1559 ed., 2 vols.; ed., J. T. McNeill; trans., F. L. Battles (Philadelphia: Westminster, 1960), 3.21.2.

[32]R. A. Muller, "Perkins' *A Golden Chaine*: Predestinarian System or Schematized Ordo Salutis?", *SCJ* 9 (1978): 71; D. K. McKim, *Ramism in William Perkins' Theology* (New York: Lang, 1987).

[33]*Geschichte des Pietismus und der Mystik in der reformirten Kirche* (Leiden, 1879), 24-26; cited in Muller, *Christ and the Decree*, 131.

[34]Fiering, *Moral Philosophy at Seventeenth-Century Harvard: A Discipline in Transition* (Chapel Hill: University of North Carolina, 1981), 4.

[35]"The Calvin Legend", in *John Calvin: A Collection of Distinguished Essays* (Gervase E. Duffield, ed., Grand Rapids: Eerdmans, 1966), 2. See, also, in the same work, Hall's "Calvin Against the Calvinists", 19f.

[36]Helm, *Calvin and the Calvinists* (Edinburgh: Banner of Truth, 1982); Woolsey, "Unity and Continuity in Covenantal Thought: A Study in the Reformed Tradition to the Westminster Assembly", 2 vols. (Ph.D. diss., University of Glasgow, 1988). Discontinuities cited by Kendall included the extent of the atonement, the *ordo salutis*, and the proper ground for assurance of salvation.

[37]*Christ and the Decree*, 130-31. Muller's order of presentation is reversed here.

[38]Muller, *Post-Reformation Reformed Dogmatics: Prolegomena to Theology* (Grand Rapids: Baker, 1987), 39.

[39]*Christ and the Decree*, 38. Muller's thesis of an incipient supralapsarianism in Calvin is unlikely in light of Calvin's rather overt infralapsarianism as will be noticed below.

[40]Which is *not* to say that they address Muller's concerns; rather they view Calvin's theology as generally (if not explicitly) anticipating the central issues of the *Westminster Confession of Faith.*

[41]Cp. Brian G. Armstrong, *Calvinism and the Amyraut Heresy* (Madison: University of Wisconsin, 1969). He argues that Calvin's views, when affirmed by Moïse Amyraut at Saumur, were viewed as heresy by later Reformed theologians who had reacquired Aristotelian assumptions. This is not unlike Cotton's status in Boston.

[42]Tipson, "The Development of a Puritan Understanding of Conversion" (Ph.D. dissertation, Yale University, 1972), 113.

[43]For an extended discussion of the issues at stake, see G. C. Berkouwer, *Divine Election* (Grand Rapids: Eerdmans, 1960), ch. 8.

[44]Beza, *A booke of Christian Questions and Answeares* (1578), 84f; cited in Kendall, *Calvin*, 30.

[45]Calvin, *Institutes*, 3.23.3. In the section following (3.23.4) Calvin acknowledges that predestination foreordains the fall but resists any impulse to explain God's purpose in allowing sin, "the last cause of which is hidden in him." Sibbes used Calvin's language at one point: "Where there is a condition

so opposite as the frame of our hearts is to God, he being holiness and we a mass and lump of sin, of necessity there must be a change." *Excellency of the Gospel*, 4.257.

[46]Calvin, *Institutes*, 3.23.11. He cites *Against Two Letters of the Pelagians*, 2.7.13-16.

[47]Perkins, *Golden Chaine*, 1.10 [177].

[48]Perkins, *Golden Chaine*, 1.16 [185-6].

[49]Perkins, *Golden Chaine*, 1.23 [197]; 1.13 [180]; cp. Beza: "God from everlasting hath purposed and decreed in Himself, to create all thing at their seasons to His glory, but namely men, and that after two sorts . . . [the elect and the reprobate]". Beza, *Treasure of Truth*, sig. B7v, B8; cited in Tipson, "Development", 114.

[50]Perkins, "Golden Chain", 1.12 [79].

[51]Breward, "Introduction" to Perkins, *Work*, 98. Nuttall's affirmation is taken from his annotated copy of Breward's edition which was donated to the Dr. Williams's Library holdings: "or the need for the God of the Quakers. cf. my *H.S.P.F.E* , 135." He refers to his *The Holy Spirit in Puritan Faith and Experience* (Chicago: University of Chicago, 1992).

[52]See Judith Rossall, "God's Activity and the Believer's Experience in the Theology of John Calvin" (Ph.D. dissertation, University of Durham, 1991).

[53]Perkins, 1.459-62. See Cohen, *God's Caress*, 218-19.

[54]See "Types of Puritan Piety", *CH* 56 (1987): 39-58; see, also, his study, "Francis Rous, Puritan Mystic, 1579-1659: An Introduction to the Study of the Mystical Element in Puritanism" (Ph.D. diss., University of Chicago, 1948).

[55]Brauer, "Types of Puritan Piety", 46.

[56]Tipson, "Puritan Understanding", 153. He cites Craig, *A Short Sum of the Whole Catechism* . . . in Thomas Torrance, ed., *The School of Faith* (London, 1959).

[57]Tipson, "Development", 138. He cites Bradford, *Writings*, ed., Parker Soc. (2 vols.; Cambridge, 1848-53), 1.5,12.

[58]Tipson, "Development", 168-70. He cites Greenham, *The Works* (London, 1612), 803.

[59]Tipson, "Development", 101-109. Tipson sees continuity between the two positions, pointing to their shared "emphasis on personal experience" (109); but our discussion of sin, below, points to a basic discontinuity of views.

[60]The term antinomist will be preferred to antinomianism to avoid associations with radical Spiritism as in the Münster rebellion. Antinomianism, as a

pejorative label, obscures an alternative use, namely, Luther's dismissal of law-keeping as a basis for justification. In the Boston Controversy neither side affirmed libertine conduct. See F. L. Cross, ed., *The Oxford Dictionary of the Christian Church*, 2d ed., s.v. "Antinomianism"; and M. Watts, *The Dissenters: From the Reformation to the French Revolution* (Oxford: Oxford University Press, 1978), ch. 1.

[61]Contemporary biographical materials for Sibbes and Perkins are limited. The Puritan hagiographers, Clarke, *Lives of Thirty-two English Divines*, and Thomas Fuller in *The Holy State and the Profane State* (1642), *Abel Redivivus* (1651), and *Worthies of England* (1662), offered discussions of the men. For Sibbes a brief but sometimes revealing memorial by Zachary Catlin is available: The "Memoir of Richard Sibbes" (three copies are held by the Univ. of Cambridge library, Add. Mss. 48 and 103; Mm. 1.49); it is provided in full by Grosart as appendix A to the "Memoir of Richard Sibbes, D.D." in Sibbes' *Works*, 1.xix-cxxxi (cxxxiii-cxli).

[62]Dever, "Moderation and Deprivation".

[63]*Works*, 1.cxv; Grosart's speculation, 1.cxvi.

[64]*Works*, 1.cxv. See Sibbes' complaints against 'formalists' who he regarded as 'the bane of the times', 6.196, 223; cf. 6.311 against ceremonialism.

[65]Sibbes would have faced questions about ecclesiology from early on in his studies at St. John's as the college, led by Whitaker, was divided by a controversy over Presbyterian polity. See Peter Lake, *Moderate Puritans and the Elizabethan Church* (Cambridge: Cambridge University Press, 1982), 191; Dever, "Richard Sibbes", 16, n. 31.

[66]*A Fountain Sealed*, 5.414.

[67]*Miracle of Miracles*, 7.111.

[68]*The Art of Contentment*, 5.191; citing Nazianzus, 5.426.

[69]Sibbes, *The Christian's End*, 5.300; cf. *Soul's Conflict*, 1.214; he cites *Confessions*, 1.1.

[70]Sibbes, despite his relatively infrequent notice of sources, cited or alluded to Augustine over 50 times (in contrast to two notices of Calvin); Bernard is noted at least 16 times.

[71]In the Song of Song sermons Sibbes cites Bernard and Augustine in what is, for him, a remarkable number of times, e.g., Bernard, 2.24, 63, 117, 121, 138, 172, and Augustine, 2.62, 121, 123, 174.

[72]Stoever, *Faire and Easie Way*, 15-18. These statements lack specific citations. Perkins, in fact, was unwilling to restrict the Spirit's motions; rather he viewed them as uncommon.

[73]Stoever, *Faire and Easie Way*, 16.

[74]For a brief narrative review of this period see Hall, *Antinomian Controversy*, 3-20.

[75]Stoever, *Faire and Easie Way*, 100-109; 108-109 are cited. Stoever's claim that the antinomians were in error by their over-reliance on "increated grace" is confused. His real target is an antinomian belief in a *direct* work of the Spirit (an *un*-created grace). These distinctions of grace will be developed below.

[76]Michael Jinkins, in "John Cotton and the Antinomian Controversy, 1636-1638: A Profile of Experiential Individualism in American Puritanism", *SJT* 43 (1990): 321-49, sees Stoever's thesis as "essentially an apology for Calvinist Scholasticism" (323, n. 8).

[77]Stephen Foster, "New England and the Challenge of Heresy, 1630 to 1660: The Puritan Crisis in Transatlantic Perspective", *WMQ* 38 (1981): 624-60; 643.

[78]Foster, *The Long Argument: English Puritanism and the Shaping of New England Culture, 1570-1700* (Chapel Hill: The University of North Carolina, 1991), 49-50; "New England and the Challenge of Heresy", 660. He cites Miller, *New England Mind*, 370.

[79]Nuttall, *Holy Spirit*, 14; his work is not chronological but analytical and topical—although his discussion of an emerging spiritual spectrum, including the Quakers, displays an implicit chronology. The result of the non-chronological approach is a blurring of Sibbes' leading role in the movement.

[80]James F. Maclear, "'The Heart of New England Rent': The Mystical Element in Early Puritan History", *MVHR* 42 (1956): 621-52; 626.

[81]Cohen, *God's Caress*, 209. John Preston (1587-1628) was one of the noted line of Puritan converts, each becoming the agent for the conversion of the next: Bayne, Sibbes, Cotton, and Preston. As such Preston would be Sibbes' "grandson" in the faith. Rous (1579-1659) graduated B.A. in 1597 from Pembroke College, Oxford.

[82]Dever, "Richard Sibbes", 119-120, n. 2. Cp. Bernard McGinn, "Love, Knowledge, and Mystical Union in Western Christianity: Twelfth to Sixteenth Centuries", *CH* 56 (1987): 7-24.

[83]Brauer, "Francis Rous", 2, 36f.

[84]Brauer, "Francis Rous", 10-18.

[85]McGinn, *The Foundations of Mysticism: Origins to the Fifth Century* (London: SCM, 1991), xviii. Cf. *Encyclopedia Britannica* (1969), s. v. "Mysticism".

[86]Oberman, "The Meaning of Mysticism from Meister Eckhart to Martin Luther", ch. 4 in *The Reformation: Roots and Ramifications*, trans., A. C. Gow (Edinburgh: T & T Clark, 1994), 88; 86 for the prior item.

[87]Rossall, "God's Activity", 131-35. Cf. Augustine, *City of God*, 14.7; *Confessions*, 10.3.4.

[88]Sibbes used the tools of the scholastic method when it suited him, e.g. in one exposition: "In the words you have *argumentum et argumenti ratio*, the argument, and the reasoning from the argument; the ground and the inference from the ground." *Christ's Exaltation*, 5.326. Dever points out Sibbes' participation in the dialectical exercise of his B.D. commencement (1610) when he stood as a "respondent" to a set of Latin inquiries about complex theological issues. "Richard Sibbes", 89-90.

[89]See, for instance, his juxtaposition of Aristotelian causal language and the ultimate priority of faith (through prayer in this case), in *The Saint's Safety in Evil Times*, 1.300-301. Human wit, he argued, is inadequate to "be our first movers" and therefore must be explained by a greater cause. The greater cause, in this case, is David's prayer that defeated Satan's "scholars" as represented by his brilliant opponent, Ahithophel (see 2 Samuel 16-17).

[90]For an overview of this development, see Gerhard Hasel, *Old Testament Theology: Basic Issues in the Current Debate*, 4th ed. (Grand Rapids: Eerdmans, 1991).

[91]*Christ's Exaltation*, 5.352.

[92]*A Glance of Heaven*, 4.194.

[93]*The Saints Safety in Evil Times*, 1.301.

[94]*Excellency of the Gospel*, 4.215. Roman Catholics, Sibbes noted, were aware of their "dark times". He located their worst abuses in the ninth and tenth centuries.

[95]E.g., Larzer Ziff, *The Career of John Cotton: Puritanism and the American Experience* (Princeton: University Press, 1962), 31; Dever, "Richard Sibbes", 88.

[96]This set of citations: *Commentary on 2 Corinthians*, 3.274.

[97]*2 Corinthians*, 3.274. Grosart attributes this to Luther's *Colloquia Mensalia* (without a page citation).

[98]*Work*, 5.7.

[99]*Work*, 5.15-16.

[100]*Soul's Conflict*, 1.176.

[101]*Life*, 5.205.

[102]Schuldiner, *Gifts*, 36-37.

[103]4.202-305. The text of 2 Cor 3:17-18 [NASB]: "Now the Lord is the Spirit; and where the Spirit of the Lord is, there is liberty. But we all, with unveiled face beholding as in a mirror the glory of the Lord, are being transformed into the same image from glory to glory, just as from the Lord, the Spirit."

[104]London, 1618; the foreword is included in Grosart's "Memoir", Sibbes' *Works*, 1.lxxxiii-vi.

[105]Dever, "Richard Sibbes", 18.

[106]H. C. Porter, *Reformation and Reaction in Tudor Cambridge* (Cambridge: Cambridge University Press, 1958), 380-381; White, *Predestination*, 116.

[107]*Works*, Grosart's "Memoir", 1.lxxxvi.

[108]Sibbes, *Privileges*, 5.254. He paraphrases Ro 8:28 here.

[109]Sibbes, *Privileges*, 5.255.

[110]Sibbes, *Privileges*, 5.264.

Chapter Two—An Affectionate God

[pages 71-113]

[1]Sibbes, *The Christian's End*, 5.298. This sermon series featured Romans 14:7-8 and God's purposes in history.

[2]Holmes Rolston, III, "Responsible Man in Reformed Theology: Calvin Versus the Westminster Confession", *SJT* 23 (1970): 129-156; and, *John Calvin Versus the Westminster Confession* (Richmond: John Knox, 1972). In the latter work, he contrasts Calvin's affectionate portrayal of God to the covenantal legalism of the *Confession* (ch. 2).

[3]*Confession*, 19.6. Duty is a primary motive in the *Confession* (e.g. 15.5; 16.3 & 5; 18.3), while Sibbes held that the renewed affections account for changes in the believer.

[4]Cf. Knight, *Orthodoxies*, 2.

[5]I owe this distinctive phrasing to a presentation by Michael Reeves.

[6]In scholastic categories the various causes ("formal cause", "material cause", etc.) all culminate in the "final cause". This assumes that, in a purposeful continuum (i.e., in the context of creation, the designed universe) the desired "end" requires specific means to achieve it.

[7]Martin Klauber, "The Use of Philosophy in the Theology of Johannes Maccovius (1578-1644)", *CTJ* 30 (1995): 367-91, misses this rejection. He argues that later theologians needed to look to "medieval models to help them integrate reason into theological discourse." 383.

[8]Oberman, "Fourteenth-Century Religious Thought: A Premature Profile", p. 7, in *The Dawn of the Reformation: Essays in Late Medieval and Early Reformation Thought* (Edinburgh: T&T Clark, 1986), helpfully places Luther within a broader context. See, also, ch. 5, "'*Iustitia Christi*' and '*Iustitia dei*': Luther and the Scholastic Doctrines of Justification". He holds that Luther's claims in the *Disputation Against Scholastic Theology* were widely applicable.

[9]"*Theologia nostra et Sanctus Augustinius prospere procedunt . . . Aristoteles descendit paulatim* . . ." in *WA Br*, I, 99 8-13; Luther to Lang, Wittenberg, 18 May 1517; cited in Oberman, "Headwaters of the Reformation: *Initia Lutheri - Initia Reformationis*", *Dawn of the Reformation*, 44.

[10]Aristotle, *Nicomachean Ethics*, trans. W. D. Ross, *GBWW* 9, 2.5 [Berlin number 1105b (30)]. Cf. 5.8 [1135a (15)]. The anthropocentric quality of this approach is acknowledged in 9.8 [1168a-69b].

[11]Oberman, *Dawn of the Reformation*, ch. 5.

[12]Aquinas, *Summa Theologiæ*, trans. C. Ernst, Blackfriars ed. (New York: McGraw-Hill, 1972), Ia2æ. 108.1, *ad* 3: *liber est qui sui causa est.* He cites *Metaphysics* 1.2 [982b26].

[13]Aquinas, *Summa*, Ia2æ. 108.1, *ad* 2: *Quia igitur gratia Spiritus sancti est sicut interior habitus nobis infusus, inclinans nos ad recte operandum, facit nos ligere operari ea quæ conveniunt gratiæ, et vitare ea quæ gratiæ repugnant.*

[14]Aquinas, *Summa*, Ia2æ. 106.1.

[15]See Steven E. Ozment, "*Homo Viator*: Luther and Late Medieval Theology", ch. 6 in *The Reformation in Medieval Perspective*, ed., S. E. Ozment (Chicago: Quadrangle, 1971), 151.

[16]"Introduction", xxiv-xxv, in Aquinas, *Summa* (Blackfriars ed.), vol. 30.

[17]See Robert F. Evans, *Pelagius: Inquiries and Reappraisals* (London: Adam & Charles Black, 1968); esp. 109-113. Augustine noted Pelagius' two categories of grace: 1) the juridical grace of forgiveness available to all, but not applied without meritorious efforts; and 2) a grace of instruction through the law.

Augustine, *A Treatise on Grace and Free Will*, trans. P. Holmes and R. E. Wallis, *NPNF*, 5.15 & 23.

[18]Augustine, *Treatise on Grace*, 5.444-43.

[19]Augustine, *Treatise on Grace*, 5.457 [32 (16)].

[20]He freely exchanges the three terms. See Norman Fiering, "Will and Intellect in the New England Mind", *WMQ* 29 (1972); cf. Fiering, *Moral Philosophy at Seventeenth-Century Harvard: A Discipline in Transition* (Chapel Hill: University of North Carolina, 1981), 117.

[21] The linkage of love and morality may be traced to the *shema* of Deut. 6:4-5 which Jesus affirmed in Mat 22:36-40. This is reinforced by other texts which affiliate love and choices of the will, e.g. John 14:15, "If you love me, you will keep my commandments."

[22]Augustine, *Treatise on Grace*, 5.457 [32 (16)].

[23]Augustine, *Treatise on Grace*, 5.457 [32 (16)]; 5.458 [33 (17)].

[24]Augustine, *Treatise on Grace*, 5.457 [33 (17)], emphasis added. This linkage of love and will is pivotal, but generally overlooked. Perkins, for instance, cites this chapter to establish his doctrine of God's "co-working grace" (*Of God's Free Grace and Man's Free Will*, 1.718). In so doing he missed Augustine's pivotal point, expressed here, as did Aquinas, *Summa*, 1a2æ. 111.2.

[25]Augustine, *Treatise on Grace*, 5.459 [38 (18)].

[26]Augustine, *The Spirit and the Letter*, 5.108 [56 (32)]. His caveat is not a denial of God's love, but a note on the grammatical use of the genitive case. In this context the question of Pelagianism versus Augustinianism is most sharply felt. John Burnaby comments, "The effect of the Pelagian controversy was to sharpen the dilemma—either God's work *or* ours." He suggests, arguably, that this is a false dilemma and that the Pauline solution is one of paradox. In his commentary on Romans, Augustine had written: "That we believe, is our own act: that we work what is good, belongs to him who gives the Holy Spirit to them that believe." He comments on this in his *Retractions* (i, 23): "I should not have said that, if I had known then that faith itself is found among the gifts of God, which are given in the same Spirit. Both therefore [faith and works] are ours, through the choice (*arbitrium*) of our will, and yet both are given through the Spirit of faith and charity." Introduction (192) in *Augustine: Later Works*, trans. J. Burnaby, *Library of Christian Classics* (Philadelphia: Westminster, 1955).

[27]Augustine, *Treatise on Grace*, 5.460 [40 (19)].

[28]Augustine, *Treatise on Grace*, 5.460-61 [40 (19)].

[29]Luther, *Werke: Kritische Gesamtausgabe, Briefwechsel*, vols. 1-18 (Weimar, 1930-85), I.88, 22-89, 29; 8 Feb. 1517; cited in H. A. Oberman, *Luther: Man Between God and the Devil*, trans. Eileen Walliser-Schwarzbart (London: HarperCollins, 1993), 121.

[30]Timothy F. Lull, ed., *Martin Luther's Basic Theological Writings* (Minneapolis: Fortress, 1989). It includes both disputations: *Disputation against Scholastic Theology* [*DST*], 13-20; *Heidelberg Disputation* [*HD*], 30-49. Oberman holds that Luther was not merely attacking nominalism, as Leif Grane argues, but the theology of all medieval schools ("'*Iustitia Christi*' and '*Iustitia Dei*'", 104). He cites Grane, *Luthers Ausinandersetzung mit Gabriel Biel in der Disputatio contra Scholasticism Theologiam, 1517* (Copenhagen, 1962), 46f.

[31]Rudolf Mau argues that Luther's reading of Galatians 5:14 is defined by *affectus*, which Luther found to be supported by Jerome and Augustine—"Liebe als gelebte Freheit der Christen, Luthers Auslegung von G 5,13-24 im Kommentar von 1519", 11-37 in *Lutherjahrbuch* (Göttingen: Vandenhoeck & Rupert, 1992).

[32]Luther, *DST*, thesis 13.

[33]Luther, *DST*, thesis 12.

[34]Luther, *DST*, theses 13-24.

[35]Luther, *DST*, theses 17, 18.

[36]Luther, *DST*, theses 21, 22.

[37]Luther, *HD*, thesis 21.

[38]Luther, *DST*, theses 76, 83, 86, 87, 88.

[39]Luther, *DST*, theses 90, 91.

[40]E.g. Aristotle, *Nicomachean Ethics*, 1.8 [Berlin nos. 1098b-99a], 5.7. Aristotle held that goodness could exist as a state of being without outward expression (see 8.5 [1157a]). Merit, a separate matter, credits any expression of goodness.

[41]Aristotle, *Nicomachean Ethics*, 2.1 [Berlin nos. 1103a-b].

[42]Luther, *DST*, theses 40-41. In his *Address to the German Nobility* (1520), Luther underlined his knowledge of Aristotle ("I know my Aristotle as well as you or the likes of you.") and argued that the *Physics*, *Metaphysics*, *Concerning the Soul*, and *Ethics* should be discarded from universities because of their flawed conception of nature and the Spirit. *Three Treatises* (Philadelphia: Fortress, 1970), 93.

[43]Ozment, "*Homo Viator*: Luther and Late Medieval Theology", points out the radical nature of Luther's message, citing Luther's belief that marital union with Christ is a reality even as a repentant believer will still sin.

[44]Melanchthon, *Loci Communes* [1521], *Library of Christian Classics*, Wilhelm Pauck, ed. (Philadelphia: Westminster, 1969). He 24 years old when he composed the *Loci* and in the first years of his embrace of Lutheran theology. This work reflected Luther's first disputations and point to Melanchthon's reliance in this early period. His position represented a dramatic shift from his prior devotion to Aristotle. He later returned to the features of scholastic theology that he confronts here. Thus the later editions of the *Loci* (e.g. the Latin edition of 1543) contradicts or ignores much of his first edition. An examination of Melanchthon's shift goes beyond the scope of this thesis. He simply serves here to illustrate the theological division over nature and grace and Luther's embrace of the Augustinian affective theology that Melanchthon effectively captures in 1521. See the preface in J. A. O. Preus, trans., *Loci Communes*, 1543 (St Louis: Concordia, 1992), 7-14, on his shifting views. Cf. Wilhelm H. Neuser, "Luther und Melanchthon—Ein Herr, verschiedene Gaben", 47-62 in *Luthers Werkung: Festschrift für Martin Brecht zum 60. Geburtstag*, eds. Wolf-Dieter Hauschild *et al.* (Stuttgart: Calwer Verlag, 1992). Neuser agrees with the widely held view that 1525 was the year when Melanchthon reverts to an Aristotelian view of the will. This led to his disagreement with Luther in the Cordatus dispute (1536). See, too, Gregory Graybill, *Evangelical Free Will: Phillipp Melanchthon's Doctrinal Journey on the Origins of Faith* (Oxford: Oxford University Press, 2010).

[45]*Loci Communes* [1521], "Introduction", 16-17. For a discussion of Melanchthon's relationship with Calvin and evidence of some reliance in the *Institutes* on the 1521 edition of the *Loci*, see ch. 13 of Alexandre Ganoczy, *The Young Calvin*, trans., David Foxgrover and Wade Provo (Edinburgh: T. & T. Clark, 1987).

[46]See R. A. Muller, "Calvin and the 'Calvinists': Assessing the Continuities and Discontinuities Between the Reformation and Orthodoxy", 2 parts, *CTJ* 30, 31 (1995-96): 345-75; 125-60. Muller is dismissive of scholars who view the revival of Aristotle in post-Reformation theology as destructive. Such scholarship displays a "strong neo-orthodox *tendenz*". Muller, however, conspicuously fails to address adequately the extensive evidence, illustrated here, of contemporary Protestant opposition to Aristotle and Aquinas (e.g. his brief and understated notice of "the relatively negative" view of medieval theology in Melanchthon and Calvin—*CTJ* 31: 132).

[47]In 1277 the bishop of Paris outlawed an Aristotelian assumption that Aquinas held: "the will necessarily pursues what is firmly held by reason, and

that it cannot abstain from that which reason dictates". Ralph Lerner and Muhsin Mahdi, eds., *Medieval Political Philosophy: A Sourcebook*, 335-54; cited in Fiering, "Will and Intellect", 526.

[48]Melanchthon, *Loci*, 23. This and subsequent citations of the *Loci* refer to the 1521 edition.

[49]See discussions of the Aristotelian-scholastic views of anthropology/psychology in Rossall, "God's Activity and the Believer's Experience", 131f; and throughout Fiering's works, cited above.

[50]Melanchthon, *Loci*, 23.

[51]Melanchthon, *Loci*, 24.

[52]Melanchthon, *Loci*, 24.

[53]Fiering, *Moral Philosophy*, 44.

[54]Melanchthon, *Loci*, 27.

[55] Augustine, *Spirit and the Letter*, NPNF 5.106 [51(29)].

[56]Melanchthon, *Loci*, 31.

[57]Melanchthon, *Loci*, 54.

[58]Melanchthon, *Loci*, 87.

[59]Melanchthon, *Loci*, 87.

[60]Melanchthon, *Loci*, 88.

[61]Calvin summarizes five senses and a symmetrical pairing of "three cognitive faculties" and "three appetitive faculties" of the soul. He comments, "Although these things are true, or are least are probable, yet since I fear that they may involve us in their own obscurity rather than help us, I think they ought to be passed over." [*Institutes*, 1.15.6] This tepid response suggests Calvin's uncertainty.

[62]Calvin, *Institutes*, 1.15.7.

[63]"Puritans and the Human Will: Voluntarism Within Mid-Seventeenth Century English Puritanism as Seen in the Works of Richard Baxter and John Owen" (Ph.D. diss., Univ. of Durham, 1989), 141. Cf. Muller, "Calvin and the 'Calvinists'", 30: 350, 31: 135; and his, *Christ and the Decree*, 1-9.

[64]Rossall, "God's Activity", ch. 3; 140.

[65]Calvin, *Institutes*, 2.4.1; cited by Rossall, 140. See Luther's use in *Werke* WA 18.635; Engl. trans., J. I. Packer & O. R. Johnston, 103-4. McNeill & Battles

link the metaphor to a variation on Pseudo-Augustine. 2.11.20 (MPL 45. 1632).

[66]Calvin, *Institutes*, 2.3.14; so, also, the citations that follow.

[67]Calvin, *Institutes*, 1.2.1; cited by B. A. Gerrish who sees God's goodness as "regulative for everything" in Calvin's theology; in *Grace & Gratitude: The Eucharistic Theology of John Calvin* (Edinburgh: T&T Clark, 1993), 26.

[68]Calvin, *Institutes*, 2.2.18.

[69]Calvin, *Institutes*, 2.2.20.

[70]Calvin, *Institutes*, 2.2.24; he cites the Pelagian view of grace in 2.2.21

[71]Calvin, *Institutes*, 2.2.24.

[72]He held Luther's distinction: sin may be necessary yet without external compulsion (2.3.5; ed. comment, n. 10).

[73]Weir, *Origins*, 137-147. Dudley Fenner promoted it in England in his *Sacra theologia* (1585).

[74]The argument that there are two contending versions of covenant theology—one more arbitrary than the other—is not addressed here. Sibbes held both positions to be orthodox. Lyle D. Bierma, "The Role of Covenant Theology in Early Reformed Orthodoxy", *SCJ* 21 (1990): 453-462; R. A. Muller, "The Covenant of Works and the Stability of Divine Law in Seventeenth-Century Reformed Orthodoxy: A Study in the Theology of Herman Witsius and Wilhelmus A Brakel", *CTJ* 29 (1994): 75-101.

[75]Musculus reflected this as cited in White, *Predestination*, 86: "while it was true God did not predestine what he did not foreknow, He did not predestine all he foreknew. Election must be attributed to the goodness of God, and we must not ask for cause of causes." Wolfgang Musculus, *Common Places of Christian Religion* (1563), f. 209r.

[76]Perkins, *Golden Chain*, pp. 185-6 [1.16].

[77]Perkins, *Golden Chain*, p. 175 [1. To the reader].

[78]A print of Perkins' one-page illustration of the Golden Chaine is offered in E. Hindson, ed., *Introduction to Puritan Theology: A Reader* (Grand Rapids: Baker, 1976), 138.

[79]Perkins, *Golden Chain*, p. 175 [1. To the reader]; the emphasis is added.

[80]*Metaphysics*, 10.6-8 [1056b-1058a]—issues of composition and division imply change.

[81]Perkins, *Golden Chaine*, 1.11.

[82]NASB translation. The context suggests an angry God whose wrath is raised against those who have spurned his love, e.g. 1:2. On God's impassibility see W. McWilliams, "Divine Suffering in Contemporary Theology", *SJT* 33 (1980): 35-53; cp. K. Surin, "The Impassibility of God and the Problem of Evil", *SJT* 35 (1982): 97-115.

[83]Perkins, *Golden Chaine*, 1.25. The problem of definition exists: is passion distinct from the affections in Perkins view, or are they synonymous as sometimes found in Sibbes? A presumed division of Christ's human and divine natures is evident in such discussions: Christ in his humanity experiences passion through his trials and death while in his deity he is passionless.

[84]Yet Perkins, inconsistently, uses the affective/relational language in his informal discussion; e.g. his "To the reader" in the *Golden Chaine* which concludes with the love benediction of Eph. 3.

[85]This point will be supported in discussing Sibbes' affective theology that is anchored in John 17.

[86]R. A. Muller questions whether the *Golden Chaine* is to be taken as a systematic theology in "Perkins' *A Golden Chaine*", or that predestination is the defining paradigm of his theology (e.g. "Calvin and the 'Calvinists'", 31: 153. However, Perkins' introduction made his purpose clear—he intended to promote a supralapsarian model of predestination while rejecting other views. Cf. Perkins' catechism, *Foundation of Christian Religion Gathered into Six Principles.* Here he put the question, "What dost thou believe concerning God?" and identified God's "chief properties" as follows: "First, he is most *wise*" . . . Secondly, he is most *holy* . . . Thirdly, he is *eternal* . . . [and] Lastly, he is *infinite*" being both omnipresent and "of power sufficient to do whatever he will." (1.3; emphasis added). Love, again, is absent. Perkins introduced God's love in the fourth of six principles, the one that explained faith. This late placement displays a structural issue in Perkins' theology. God's love is only for the elect; it is mentioned, therefore, only when the elect are revealed in the theological map of the *ordo salutis*. God is a lawgiver who confronts humans with moral requirements to prepare the elect for salvation by first "bruising them".

[87]Perkins, *Golden Chaine*, 1.109.

[88]Perkins, *God's Free Grace*, 1.723.

[89]Perkins, *God's Free Grace*, 1.703.

[90]Perkins, *Exposition of the Symbol*, 1.278.

[91]Perkins, *Foundation*, 1.6 [157-58].

[92]Perkins, 1.720; he cites the *Summa*, 1.1 Q.105.5 (transl.--*GBWW*).

[93]Perkins, *Symbol*, 1.299.

[94]Perkins, *Golden Chaine*, 1.25 [198].

[95]Perkins, *Symbol*, 1.301.

[96]Perkins, *Golden Chaine*, 1.15-16 [184-85].

[97]Knight, *Orthodoxies*, 97. The context for her statement is that of a Perkins disciple, Thomas Hooker, who linked God's prevenience and human obedience; the latter task is "answerable to that grace bestowed."

[98]Sibbes, *Bowels Opened*, 2.181.

[99]Sibbes, *Salvation Applied*, 5.388.

[100]Sibbes, *Faithful Covenanter*, 6.3.

[101]Kendall, *Calvin*, 103, 109.

[102]Dever, "Richard Sibbes", 96-97.

[103]Sibbes, *Successful Seeker*, 6.113. Cf. 4.144. Knight (*Orthodoxies*, 136) notices this purpose as well but fails to elevate its significance.

[104]Sibbes, *Christian's End*, 5.300. He cites the *Confessions*, 1.1; cf. Sibbes, *Soul's Conflict*, 1.214: "For the soul is made for God and never finds rest till it returns to him again."

[105]Dever, "Richard Sibbes", 125; ch. 6 examines Sibbes' affectionate theology but one is left to infer from the discussion that Sibbes' emphasis is a matter of preference rather than an alternative position. Cf., Grosart's "Memoir" in Sibbes' *Works*, 1. xix.

[106]Sibbes, *Description of Christ*, 1.5.

[107]Sibbes, *Matchless Love*, 6.386.

[108]Sibbes, *Matchless Love*, 6.387.

[109]Perkins, *Golden Chain*, 1.70 [213].

[110]Sibbes, *Faithful Covenanter*, 6.4.

[111]Sibbes, *Matchless Love*, 6.387. Sibbes cited John 17:28 in this context. This priestly prayer of Christ is the principal text for Sibbes' teleology.

[112]Sibbes, *Fountain Opened*, 5.462-3.

[113]Sibbes, *Fountain Opened*, 5.483-4.

[114]Sibbes, *Description of Christ*, 1.12.

[115]Sibbes, in *Salvation Applied*—a sermon that defended limited atonement—addressed to the problem with pastoral pragmatism: "Reason not this, whether God hath elected, or Christ hath died for thee. This is the secret will of God. But the commandment is, to believe in Christ. This binds. Therefore, yield to Christ when thou art called and bidden to cast thyself upon him; then thou shalt find, to thy soul's comfort, the fruit of his death." (5.391; cf. his *Commentary on 2 Cor.*, 3.156).

[116]Sibbes, while conversant with Eastern theology, held the Western view of the procession of the Spirit: "[H]e is both breathed from the Father and the Son, as proceeding from them both; and by office, breatheth into all that God hath given Christ to redeem and him to sanctify." In *Fountain Sealed*, 5.412.

[117]Sibbes, *Fountain Opened*, 5.444.

[118]Sibbes, *Soul's Conflict*, 1.137.

[119]Sibbes, *Fountain Opened*, 5.444.

[120]Sibbes, *Fountain Opened*, 5.444.

Chapter Three—Defining the Problem: What is Sin?

[pages 115-149]

[1]Was Sibbes influenced by Melanchthon's early *Loci Communes*? If so we have no direct evidence of it. He was, however, alert to Melanchthon's affective themes. Sibbes, for instance, cited him to show that affections motivate prayers: "As Melanchthon said well, 'If I cared for nothing, I would pray for nothing, *Si nil curarem nil orarem*."—Sibbes, *The Soul's Conflict*, 1.158. Grosart locates this quotation in *Dicta Melancthonis*, in Melchoir Adam, *Vitæ Germ. Theolog.* (Frankfort, 1653). Sibbes also noted Melanchthon's moderate temper: "[Christ] sent Augustine and Jerome, Luther and Melanchthon . . . Luther, hot and fiery; Melanchthon, of a soft and mild spirit."—*Of the Providence of God*, 5.38.

[2]Sibbes, *Soul's Conflict*, 1.159.

[3]A history of the doctrine of sin may be traced before Augustine but many of the subsequent categories such as original and actual sin; privative and positive sin; questions of transmission; and discussions of the relationship between sin and salvation were fragmentary. Athanasius, Ambrose and Ambrosiaster explored questions of the fall and transmission of sin, for instance, but it was

left to Augustine to press issues at length, given his Manichean exposure and his debate with the Pelagians. See, for a summary of early views, J. N. D. Kelly, *Early Christian Doctrines*, fifth, revised ed. (London: A & C Black, 1977), ch. 13; also, F. R. Tennant, *The Concept of Sin* (Cambridge: Cambridge University Press, 1912).

[4]E.g. Augustine, *Confessions*, 7.12&13: *"itaque vidi et manifestatum est mihi, quia omnia bona tu fecisti"* and *"Et tibi omnino non est malum".*

[5]Augustine, *De Libero Arbitrio*, trans. Dom Mark Pontifex (London: Longmans, Green and Co., 1955), 2.20.54.

[6]Evans, *Augustine on Evil* (Cambridge: Cambridge University Press, 1982), 33. Calvin, in a rare disagreement with Augustine, challenged the Bishop's privative framework (and, with it, any secondary indeterminacy), while still affirming Augustine's intention. The whole scheme, Calvin believed, violated explicit biblical data: "[T]he will of God is the great cause of all things that are done in the whole world; and yet, that God is not the author of the evils that are done therein. But I will not say, with Augustine—which, however, I readily acknowledge to have been truly said by him—"In sin or in evil, there is nothing positive." for this is an acuteness of argument which, to many, may not be satisfactory. I would rather assume another principle of argument, and say, "Those things which are vainly or unrighteously done by man are, rightly and righteously, the works of God!" And if this should appear to some, at first sight, to be paradoxical or self-contradictory, let not such be so fastidious or hasty as not to inquire, with me, into the word of God, and see how the Divine matters stands as viewed in that glass." Calvin, *Calvin's Calvinism: The Eternal Predestination of God and The Secret Providence of God*, trans., Henry Cole (London: Sovereign Grace Union, 1927), 233.

[7]Berkouwer, *Sin* (Grand Rapids: Eerdmans, 1971), 261.

[8]G. Vandervelde, *Original Sin: Two Major Trends in Contemporary Roman Catholic Reinterpretation* (Amsterdam: Rodopi N.V., 1975), 27; cf. Evans, *Augustine*, 95. Vandervelde's introduction, 1-54, includes a survey of this development. This polarity continues to exist although the terminology shifts. In the early twentieth century F. R. Tennant conceived sin to be privative ('. . . sin may be defined as moral imperfection for which an agent is, in God's sight, accountable."). Later his pupil, Frederic Greeves, argued that sin was ignorance (i.e. privation of knowledge). Tennant, *Concept of Sin*, 245; Greeves, *The Meaning of Sin* (London: Epworth Press, 1956), ch. 2. See, concerning the affections and the will, Augustine's discussions of sin in his *Confessions* in which love shapes the will by its desires, a view which anticipates Sibbes' elevation of the affections; e.g. 8.5, "I was quite sure that it was better for me to give myself

up to your love [*tuae caritati me dedere*] than to surrender to my own lusts [*cupiditati*]." Cf. *De Libero Arbitrio*, 1.16.34.

[9]Evans, *Augustine*, 113.

[10] Compatibilism holds that freedom is the power to do what one desires to do, even within a determined universe. Another option—held by Perkins—is secondary indeterminacy in which God permits free-will, self-moved choices within his larger plan. In contrast to this view, compatibilism assumes that the elect desire God's intended purposes. The question, of course, is how two truly free wills achieve full correspondence. The answer of the affective tradition is located in the conforming power of captured affections—believers are, in the Pauline terms of Rom. 6 free to be "enslaved" to righteousness from the heart. See Paul Helm, *The Providence of God* (Leicester: Inter-Varsity, 1993), 66f, for a survey of options related to providence.

[11]Augustine, *Retractions*, 2.42. Cf. Evans, *Augustine*, 128.

[12]Augustine, *On Nature and Grace*, trans. P. Holmes, *et al.*, *NPNF*, 5, 80 [67].

[13]Augustine, *Nature and Grace*, 21 & 22 [19 & 20].

[14]Augustine, *Nature and Grace*, 25 [23].

[15]Augustine, *Nature and Grace*, 29 [26].

[16]Augustine, *Nature and Grace*, 37 [33].

[17]Augustine, *Nature and Grace*, 49 [42]; 67 [57]; 70 [60]; 77 [64]; 79 [66].

[18]Augustine, *Nature and Grace*, 83 [69], 84 [70].

[19]Vandervelde, *Original Sin*, 26-32, esp. 32. Before Augustine, Athanasius held a version of privative sin: Adam and Eve's were distracted from their prior gaze of faith; deprived of the grace of God's image, they fell. See Kelly, *Early Christian Doctrines*, 346-8.

[20]Aquinas, *Summa*, 1a2æ.82.1.

[21]Aquinas, *Summa*, 1a2æ.81.2.

[22]McGrath, *Iustitia Dei*, 1.78-79; cf. sect. 9. See, also, Ernst, "Introduction", xvi, *Summa*. He identifies Aquinas' commentary on Lombard, (*In* II *Sent.* 28, 1.1 ad 1) as the primary reference for this development.

[23]Perkins, *Golden Chain*, 1.18. Chapter title 10 begins: "Of sin and the fall of angels". Ch. 11 is: "Of man's fall and disobedience". It begins, "Adam's fall was his willing revolting to disobedience by eating the forbidden fruit." Thus Perkins may have portrayed angelic sin as privative and human sin as positive. Sibbes did this as well. Perkins, however, states later in ch. 10, "The fall is of

men and angels . . ." When he first introduces privation in ch. 6, he fails to identify men or angels: "And he forsaketh his creature either by detracting the grace it had, or not bestowing that which it wanteth." The reader must assume he is speaking of humans. The key issue in using the privative argument is not effected by this uncertainty, i.e. did God withdraw his grace in order to cause sin in his creation?

[24]Perkins, *Golden Chain*, 1.18. This doublet was also argued by Aquinas: *Summa*, 1a2æ.82.1.

[25]Ursinus, "Briefe Discourse" in Perkins, *Works*, 1. 429-38; Ursinus, *Commentary . . . on the Heidelberg Catechism*, trans. G. W. Williard (Phillipsburg, NJ: Presbyterian and Reformed, 1985; orig. Latin ed., Geneva, 1587), 35, 39.

[26]Perkins, *Golden Chaine*, 1.18.

[27]Perkins, *Golden Chaine*, 1.70.

[28]Hall, *Antinomian* 133 (Cotton's "Rejoynder"). Cited above, 12.

[29]Perkins, *Foundation*, 1.3-8.

[30]Perkins, *Golden Chaine*,1.21.

[31]Perkins, *Golden Chaine*,1.20-21.

[32]Bayne, *Briefe Directions unto a Godly Life* (London, 1637), 201-3.

[33]Perkins recognized the power of the affections--so much so that, in an attack on the Aristotelian doctrine of the golden mean, he concluded: "All virtues that are not joined with a renovation and change of affections, are no better than sins." In *William Perkins, 1558-1602: English Puritanist*, ed., Thomas F. Merrill (Nieuwkoop: B. De Graaf, 1966), 163. Cf. Ames in his *Commentary on 1 Peter*, v. 22, reason 4; in his *Workes* (London, 1643), 28.

[34]Concupiscence, from *concupisco*, denoted inordinate desires, e.g. coveting, lusting, etc. Sexual desire is only one aspect of concupiscence but, from Augustine until the Reformation, it accounted for the view that sin is transmitted through procreation, with Ps 51:5 as a prooftext: "I was brought forth in iniquity and in sin my mother conceived me." Concupiscence, as it related to Adam's fall, was the coveting of God's authority and glory. It displayed arrogance and pride, with disobedience or law breaking as a consequent behavior.

[35]Sibbes, *Commentary on 2 Cor 4*, 4.354.

[36]Sibbes, *Christ's Exaltation Purchased by His Humiliation*, 5.342.

[37]Sibbes, *Soul's Conflict*, 1.172. The *donum gratiæ* is implicit in the "accessory and supernatural" quality; the phrase itself is not used.

[38]Sibbes, *Soul's Conflict*, 1.173. The absence of dates and sequence for the majority of Sibbes' works usually disallow any possibility in tracing the maturation of his thought and, therefore, to display a diminishing presence of Perkins' categories, including original privation. However in a rare exception Sibbes himself in the week of his death recorded that he began this series twelve years earlier (i.e. in 1623; see 1.126). Thus it represents a position held in his maturity. The dissonance between this view and that of angelic privation almost certainly reflects an earlier composition of the latter position. Apart from that, the discussion here is certainly more extended (1.171-3) and careful than the relatively brief and passing point made in the Corinthians *Commentary* (4.354).

[39]See Ernst, "Introduction", xvii, Aquinas, *Summa*. Ernst notes Aquinas' reading of Aristotle's *Eudemian Ethics* as the ground for this shift. Ernst suggests that after this insight Aquinas shifted toward a more Dionysian solution in which grace returns to its source by assimilation. This offers a ground for movement in the soul that receives grace (xviii).

[40]Sibbes, "Commentary on 2 Cor 1", 3.430-31 [including subsequent citations.]; cf. a similar critique of human self-deification in 5.422, cited in ch 4.

[41]Sibbes, *Soul's Conflict*, 1.268.

[42]Knight sees Sibbes' doctrine of sin as privative, apparently measuring it against the view promoted in Perkins' theology. Her approach misses the positive violation described here. *Orthodoxies*, 113.

[43]Sibbes, *The Spiritual Jubilee*, 5.228.

[44]Sibbes, *Soul's Conflict*, 1.279. Sibbes regularly uses sight as descriptive of faith, e.g. 4.483, 4.251, 4.270, 7.349.

[45]Sibbes, *Soul's Conflict*, 1.154; *Saints Safety*, 1.304; *A Fountain Sealed*, 5.422 (original emphases).

[46]Sibbes, *Excellency of the Gospel*, 4.252.

[47]Sibbes, *Excellency*, 4.252.

[48]Sibbes, *Excellency*, 4.231.

[49]John Rogers, *Ohel or Bethshemesh, A Tabernacle for the Sun* (London, 1653), 410; this is a collection of Puritan testimonials. Susan Hardman Moore alerted me to this citation.

[50]See Jesper Rosenmeier, "The Image of Christ: the Typology of John Cotton" (Ph.D. dissertation, Harvard University, 1965). Rosenmeier attributes the division in the Antinomian Controversy to a disagreement over the nature of the elect after conversion. John Winthrop, Thomas Shepard, Thomas Hooker, and Peter Bulkeley all held that the "image of Christ" was a restoration "to the natural law which God had given to Adam and redrafted in the law of Moses" as opposed to Cotton's view which "relied on the immediate revelation of the Holy Spirit which stamps a man with the seal of Christ's Crucifixion and Resurrection" (139). Rosenmeier's work fails to capture the differing views of grace and sin that divided the participants; instead he elevates what was a secondary feature in the debate, the use of typology among Puritans to support their arguments.

[51]E.g. Perkins, *Golden Chaine*, 1.17-18.

[52]See the *Westminster Confession of Faith*, 5.5, where God is said to leave saints "for a season" to "manifold temptations and the corruption of their own hearts" for a number of positive reasons including the person's punishment, self-discovery of sin, enlargement of dependence, and the like. How God does this is not explained but the idea may reflect a Perkinsonian duality of grace. If the authors viewed grace as a supplied resource, it would be a privative action similar to the grace withdrawal of "new grace" which caused Adam's fall in Perkins' scheme (in the *Confession* there is no explanation for Adam's choice to sin, apart from a statement that the first couple was "seduced"—6.1). Support is found in the subsequent section, 5.6, where hardened hearts in reprobates, "for their former sins", are explicitly attributed to the withholding of God's grace.

[53]Bayne, *Briefe Directions unto a Godly Life . . .* (London, 1637), 3-4. By "the present keeping of the law" Bayne apparently meant the ability to keep accessible laws (to use Perkins' category--below), which are also beyond human ability apart from the work of the Spirit: "it is not to be sought for in ourselves . . . . It being appointed by the Father, was undertaken and wrought by Christ, and is sealed in men's hearts by the holy Ghost."

[54]Perkins, *Golden Chaine*, 1.86. Cf. Stoever, who sees the Puritan doctrine of regeneration as "the renovation and reordering of human nature" (*Faire and Easie Way*, 8).

[55]Perkins, *Discourse of Conscience*; in Merrill, *Perkins*, 21-22.

[56]Perkins, *A Discourse of Conscience*; in Merrill, *Perkins*, 21.

[57]Sibbes, *Christ's Exaltation Purchased by Humiliation*, 5.329.

[58]Sibbes, *Christ's Exaltation*, 5.336.

[59]Sibbes, *Description of Christ*, 1.14; cf. *Miracle of Miracles*, 7.111.

[60]Sibbes, *Description of Christ*, 1.14.

[61]Sibbes, *Exaltation*, 5.344.

[62]Sibbes, *Exaltation*, 5.334.

[63]Sibbes, *Exaltation*, 5.339; the sequence of citations above began on 338.

[64]Sibbes, *Exaltation*, 5.340. This recalls Luther's similar elevation of all vocations for believers.

[65]Paul Bayne, a nomist, illustrates this tendency when he, despite the Pauline teaching to the contrary (1 Tim 2:14), attributes Adam's fall to Satan's deception: "God created man happy, yet mutable; but Satan by deceit did cast him from that happy condition." In *Briefe Directions*, 1.

Chapter Four—Mystical Marriage

[pages 151-185]

[1]See R. Tudor Jones, "Union with Christ: The Existential Nerve of Puritan Piety", *Tyndale Bulletin* 41 (1990): 186-208. He notes Sibbes' place of prominence among Puritans addressing this topic.

[2]Sibbes, *Fountain Opened*, 5.479.

[3]Sibbes, *Descriptions of Christ*, 1.6.

[4]Eph. 5: 31-32, "'For this reason a man shall leave his father and mother and be joined to his wife, and the two shall become one.' This is a great mystery, and I take it to mean Christ and the church." [RSV]

[5]E.g. *Golden Chaine*, 1.82; *Grain of Mustard Seed*, 1.637. See Herman Ridderbos, *Paul: An Outline of His Theology*, trans., J. R. De Witt (Grand Rapids: Eerdmans, 1975), who points to the importance of union in Paul's theology (58) but argues that the question of whether this is a union of participation or one of Federal imputation is not clearly defined by Paul (59-62; 363).

[6]*Faire and Easie Way*, 41. This represented the Federalism of John Cotton's opponents in New England's Antinomian Controversy. Stoever cites three contemporary theologians: William Ames, *The Marrow of Sacred Divinity* (London, 1642), I.26; Edward Leigh, *A System or Body of Divinity* (London, 1654), 490-91; John Ball, *A Treatise of Faith* (London, 1631), 6, 11.

[7]Stoever, *Faire and Easie Way*, pp. 83-84.

[8]McGrath, *Iustitia Dei*, 1.145-6; he cites Aquinas, *I Sent.* dist. 17 q. 1 a.1. Aquinas, using Aristotle's categories of causation, identified two measures by which God is "in all things": he is the ground of their being and the power which rules them. In his power God is "especially in the rational creature who knows and loves him actually or habitually" (*Summa*, 1a. 8,3).

[9]Augustine, *On the Predestination of the Saints* [*De prædestinatione Sanctorum*], *NPNF*, 5.15, 31. See J. N. D. Kelly, *Early Christian Doctrines*, chs. 10-11 for a discussion of Christological issues in Augustine's era. A distinction between "Word-flesh" and "Word-man" Christologies denotes the degree to which a real humanity existed in Christ (e.g. 301-9).

[10]Augustine, *Predestination of the Saints* 5.15, 31.

[11]Aquinas, *Summa*, vol. 30, "Introduction", xxii; Ernst cites 3a.2, 10; 7, 13 ad I; 23, 4 ad 2; cf 2, II *sed contra*; 24, I ad 3; 2 *sed contra, corp.*, ad I; 3 *sed contra.*

[12]Above, 78.

[13]Ernst, "Introduction", in Aquinas, *Summa*, vol. 30. McGrath, in *Iustitia Dei*, 1.78-79, points to the *Summa Fratris Alexandri* as the first systematic exposition of the dichotomy; cf. sect. 9, esp. 108.

[14]Perkins, *Exposition*, 1.298-99.

[15]Perkins, *Exposition*, 1.299 (emphasis added).

[16]Augustine, *On the Predestination of the Saints*, 15, 31.

[17] Perkins' reliance on adoption as the primary mechanism of spiritual union is a logical concomitant to his juridical theology. Given his strong doctrine of incommensurability, God offers himself to the elect through benefits rather than by real union. His discussions of adoption are widespread: e.g., in Breward's editions of his *Works*, 198, 201, 219, 234, 394.

[18] E.g. Sibbes, *A Fountain Sealed*, 5.425; also 7.447.

[19]Perkins, *Golden Chaine*, 1.77.

[20]Perkins, *Golden Chaine*, 1.77, 78 (emphasis added).

[21]Perkins, *Golden Chaine*, 1.78.

[22]Perkins, *Golden Chaine*", 1.30.

[23]Breward, in his "Introduction" to Perkins' *Works* notes this "oversharp account of the distinction between Christ's divinity and humanity", 98. Breward also notices the differences between Perkins' more systematic works and his pastoral expositions such as *A Declaration of the True Manner of Knowing Christ Crucified* that presents a Christology more aligned with the definition of

Chalcedon. This inconsistency is found between 'kinds' of literature; Perkins remains generally consistent in the formal expositions featured in this thesis.

[24]Perkins, *Exposition*, 1.299.

[25]Perkins, *Golden Chaine*, 1.79.

[26]Perkins, *Exposition*, 1.308. Perkins was not alone in holding this theology, which suggests his effectiveness in its propagation. Two of his most noted students, Paul Bayne and William Ames, also affirmed *habitus* in their own theologies, as did Sibbes, although in a modified form which will be discussed below. Ames, for instance, in his widely read *Marrow of Sacred Theology*, spoke of "the habit whence faith flowes" (*habitus ex quo fluit fides*), 6, in *Workes* (London, 1643); Latin text, *Medulla S.S. Theologiae*, 3d ed., (London, 1629), 6. Bayne also spoke of Christian obedience as accomplished through the two forms of grace working together, "*gratia increata* (increated) and *gratia adiuvans* (assisting)." Bayne explained God's prevenience in salvation by *habitus*: "Not that God doth force the will, but by an habite of grace maketh it willing, and by light in the understanding maketh it determine it selfe in following him." Bayne, *Lectures* [Phil. 2:13], and [II Tim. 1:9]; in Paul R. Schaefer Jr., "The Spiritual Brotherhood on the Habits of the Heart: Cambridge Protestants and the Doctrine of Sanctification from William Perkins to Thomas Shepard" (Ph.D. diss., Oxford University, 1994), 102 (n.73), 105.

[27]Aquinas had been alert to their definition: "Thus if we were to speak of God's grace not as some habitual gift but as God's very mercy itself [*misericordiam Dei*] by which he works from within the movements of the mind and ordains external affairs to man's salvation, *in this sense man cannot perform any good work without God's grace*." From *quæstio Disputata de veritate* (xxiv, 14); cited by Ernst in Aquinas, *Summa*, vol. 30, "Introduction", xv. Emphasis added.

[28]McGrath, *Intellectual Origins*, 89.

[29]See McGrath, *Intellectual Origins*, 79-82, for a review of how this paradigm developed and how the Ockhamist critique developed which then provided an intellectual context for its denial by Luther.

[30]Gerrish, *Grace*, 96.

[31]Martin Luther, *Werke. Kritische Gesamtausgabe*, II, 509; cited in Gottfried W. Locher, *Zwingli's Thought: New Perspectives*, vol. 25 of *Studies in the History of Christian Thought*, ed. Heiko A. Oberman (Leiden: E. J. Brill, 1981), 13.

[32]Huldrych Zwingli, *Huldreich Zwinglis Werke. Erste vollstandige Ausgabe*, ed., Melchior Schuler and Johannes Schultess, IV, 10; cited in Locher, *Zwingli's Thought*, 13.

[33]Locher, *Zwingli's Thought*, 178.

[34]Calvin, *Institutes*, 3.11.15.

[35]Calvin, *Institutes*, 3.1.1; 3.1.2. Cf. 75 above.

[36]Calvin, *Institutes*, 3.1.3. "*Corda nostra incendit amore Dei et studio pietatis.*"

[37]Calvin, *Institutes*, 3.2.8. Aquinas had asked whether the distinction is grounded in differing habits of grace in the *Summa*, 2. 2ae.4,4

[38]Calvin, *Institutes*, 3.2.38; 3.2.14. Cf. Aquinas, *Summa*, 1. 2ae.112,5—"Whether a man can know that he has grace").

[39]Calvin, *Institutes*, 3.2.23; 3.2.24. Edward A. Dowey, *The Knowledge of God in Calvin's Theology* (New York: Columbia University, 1952), cites this section in introducing a section on "Faith as mystical union with Christ". Dowey's useful distinction between Calvin's knowledge of God as Creator and as Redeemer is vividly illustrated in Calvin's discussion in the following section of the *Institutes* (3.2.25) where Bernard of Clairvaux is cited to support Calvin's assertion that any introspection of the heart is futile.

[40]Calvin, *Institutes*, 3.11.16.

[41]Bernard McGinn, *Foundations of Mysticism*, 118.

[42]This approach solved a problem for both the early Jewish exegetes and later Christians--celebration of a merely human love relationship was assumed to be inferior to the purposes of biblical revelation.

[43]Revelation 22:13-17, 19:7-10; cp. Ephesians 5:22-33.

[44]Theodore Beza, *Master Bezaes Sermons Upon the Three First Chapters of the Canticle of Canticles*, trans., John Harmar (Oxford, 1587). Unlike those who used *Canticles* in arguing for a real union of Christ and the Church, Beza emphasized incommensurability in terms similar to those Perkins later used. He identified three "unions of God with man"—Christ's incarnation, his hypostatic union and "a third conjunction" in which the church is spiritually married to Christ. His caveat followed: "Not that the body of Christ is really within our bodies, or his soul within our soul . . . [but by the] virtue of his Holy Spirit, and by the means of his human nature, by the which he . . . agrees in one part with us, is so near and so powerfully joined with us, by the means of faith which apprehends him, that he quickens us to life eternal, working in our understanding and will to repair in us by little and little the image of God . . . ." (7).

[45]Gifford, *Exposition on the Canticles* (London, 1612); idem, *Fifteene Sermons upon the Song of Salomon.* (London, 1620), preached before 1599; idem, *Sermons upon*

the Whole Booke of the Revelation (London, 1599); John Cotton, *A Brief Exposition of the Whole Book of Canticles* (London, 1642); F[rancis] Rous, *The Mysticall Marriage* (London, 1635). Gordon S. Wakefield, "Mysticism and Its Puritan Types", *London Quarterly and Holborn Review* 191 (1966): 34-45, characterizes Sibbes' view of the bride as corporate while Rous' view is individualistic, leaning upon "pseudo-Dionysius, Bernard and Gerson" (41). Wakefield's broader discussion differentiates the more radical quality of Dionysian mysticism from Bernard's more affective approach.

[46]At least one of Bernard's works was available in English translation in Sibbes' era: *Saint Bernard, His Meditations: or, Sighes, Sobbes, and Teares, upon our Saviours Passion* (London, 1611).

[47]Theo Bell, *Divus Bernhardus: Bernhard von Clairvaux in Martin Luthers Schriften* (Mainz: Verlag Philipp von Zabern, 1993); cf. review by D. Bielfeldt in *SCJ* 26 (1995): 207-8. See, also, Franz Posset, "*Divus Bernhardus*: Saint Bernard as Spiritual and Theological Mentor of the Reformer Martin Luther", 517-32 in *Bernardus Magister*, J. R. Sommerfeldt, ed. (Kalamazoo: Cistercian, 1992).

[48]Nineteen citations—see the Index, *Institutes*, McNeill & Battles ed. For discussions of Calvin's use of Bernard, see A. N. S. Lane, "Bernard of Clairvaux: A Forerunner of John Calvin?", 533-45 in *Bernardus Magister*; also, Dennis E. Tamburello, "Christ and Mystical Union: A Comparative Study of the Theologies of Bernard of Clairvaux and John Calvin" (Ph.D. diss., Univ. of Chicago, 1990); and Jill Raitt, "Calvin's Use of Bernard of Clairvaux", *ARH* 72 (1981): 98-121.

[49]See S. J. Eales in *Life and Works of Saint Bernard, Abbot of Clairvaux*, vol. 4, trans. & ed., Eales (London, 1896), 8.

[50]Martin Luther, *Luther's Works*, v. 26, *Lectures on Galatians, 1535*, Jaroslav Pelikan, ed., (St Louis: Concordia, 1963), 2:20 (167, 168).

[51]Luther, *Galatians, 1535*, 2:20 (172).

[52]He apparently resists the Origen-Bernardian use of an allegorical application to Christ and the Church. In his many citations of Bernard's work, no elements of the allegorization are to be found.

[53]Calvin, *Institutes*, 4.12.24.

[54]Calvin, *Institutes*, 4.17.9.

[55]Calvin, *Institutes*, 4.19.35.

[56]A. McGrath, *Intellectual Origins*, 82, points to a "general transition from a concept of *ontological* to *covenantal* causality" in the doctrine of justification during the later medieval period.

[57]Sibbes, *Spouse*, 2.200-208; *Church's Blackness*, 7. 93-104. The latter work was published in 1629.

[58]Sibbes, *Bowels Opened*, 2.5-193. The awkward title reflects the biblical identification of deep feelings with the bowels. Cp. Sibbes citation of 1 Pet 3:18, "Therefore, 'as the elect of God,' saith the apostle, 'put on bowels of compassion,' . . . (*The Returning Backslider*, 2.264).

[59]He cites sermon two of Bernard's Canticles: "as Bernard saith, I go willingly to a Mediator made bone of my bone, my brother." [*A Christian's Portion*, 4.33] Even in his two separate sermons on the Song of Songs where Sibbes did cover some common textual ground in chapter one with Bernard, it is evident that his expositions were distinctly his own. Also, there is no apparent relationship between Sibbes' sermons and Beza's. Like Bernard, Beza's sermons extended only through chapter three.

[60]He was constrained by some, but not many, consensual matters: the kisses of chapter one, verse two, for instance, were always understood as God's activities of self-revelation. God's "speech," Bernard wrote, "living and powerful is to me as a kiss . . . [with] peace in the heart . . . joys . . . revealing of things hidden . . ." [*Life and Works of Saint Bernard*, 4.13]. Similarly, but with less drama, Beza saw them as "the preaching of his word accompanied with the virtue and working of his holy Spirit" [Beza, *Sermons*, 19], and for John Cotton, "the voice of his word . . . the breath of his Spirit . . . [his] grace . . . [and] comfort". Sibbes and Gifford both viewed the plural construction, "kisses", as God's self-disclosure through the progression of Bible covenants, thus combining both relational and historical models of interpretation on this point [Sibbes, *Spouse*, 1.202-3; Gifford, *Fifteene Sermons*, pp. 12-14. The latter work was posted in the *Stationer's Register* on 21 March 1598 and thus seems to be one of the earliest of the spate of Puritan sermon series after the publication of Beza's work]. In another case, verse five, "I am black but lovely", was always understood to characterize the "imperfection", or blackened "estate" of the church, "partly through sins . . . partly through afflictions", and "subject to sin" [Beza, *Sermons*, 87; Cotton, *Brief Exposition of . . . Canticles*, 22; Gifford, *Fifteene Sermons*, 34; Sibbes, *Church's Blackness*, 7.95]. Within such interpretive limits, Sibbes and the other ministers were free to display important elements of their theologies—e.g. the issues of covenant for Sibbes and Gifford—by linking them allegorically, and often very arbitrarily, to points in the narrative.

[61]Sibbes, *Spouse*, 2.201; italics are original.

[62]Sibbes, *Spouse*, 2.201.

[63]McGinn, "Love, Knowledge, and Mystical Union", 7-24; he cites, especially, *Sermones in Cantica*, 83.4-6.

[64]Sibbes, *Spouse*, 2.203.

[65]Sibbes, *Faith Triumphant*, 7.423: "Faith sees things in heaven; it sees Christ there; it sees our place provided for us there; it sees God reconciled there; by it we see ourselves there, because we shall be there ere long."

[66]Sibbes, *Excellency of the Gospel*, 4.257.

[67]*Theosis* presumes a degree of oneness between God and believers. It serves as an alternative ground for salvation functions that are explained by adoption and imputed righteousness in Western juridicism. Luther may have been a bridge for Sibbes' thought. For Luther's position, see Michael C. D. McDaniel, "Salvation as Justification and *Theosis*", in *Salvation in Christ: A Lutheran-Orthodox Dialogue*, John Meyendorff and Robert Tobias, eds. (Minneapolis: Augsburg, 1992), 67-83.

[68]Sibbes, *Excellency*, 4.271.

[69]Sibbes, *Faith Triumphant*, 7.424. Sibbes, in other settings, also spoke of faith as an active capacity, using the imagery of a hand, for instance, in *2 Corinthians* (3.518). But Sibbes, while acknowledging the activity of faith, once regeneration has occurred (as Calvin did in identifying the soul's embracing of the truth), was generally consistent in attributing a passivity to the human role in the first step of regeneration, e.g. his discussion of human "assent" in the context just noted (3.519).

[70]Sibbes, *2 Corinthians*, 3.519.

[71]Sibbes, *2 Corinthians*, 3.488; cf. 3.485: "And God himself was suspected of Adam in innocency. The devil is so cunning that he calls God himself into question, as if he had not meant so well to him. What will that impudent spirit do, that will bring the creature into suspicion of him that is goodness itself?"

[72]Sibbes, *Faithful Covenanter*, 6.8. This displays the underlying motive structure of the covenant as affective rather than volitional. Dever, in "Richard Sibbes", fails to capture this as the fundamental difference in emphasis between Sibbes and other Federalists. As a result Dever understates the importance of this discussion by Sibbes, listing it under the rubric of "benefits" offered by the covenant rather than identifying it as the foundation and guiding purpose of Sibbes' covenantal thought (101).

[73]Sibbes, *2 Corinthians*, 3.488.

[74]Sibbes, *Saint's Happiness*, 7.68.

[75]Sibbes, *David's Conclusion; or the Saint's Resolution*, 7.88.

[76]Sibbes, *Faith*, 7.439. Citations that follow are also from this source. Cf. 6.9.

[77]Sibbes, *Soul's Conflict*, 1.220.

[78]Sibbes, *Soul's Conflict*, 1.221.

[79]The relationship of this spiritual enlightenment of the desires to faith and love should be noticed. By such transformed desires the soul is persuaded to devotion. Devotion is common to both faith and love. Tamburello, in "Christ and Mystical Union", characterizes Bernard's doctrine of union with Christ as defined by love, while Calvin's is defined by faith. Sibbes' view is that faith and love are simply two aspects of the same function of personal entrustment of one person to another. This would be true of Calvin's position as well, a view that Tamburello almost reaches: "Calvin more characteristically speaks of union with Christ (or God) in relation to faith than to love; but love is definitely a part of the picture." (165).

[80]Sibbes, *Faith*, 7.439.

[81]Sibbes, *Faith*, 7.445.

[82]Sibbes, *Successful Seeker*, 6.113.

[83]Sibbes, *2 Corinthians*, 3.488.

[84]Sibbes, *2 Corinthians*, 3.489. This mutuality of love also stood behind Sibbes' challenges against the "violent" quality of preaching among his peers: "He is rather a butcher than a physician, that loves to torment his patient." Instead, he believed, listeners are to "be led, and not forced." The embracing of God by the elect is a result of God's love, "because God's aim is to gain our love, and which way can that be, but by a way of love? For the nature of man is such, that it will never love till it know it be loved first." (3.490).

[85]Sibbes, *Art of Contentment*, 5.182.

[86]Sibbes, *Excellency of the Gospel*, 4.274-5. Of the major studies to consider Sibbes, Harold P. Shelly, "Richard Sibbes: Early Stuart Preacher of Piety" (Ph.D. diss., Temple University, 1972), is virtually alone in capturing the importance of the affections in Sibbes' theology (ch. 3, "Warm Hearted Divinity") but even he understates the case (106-7). Against this awareness, Dever, "Richard Sibbes", is rather dismissive of Shelly's contribution (120, n. 2, 125f), which reflects Dever's emphasis on rational and volitional theology (129-30).

[87]Pettit, *The Heart Prepared: Grace and Conversion in Puritan Spiritual Life*, 2d ed. (Middletown: Wesleyan University, 1989), 73. Pettit mistakenly assumes that

people can move from a non-elect to an elect status in Reformed categories. This error, however, illustrates an inference easily drawn from the cooperative rhetoric of Federalism.

[88]Sibbes, *Spouse*, 2.203.

[89]Sibbes, *Spouse*, 2.204.

[90]As it also strikes some modern historians who express strong affinities for the scholastic syntheses; e.g. R. A. Muller, *God, Creation, and Providence in the Thought of Jacob Arminius: Sources and Directions of Scholastic Protestantism in the Era of Early Orthodoxy* (Grand Rapids: Baker, 1991), esp. 277-78.

[90]Muller, *God, Creation, and Providence*, p. 276; Gründler, "Thomism and Calvinism in the Theology of Girolamo Zanchi (1516-1590)" (Th.D. diss., Princeton Theological Seminary, 1961), 23.

[91] Muller, *God, Creation, and Providence*, p. 276; Gründler, "Thomism and Calvinism in the Theology of Girolamo Zanchi (1516-1590)" (Th.D. diss., Princeton Theological Seminary, 1961), 23.

Chapter Five—Sibbes' Anthropology

[pages 187-223]

[1]Sibbes, *The Soul's Conflict*, 1.173. He alludes here to the belief that the soul operates through an equilibrium of bodily fluids or humours: these are blood, phlegm, yellow bile and black bile. Cp. Aristotle, *On Sleep and Sleeplessness*; Berlin no.s 453b-458a.

[2]Sibbes, *Saint's Safety in Evil Times*, 1.298.

[3]Sibbes, *Soul's Conflict*, 1.160.

[4]For discussions of faculty psychology as used by the Puritans, see Miller, *New England Mind*, vol. 1, ch. 9, "The nature of Man"; and Dever, "Richard Sibbes", 122-23. R. A. Muller, *God, Creation, and Providence*, identifies the original distinctions of the Aristotelian model as fourfold: intellect, will, sensitive power, and vegetative power (143). This model characterized the intellectual and volitional capacities as primary; it also rejected a place for the passions that Aristotle (as noticed already) saw as a reactive rather than directive function of the soul. The Puritans, however, regularly included the affections as a primary feature of the soul. This included Perkins (e.g. 1.187, 193, 194, 196, 311, 392) despite his occasional subordination of the affections to a function within the will (e.g. 1.23) and his addition of the conscience as a fourth faculty on occasions (e.g. 1.20, 637).

[5]Muller comments that early orthodox Protestants, using Aristotelian faculty psychology, developed it "in considerable speculative depth"; *God, Creation, and Providence*, 143.

[6]Miller, *New England Mind*, 1.245.

[7]Sibbes, *Soul's Conflict*, 1.159.

[8] Perkins, *Reformed Catholike*, 1.557-58.

[9]Dever, "Richard Sibbes", 139. In a relatively brief chapter on Sibbes' affectionate theology Dever addresses Sibbes' main theological concerns, including the topics of sin, salvation, backsliding, assurance, and sanctification. He is explicit in his concern that Sibbes elevated sanctification over justification because of this emphasis on love (140-41). Here Dever displays his own commitment to a more juridical than ontological theology of union. For a positive assessment of Sibbes' interiorization, see B. R. White, "Echoes of Medieval Christendom in Puritan Spirituality", *One in Christ* 16 (1980): 78-90; 81.

[10]Sibbes, *Soul's Conflict*, 1.136; and *Bowels Opened*, 2.40. Cp. Aristotle's "On Sleep".

[11]Sibbes, *Bruised Reed*, 1.82; *Last Two Sermons: the First*, 7.347; *2 Corinthians 1*, 3.519.

[12]Fiering, *Moral Philosophy*, 53.

[13]Fiering, *Moral Philosophy*, 5.

[14]Fiering, *Moral Philosophy*, 44.

[15]Fiering, *Moral Philosophy*, 159; he cites Fenner's "To the Reader".

[16]Fiering, *Moral Philosophy*, 164; he cites Fenner, *Affections*, 51 (emphasis in the original).

[17]Fiering, *Moral Philosophy*, 4.

[18]Fiering discusses aspects of the confusion that emerged "between the Molinist liberty of the will and the Augustinian liberty that subordinates the will to either divine or satanic influence." *Moral Philosophy*, 137.

[19]Fiering, *Moral Philosophy*, 161.

[20]Gerrish, *Grace and Reason*, 49.

[21]Gerrish, *Grace and Reason*, 13, 15, 18.

[22]Calvin, *Institutes*, 1.4.1.

[23]Sibbes, *Marriage Feast*, 2.460.

[24]Sibbes, *Marriage Feast*, 2.463.

[25]Sibbes, *Soul's Conflict*, 1.243.

[26]Sibbes, *Bruised Reed*, 1.82.

[27]E.g. *Spiritual Jubilee*, 230: "Our will was given to us to cleave to God and the best things; to make choice of the best things . . ."

[28]Pettit, *The Heart Prepared*, 73; Kendall, *Calvin*, 108-9; Beck, "*gratia praeparans*", 167-68.

[29]Perkins, *Reformed Catholike*, 1.553; 2.178.

[30]Sibbes, *Description of Christ*, 1.20-21.

[31]Sibbes, *Soul's Conflict*, 1.197; the marginal reference: "*Ergone ita liberi esse volunt, ut nec Deum volunt habere Dominum?*"--Aug. *de Spir. et Lit.*

[32]Sibbes, *Soul's Conflict*, 198; the marginal reference: "*Certum est, nos velle cum volumus, sed ille facit ut velimus*--Aug."; Grosart attributes the thought to *Confessions*, 7.3.5.

[33]Sibbes, *Faith Triumphant*, 7.440.

[34]Sibbes, *Saint's Happiness*, 7.69.

[35]Sibbes, *Faithful Covenanter*, 6.10-11. Knight, *Orthodoxies*, 82.

[36]Francis Rous (1579-1659), for instance, as a Dionysian mystic among the Puritans, held an extreme position: "In these accesses of Christ there are heights of union, and the increases of union bring with them increases of uniformity. The Spirit of union is fire, and fire turns that into itself to which it is united; and the fuller and closer this union is, the more is this turning. So Christ Jesus the more he comes into a soul by his Spirit, the more spiritual he makes her; yea, the more doth he melt a soul into himself; the more doth he turn her will into his will . . ." *Mysticall Marriage*, 255. Thomas Taylor (1576-1633), on the other hand, identified the will and affections as twin components of the soul (as opposed to the spirit which consists of mind and conscience); the affections is the lesser of the two, "being guided and carried by the mind and will renewed." *The Progresse of Saints to Full Holinesse*, (London, 1630), 197.

[37]Perkins, *God's free grace*, 1.717. Fiering comments that Perkins' position--in describing the Spirit's work of "inlightening the mind and conscience with spiritual and divine light" is "hardly a step away from the 'candle of the Lord'" that Benjamin Whichcote and other Cambridge Platonists used to describe a universal divine light. *Moral Philosophy*, 58.

[38]Perkins, *Golden Chaine*, 1.87.

[39]Perkins, *God's free grace*, 1.717 (original emphases).

[40]Perkins, *God's free grace*, 1.716-17. This may be an allusion to the story of Buridan's ass, a paradox in which the ass stands equidistant from two stacks of hay; lacking a reasoning capacity by which it could resolve the dilemma of choosing between two equal goods, the animal starves.

[41]Sibbes, *Bruised Reed*, 1.82.

[42]Sibbes, *Bruised Reed*, 1.83.

[43]Perkins, *A Warning Against the Idolatry of the Last Times*, 311 [1.701].

[44]Sibbes, *Matchless Love and Inbeing*, 6.403.

[45]See, in chapter 2, a discussion of his commitment to many aspects of Federal theology but his denial of its most important aspect, the bilateral nature of a testament. Knight comments on the incorrect placement of Sibbes by historians: "[Perry] Miller took this position to be representative of the whole of the Puritan spectrum, joining Sibbes with Ames, Cotton with Hooker in a falsely monolithic wedding of sensibilities." *Orthodoxies*, 90; she cites Miller and Kendall (n. 7 & 8, 250).

[46]Stoever, *Faire and Easie Way*, 61; Sibbes, *Excellency*, 4.248.

[47]Dever, "Richard Sibbes", 117; Sibbes, *Bruised Reed*, 1.50.

[48]Kendall, *Calvin*, 109; Sibbes, *Matchless Love*, 6.393.

[49]Sibbes, *Bruised Reed*, 81-82.

[50]"His divine power has given us everything we need for life and godliness through our knowledge of him who called us by his own glory and goodness. Through these he has given us his very great and precious promises, so that through them you may participate in the divine nature and escape the corruption in the world caused by evil desires." [NIV]

[51]Sibbes, *Bruised Reed*, 1.80.

[52]Perkins, *Golden Chaine*, 1.113 [257]. The Romans citation addresses the witness of the Spirit who "testifies with our spirit that we are God's children." [NIV]

[53]Perkins, *Golden Chaine*, 1.113 [257]; this is taken from article four, and the prior citation from article two, of ch. 58, "Of the Application of Predestination".

[54]Taylor, *The Progresse of Saints to Full Holiness* (London, 1630), 211.

[55]Sibbes, *The Saint's Happiness*, 7.72.

[56]Sibbes, *Saint's Happiness*, 7.72

[57]Sibbes, *Christ's Exaltation Purchased by His Humiliation*, 5.347.

[58]Sibbes, *Second Sermon*, 7.354.

[59]Sibbes, *Description*, 1.19.

[60]Sibbes, *Description*, 1.23.

[61]Sibbes, *Description*, 1.61-62; he cites 1 Cor. 10:31.

[62]Sibbes, *Description*, 1.82.

[63]Sibbes, *Description*, 1.78.

[64]Sibbes, *Description*, 1.78.

[65]Sibbes, *Description*, 1.79-80.

[66]Sibbes, *The Witness of Salvation*, 7.369.

[67]Sibbes, *Witness*, 7.369-70.

[68]Sibbes presented this in *Description*, 1.17: "God the Father and the Son put the Spirit upon the manhood of Christ; so Christ both gives and receives the Spirit in diverse respects. As God, he gives and sends the Spirit. The spiration and breathing of the Spirit is from him as well as from the Father, but as man he received the Spirit." This synthesis honored the Western tradition of the *filioque* in which the Spirit proceeds from both the Father and the Son.

[69]Sibbes, *Description*, 1.17

[70]Sibbes, *Description*, 1.5.

[71]Sibbes, *Description*, 1.6-7.

[72]Sibbes, *Description*, 1.7.

[73]Dowey, *Knowledge of God in Calvin's Theology*, and Mary Potter Engel, *John Calvin's Perspectival Anthropology* (Atlanta: Scholars, 1988), both notice an ongoing duality of perspectives in Calvin; Dowey in the issues of God's revelation as creator and as redeemer, and Engel in matters of anthropology. Sibbes adopts a similar strategy but fails to link it to Calvin.

[74]Sibbes, *Description*, 1.9.

[75]Sibbes, *Description*, 1.9.

[76]Perkins' reliance on adoption as the primary mechanism of spiritual union is a logical concomitant to his juridical theology. Given his strong doctrine of

incommensurability, God offers himself to the elect through benefits rather than real union. His discussions of adoption are widespread: e.g., in Breward's edition of his works, 198, 201, 219, 234, 394.

[77]E.g. Sibbes, *A Fountain Sealed*, 5.425; also 7.447.

[78]Sibbes, *Miracle of Miracles*, 7.111. Cf. Blackham, "Pneumatology", who examines the views of Goodwin on these very matters. It is apparent that Goodwin shares much in common with his friend and mentor, Sibbes, on this subject. Blackham, with greater interest in modern theological matters than in historical theology, notices Sibbes but fails to explore his impact on Goodwin.

[79]Sibbes, *2 Corinthians*, 3.275.

[80]Sibbes, *Soul's Conflict*, 1.159.

Chapter 6—God's Work in Forming Faith

[pages 225-260]

[1]Sibbes, *Commentary on 2 Corinthians*, 4.444.

[2]Sibbes' theology of the Spirit and the Word receives attention in most studies that address his theology, e.g., Bert Affleck, Jr., "The Theology of Richard Sibbes, 1577-1635" (Ph.D. diss., Drew University, 1968), ch. 3; and, most recently, Beck, "*gratia praeparans*", 187-196, 224.

[3]The place of promises in Puritan covenantal thought is crucial but rarely receives special attention. An exception is Knight's *Orthodoxies*, 100-104, where she underscores the importance of the issue as part of the debate between Peter Bulkeley and Cotton in New England.

[4]E.g. the conditionality of Deut. 30:19, "I have set before you life and death . . . So choose life in order that you may live"; and the unconditional promise received by Abraham in Gen 15:5 which Paul uses as the paradigm for saving faith in Gal 3:1-7.

[5]E.g. "God infuseth supernatural grace and knowledge unto us", *Commentary on 2 Cor*, 4.352; cf. 4.517, 7.225.

[6]Sibbes, 1.18, 22.

[7]Sibbes, *Excellency of the Gospel Above the Law*, 4.213. Affleck, in "Theology of Richard Sibbes", has taken this Spirit-Christicism as evidence that Sibbes' doctrine of the Spirit represented an almost Barthian Christocentricism: "God is known as He works, and the content of His work as the Spirit of Life is the truth of His love for us in Christ Jesus; to know the God who reveals Himself

in this work is to know the Power of all life." (p. 149-50). Affleck concludes, then, that Sibbes has interpreted God's attributes "as inseparable dimensions that reveal the one God, whose nature is 'pure act' defined by the Spirit of life . . ." He also finds Sibbes to be something of a demythologizer (68). Sibbes, however, hardly anticipated such modern issues, given the precritical assumptions of his era.

[8]Sibbes, *Excellency*, 4.214.

[9]Sibbes, 5.426.

[10]What did Sibbes have in mind when he spoke of motions? His descriptions suggest, generally, an inward impression or modest inclination, rather than a dominating experience or impulse: "The motions of the Spirit are sweet and mild, and lead us gently on. They are not ordinarily violent raptures, removing the soul from itself, but leave in the soul a judgment of them, and of other things." (*A Fountain Sealed*, 5.427). Remarkably, Sibbes also held that spiritual motions are offered to reprobates. This reflected his view that the Word, both general and specific, is a grace of God available to all (*Description of Christ*, 1.25).

[11]Sibbes, *Fountain Sealed*, 5.427.

[12]Sibbes, *Fountain Sealed*, 5.427.

[13]Nuttall, in *Holy Spirit*, misses this distinction in Sibbes (as Affleck points out) and wrongly concludes: "The question whether the Holy Spirit ever speaks apart from Scripture . . . hardly raises it head; but it is clear that, if it had, Sibbes would have answered it decidedly in the negative." (24).

[14]Above, 29-30.

[15]Hall, *Antinomian*, 133-34 (Cotton's "Rejoynder"); cited above, 12.

[16]Cotton, *A Treatise of the Covenant* (London, 1659), 22-23; the marginal cit. is *Institutes*, 3.2.29.

[17]Calvin, *Institutes*, 3.2.29. It is notable that, before Calvin, Luther's moved away from a view of synergistic human responsibility under covenant (representing nominalist influences) to his later commitment to an explicitly monergistic stance which was expressed in terms of God's unilateral promises. See Lillback, "The Binding of God", ch. 4, esp. 112-135. Lillback, however, suggests that Luther's resulting position is to be differentiated from Calvin's, a view which is unacceptable in light of Calvin's use of God's unilateral promises as the foundation for faith.

[18]Calvin, *Institutes*, 3.2.29.

[19]Hall, *Antinomian Controversy*, 36-37.

[20]Hall, *Antinomian*, 36.

[21]Cotton responded: "These scriptures [which follow] seem to me as thunderbolts to cast down all contrary imaginations. We must be abiding in Christ, or else without him (to wit, without his abiding in us) we can do nothing, John 15:5. . . . And how we can be good trees, before we be engrafted into Christ, we must look for it in Aristotle's [1 word unintel.]: for it is not revealed in the Gospel of Christ." (Hall, *Antinomian*, 40). The missing word in the original mss at the Boston Public Library is, in fact, legible as either "Ethices" or "Ethicos"—recalling Luther's critique of Aristotle's *Nicomachean Ethics*.

[22]While Calvin spoke on occasions of faith as if it were an act of human will which "lays hold of the goodness of God", he still presents God as the one initiating the embrace. See his work on Rom 4:4; *Calvin's Commentaries: The Epistles of Paul The Apostle to the Romans and to the Thessalonians*, trans. Ross Mackenzie, eds. D. W. and T. F. Torrance (Grand Rapids: Eerdmans, 1960).

[23]Cp. Perkins, in *Reformed Catholicke*, who described faith by its function of "receiving" in a manner that implies a mental action—to take hold of by the will—rather than an affective response: "Indeed love, hope, the fear of God and repentance have their several uses in men, but none serve for this end to apprehend Christ and his merits; none of them all have this receiving property, and therefore there is nothing in man that justifies as a *cause* but faith alone" (1.565, emphasis added). Perkins, paradoxically, also speaks of faith as "unfallible assurance" in this treatise; but assurance, in the context, is gained by the efforts of faith as it seeks to "apprehend and apply the promise and the thing promised" (1.557).

[24]Woolsey, "Unity and Continuity", argues strenuously but unconvincingly that Calvin was a wholehearted bilateralist in applying the unconditional promise of salvation only to those who disclose themselves as elect through legal obedience: "Calvin [taught] that with respect to the initiation, establishment, and ultimate intention of the covenant, the promise was gratuitous, unilateral and inviolable; but with respect to participation in the blessings of the covenant, it was conditional and bilateral." (2.13). This reflects what has become a commonplace among scholars who wish to maintain continuity between deistic monergists such as Calvin and the modified synergism of later Federalists: e.g. "the covenant of grace is monopleuric or unilateral in its origin, but dipleuric or bilateral in its fulfillment", in Anthony Hoekema, "The Covenant of Grace in Calvin's Teaching," *CTJ*, 2 (1963), 140; also cited in Dever, "Richard Sibbes", 106-7. This solution, however, fails to address Calvin's belief that human boasting, which reflects sin, is rooted in the

attribution of *any* initiative for salvation to the human will. His position, consistently, is that any meaningful initiative towards God reflects regeneration as already initiated. Woolsey resolves this by conflating Calvin's views of the law and gospel, seeing them as parallel in their covenant operation (2.3) and, by this means, *as investing in the gospel all the conditional elements of the Old Testament covenantal law*. Thus, Calvin could be seen as making the gospel "in some sense conditional" because his *Old* Testament expositions confronted broken covenants as sinful (2.6). Calvin's Old Testament commentaries do, in fact, address the obviously conditional elements found there, but that fails to address the fact of his regular discrimination between the elect who respond to unconditional promises and the reprobate who fail to respond from the heart to either the conditional or unconditional promises (e.g. *Commentary on Romans* 3:27; 7:6, 14; *Galatians* 3:25; *Ephesians* 2:9). Woolsey, throughout his work, fails to address Calvin's recognition that the motive force of sin is found in the corrupted affections as part of the pride and unbelief (e.g. *Commentary on Genesis* 3:6), so that he relates virtually all covenantal obligations to the human will, despite even citing one of Calvin's common expressions about the place of transforming love (e.g. Woolsey, 2.13).

[25]A. McGrath, in *Reformation Thought*, suggests that Calvin's "rejection of the role of intermediaries, such as 'created habits of grace'" represented an application of Ockham's razor (84). While that may be an outcome, Calvin's rejection is best linked to his belief that *habitus* gives nature a false status.

[26]Calvin, *Institutes*, 3.2.7; the following citations are drawn from this section.

[27]Calvin, *Institutes*, 3.2.7.

[28]Calvin, *Institutes*, 2.2.12.

[29]Calvin, *Institutes*, 2.2.11 & 10.

[30]Calvin, *Institutes*, 3.2.7.

[31]Calvin, *Institutes*, 3.2.30.

[32]Calvin, *Institutes*, 3.2.30.

[33]Calvin, *Institutes*, 3.2.32.

[34]Calvin, *Institutes*, 3.2.32. Rossall affirms the crucial function of the affections in Calvin's theology in "God's Activity and the Believer's Experience in the Theology of John Calvin", pp. 126-7. Similarly William J Bouwsma comments that Calvin's "the affective knowledge of faith is the deepest of all experiences." In *John Calvin: A Sixteenth Century Portrait* (Oxford: Oxford University Press, 1988), 158-9. This discussion also gives credibility to

Kendall's general premise in *Calvin* that Calvin held that God's grace is universally available but is effective only for the elect.

[35]God's self-revelation, according to Calvin, was characterized by love and applied in mercy and grace through Christ: "faith is a knowledge of the divine benevolence toward us and a sure persuasion of its truth" (*Institutes*, 3.2.12). His doctrine of temporary faith was an affirmation that even the reprobate could gain brief and limited perceptions of this divine goodness: "For nothing prevents God from illumining some with a momentary awareness of his grace, which afterward vanishes." (*Institutes*, 3.2.11). It was this caveat (whether generated by Calvin's theology or by Biblical texts such as the parable of the Soils, Mat 13:1-23, and Heb 6:4-8) that motivated the Puritans in their great quest for assurance of salvation. Calvin, however, seemed confident that the clarity of this illumination in the elect would largely, if not completely, resolve such a concern.

[36]Calvin, *Institutes*, 3.2.34.

[37]Calvin, *Institutes*, 3.2.35. Luther, in his emphasis on justification by unconditional faith, displaced any role for human works. This produced his truncated view of sanctification. Zwingli attributed justification to moral regeneration that displayed itself in works. Calvin held to the unconditionality of faith but linked the origination of faith to regenerative union with Christ. See A. E. McGrath, *A Life of John Calvin: A Study in the Shaping of Western Culture* (Oxford: Blackwell, 1990), 166.

[38]Perkins, *Exposition of the Creed* in *Works*, 1.165.

[39]Knight, *Orthodoxies*, 78.

[40]Perkins, *Golden Chaine*, 1.32.

[41]Perkins, *Golden Chaine*, 1.32; 1.70.

[42]P. Helm, "Was Calvin a Federalist?", rejects assertions that Perkins equated the covenant of works with the Adamic covenant (49; the connection is made only later in the *Westminster Confession*), or that Perkins believed that the covenant of grace is conditional (49-50). In Helm's construction Perkins portrays the two covenants as operating in "a parallel fashion, in both the Old Testament and the New, and each is to be distinguished from the original arrangement with Adam" (49). The two covenants are from Moses and co-exist; one is beyond human ability to fulfill, and the other is gratuitous and received by faith. Helm's article anticipates criticisms of the synergistic (even Pelagian) quality of Perkins' Federalism that arise if the guiding relational structure of the God-human nexus is shaped by a conditional covenant as, indeed, this study argues. Perkins himself may have recognized the weakness

in his approach, as suggested by an apparent reversal evident in his commentary on Galatians (see a discussion of this in M. McGiffert, "The Perkinsonian Moment"). Helm's case is unconvincing in two respects. First, he argues that Perkin's failure to speak of a covenant of works in Adam's fall (in ch. 11 of *A Golden Chaine*) is evidence that Perkins reserved the title for the later Mosaic covenant. Against this, Perkins in ch. 9 spoke of the conditions for eternal life given Adam: "to will and perform the commandment". This matches the condition of the covenant of works in ch. 19. Perkins also described the covenants of ch. 19 as the "outward means" of election and God's "contract with man", language which implies something more fundamental than the lesser function seen in the Mosaic covenant. Second, Perkins' language in the covenant of grace is clearly conditional in that it "exacts" faith and repentance. He knew that covenant always denotes conditions, a matter inadvertently confirmed by his caveat that, although a covenant, it is "partly" a testament (since it depends on Christ's work and is merely an act of will rather than a behavioral obligation; nevertheless, faith and repentance remain qualifying conditions).

[43]Even Woolsey, who is quick to notice any evidence of continuity between Calvin and later Reformed theology, acknowledges that covenant failed to reach a "titular place in Calvin's work" ("Unity and Continuity", 1.316), although he argues that the ideas of covenant are widely present in the Genevan's writings. That point, of course, is easily explained by the broad biblical usage of covenantal language. The question to be answered is whether Calvin believed that covenantal theology is the defining structure for salvation. It seems clear, against Woolsey's contentions, that the function of unconditional promises are always prior to covenant for Calvin and serve as the ground for individual salvation; the Abrahamic covenant, Calvin believed, is subsequent and complementary to faith, laying the ground for corporate relations with national Israel and the Church. Arminius, over against Perkins, recognized this important distinction: "The confusion of the promise with the Old Testament is productive of obscurity in Christian Theology, and is the cause of more than a single error." Jacob Arminius, *Disputationes privatae*, LI.viii; cited in R. A. Muller, "The Federal Motif in Seventeenth Century Arminian Theology", *Nederlands Archief voor Kerkgeschiedenis* 62 (1982):102-122; 106.

[44]Perkins, *Golden Chaine*, 1.70.

[45]Perkins, *Golden Chaine*, 1.70.

[46]Lillback, "The Continuing Conundrum: Calvin and the Conditionality of the Covenant", *CTJ* 29 (1994): 42-74; 49.

[47]Luther, *Luther's Works*, 3.76-77; cited in Lillback, "The Binding of God", 194. Dismissing this resistance by Luther, Lillback later presents his central thesis, that Calvin also held to a covenantal mutuality and was "truly one of the key links between medieval covenant theology and the later mature Reformed covenant theology." (330). Lillback, however, overlooks the crucial role of chronological issues and misreads Calvin as a result. In his exposition of Galatians 3:17, Calvin had confronted "scholastic theologians" for their attempts to find merit in their obedience to the law, as based "on the ground of a covenant". Using the argument that, chronologically, the law was not yet given at the time of the Genesis narrative to which Paul refers in Galatians, Calvin concludes: "Hence the law which came [430 years] after could not abolish the promise." In this argument Calvin had entertained the scholastic premise that "except by a covenant with God, no reward is due to works"; Lillback takes this to mean that Calvin held "the idea of the covenant as the means of the divine acceptance of men's works." This is *not* Calvin's point. Calvin uses "promise" and "covenant . . . through Abraham" interchangeably in this context, but nothing in his discussion suggests that by this he means to conflate the "promise" with the covenant of Genesis 17. Instead, given his concern displayed already with the sequence of salvation history, he would certainly identify the promise (also called the "covenant of Christ"), with the blessing to the nations in 12:3 and to the seed in 15:6. Thus only Christ is able to fulfill the covenant conditions, not the individual believer. Calvin, *Commentary on Galatians* 3:17.

[48]Sibbes, *Yea and Amen*, 4.114-149.

[49]Dever, "Richard Sibbes", pp. 102-104, notices Sibbes discussion of absolute and conditional promises. Dever uses it to try to resolve the bilateral and unilateral distinctions made elsewhere by Sibbes concerning covenants and testaments. By implying that Sibbes understood that Christ's fulfillment of the covenant conditions modifies it, functionally, into a testament, Dever attempts to mitigate Sibbes explicit differentiation of the Old and New Testaments (see Sibbes, 5.342).

[50]Sibbes, *Yea and Amen*, 4.118.

[51]Sibbes, *Faith Triumphant*, 7.414.

[52]Sibbes, *Faith Triumphant*, 7.421.

[53]Sibbes, *Christ's Exaltation Purchased by His Humiliation*, 5.336.

[54]Sibbes, *Yea and Amen*, 4.118-19.

[55]Sibbes, *Yea and Amen*, 4.120.

[56]Sibbes, *Yea and Amen*, 4.125.

[57]Sibbes, *Yea and Amen*, 4.118-19.

[58]Sibbes, *Yea and Amen*, 4.119.

[59]Sibbes, *Yea and Amen*, 4.120.

[60]Sibbes, *Yea and Amen*, 4.121.

[61]Sibbes, *Yea and Amen*, 4.122. He offers the same distinctions in *2 Corinthians*. God's promises, in both settings, are listed as: A. Universal, such as the Noahic promise that the earth would not be destroyed again; B. For the Church, which are both 1. Outward—dealing with tangible needs—and 2. spiritual. Within this category he notes absolute and conditional promises. His illustration of an absolute promise was the incarnation: "God promised Christ, let the world be as it will, Christ did and would have come." Eschatological matters are placed here (3.394).

[62]Sibbes, *Yea and Amen*, 4.122; Phil. 2:12b-13: "continue to work out your salvation with fear and trembling, for it is God who works in you to will and to act according to his good purpose." [NIV]

[63]Sibbes, *2 Corinthians*, 3.394.

[64]Sibbes difficulty is captured in a slightly different manner by Beck, "*gratia praeparans*", 250: "How could someone in Adam, fallen with an inclination to the evil be inclined to ask for the good? Sibbes has not answered the question. It is our thesis that Sibbes has not answered the question because it is at both ends insoluble." I argue, however, that Calvin's or Perkins' views were both coherent possibilities: one elevating grace, the other nature. Sibbes fails because he attempts to combine the two.

[65]Perkins, *Symbole*, 1.125; *Golden Chaine*, 1.113.

[66]Bulkeley, *The Gospel-Covenant, or The Covenant of Grace Opened* (London, 1646), pp. 256, 259. This sermon series was clearly offered as a corrective to John Cotton's antinomist theology, which included a rejection of the practical syllogism, e.g. "Mr. Cotton's Rejoynder", p. 94f, in Hall, *Antinomian Controversy*. On Bulkeley's theology, see my "John Cotton", 98-102.

[67]Bulkeley, *The Gospel-Covenant*, 265-270. The second of these was "a closing with the whole will of God, without exception or reservation. When God writes his Law in our hearts, he writes all his Commandments there, as he wrote all of them before in the tables of stone . . ." (265).

[68]Wilhelm Niesel, *The Theology of Calvin*, trans., Harold Knight (Grand Rapids: Baker, 1980; first published as *Die Theologie Calvins*, Munich: Chr. Kaiser Verlag, 1938), pp. 178, 180-1.

[69]The following discussion will raise some of the key issues of the discussion. See, also, Muller, *Christ and the Decree*, p. 25, n. 71; cf. Barth, *CD* 2.2 (333-340) and Berkouwer, *Divine Election*, 279-306.

[70]Lynn Baird Tipson, Jr., "The Development of a Puritan Understanding of Conversion" (Ph.D. diss., Yale University, 1972), 99. He cites Barth, *Church Dogmatics*, 2, 2, 330 (100, n. 216).

[71]Tipson, "Puritan . . . Conversion", 100-1; he cites the *Institutes*, 3.24.2, and 3.2.12. Tipson, again, draws on Barth to make the point that Calvin's doctrine, if pressed, would "ultimately result in increased emphasis on human piety at the expense of Christ's objective work." (101).

[72]Tipson, "Puritan . . . Conversion", 108; he cites the *Institutes*, 4.1.3. He explicitly rejects Niesel's assumption that the key question of assurance is one of works (102, n. 220), again relying in Barth's critique of Niesel for support (*Church Dogmatics*, 2.2, p. 333f).

[73]*Institutes*, 3.24.12. Cf. Charles Partee, "Calvin and Experience", *SJT* 26 (1973):169-181, 180.

[74]Calvin, *Institutes*, 3.2.12; italics added.

[75]Tipson, "Puritan . . . Conversion", 108-9.

[76]Kendall, *Calvin*, 28, n. 7. It is at this very point in his study that Kendall makes a mistake, not related to Dever's critique, that misdirects the balance of his thesis. He concludes that faith and assurance is based by Calvin "in the 'heart' . . . . [by which] Calvin means a fully persuaded mind." As has been seen already, Calvin was *not* reverting to the intellectualist tradition as implied by Kendall, but in his doctrine of faith and assurance was asserting the priority of an affective experience of God, a tradition associated with moderate Bernardian mysticism. Because of this misstep Kendall presses on in his work to identify the distinctions between Calvin and subsequent Federal theology on the basis of a purely rational issue, namely, the extent of the atonement. In that pursuit he appears to overstep the evidence, a matter shown by Roger Nicole, "John Calvin's View of the Extent of the Atonement", *WTJ* 47 (1985): 197-225.

[77]Dever, "Richard Sibbes", p. 146-7, n. 21. This is an underlying argument in Schaefer's "The Spiritual Brotherhood", which also challenges Kendall's work (e.g. 63).

[78]Calvin, *Institutes*, 3.14.18; cited in Dever, "Richard Sibbes", 149. Stoever, as Dever notes (n. 31), offers this passage as Calvin's version of the practical syllogism, in *'A Faire and Easie Way to Heaven'*, 223, n. 16.

[79]Calvin, *The Sermons of M. John Calvin upon the Fifth Booke of Moses Called Deuteronomie*, , trans. Arthur Golding (London, 1583), 440.a.30; cited in Dever, "Richard Sibbes", 149-50.

[80]E.g. *The Unprosperous Builder*, 7.17-31, a powder-plot sermon which also celebrates the failure of the "Spanish match" for Prince Charles (p. 28), an event which aroused fears of incipient papal influence over the throne. Cf. 1.77; 3.500-505; 4.428; 7.517f.

[81]Calvin's point concerning the witness of sanctifying works "before men" was also made in his exposition of 2 Peter 1, as will be noted below.

[82]Muller, *Christ and the Decree*, offers a further challenge to the Niesel thesis. He believes that Calvin affirmed a proper use of the practical syllogism (p. 26) citing the *Inst.* 3.24.4, "we cling to those latter signs [of election] which are sure attestations of it." Calvin, however, was *not* suggesting that the "latter signs" are evidences of sanctification. This discussion develops the prior section (3.24.3) in which he challenges two "errors": 1) synergism on the basis of being "given an ability to believe, and not, rather, faith itself!", implying the Thomistic duality of *habitus* and *actus*; and, 2) a view that election is based on faith (anticipating the Arminian formula). Against these Calvin insists that "Scripture teaches us we are illumined according as God has chosen us . . ." This means that for assurance "we must begin with the Word" but from "his outward Word God may sufficiently witness his secret grace to us, provided only the pipe, from which water abundantly flows out for us to drink, does not hinder us from according its due honor to the source." The "latter signs", referred to in the next sentence, identify the inward (subjective) illuminations of the Spirit that accompany the prior (objective) Word in the elect.

[83]Sibbes, *Matchless Love*, 6.389.

[84]Sibbes, *Matchless Love*, 6.388.

[85]This is the ground for Sibbes' version of preparationism. That is, while he rejected any notion that that people can prepare themselves for salvation, Sibbes also believed that the invisible and silent presence of the Spirit would use his exhortations in *his* work of preparing ("framing") the future saint for the moment of conversion: "When the Holy Ghost hath framed our hearts to believe, then we believe . . . . It is true, the grace is from the Spirit, but when the grace is received, the act is from ourselves, not only from ourselves, but immediately from ourselves." (4.449). Cf. 6.522: "God usually prepares those that he means to convert . . . Therefore preparations we allow, and the necessity of them. But we allow this, that all preparations are from God." Kendall, in *Calvin*, is correct in assessing the uncertain boundaries presented by Sibbes in defining the Spirit's work prior to conversion, the event itself, and

the aftermath, as a "weakness in his theology [that] . . . keeps him from lucidly espousing a doctrine of full assurance". (106).

[86]Sibbes, *2 Corinthians*, 3.466-7. Sidney H. Rooy, in *The Theology of Missions in the Puritan Tradition* (Grand Rapids: Eerdman's, 1965), summarizes the necessity of both human and divine functions in Sibbes' theology at this point; he later concludes that Sibbes' full theology "constitute[s] the Biblical way of ascribing redemption completely to God." (18-21; 60).

[87]Sibbes, *Yea and Amen*, 4.140. He offers the same list with its own exposition but without "stablishing" in *2 Corinthians*, 3.464.

[88]Sibbes, *Yea and Amen*, 4.134.

[89]Sibbes, *Yea and Amen*, 4.134-5. In discussing the seals, Cary Weisiger in "The Doctrine of the Holy Spirit in the Preaching of Richard Sibbes" (Ph.D. diss., Fuller Theological Seminary, 1984), comments: "There is some difficulty in understanding the thought of Sibbes in regard to persuasion and sealing." (295). Weisiger confuses persuasion with assurance which accounts for his difficulty. As noted already, Sibbes viewed persuasion as a step in *coming to* original faith Christ; assurance occurs only at, or after the point when faith occurs.

[90]Sibbes, *Salvation Applied*, 5. 400; cf. 4.175, 279; 5.450-1.

[91]Cotton and his followers in the Antinomian Controversy adopted this distinctive version of conversion. But, as Knight correctly points out, conversions were not, typically, instantaneous events for the antinomists: "[T]hey too, suffered periods of spiritual doubt and anguish in the early phases of their conversion, the Brethren [antinomists] more often achieved an assurance that was full and complete." (*Orthodoxies*, 38). See also Patricia Caldwell, *The Puritan Conversion Narrative: The Beginnings of American Expression* (Cambridge: Cambridge University Press, 1983).

[92]Sibbes, *Second Sermon*, 7.352.

[93]Sibbes, in *The Soul's Comfort*, 1.138, denied the main premise of the practical syllogism: "[M]en by a natural kind of popery *seek for their comfort too much* [from] *sanctification*, neglecting justification, relying too much upon their own performances. . . . Satan joining together with our consciences will always find some flaw even in our best performances; hereupon the doubting and misgiving soul comes to make absurd demand . . ."

[94]Cotton sought to demonstrate that in the sequence of the textual material of 1 Peter, the readers' salvation is presumed in verse nine; the conditional statements build upon that as a prior assumption. Thus Cotton concluded: "The place you quote in Peter doth not argue it to be a way of God for men to

seek to see Christ in their Justification by clearing up their Sanctification and by abundant exercise in that way. . . . And for the 11th verse . . . it only holdeth forth that which no man denieth, to wit, that the way of faith and of the fruits thereof is the Royal way . . . and so Piscator maketh it a fifth Argument used by the Apostle to persuade to grow in faith . . . ." Cotton is cited from his "Rejoynder", in Hall, *Antinomian Controversy*, p. 131, (cf. 185 re. Calvin). Cotton refers to Johannes Piscator, *Analysis Logica Septem Epistolarum Apostolicarum* (Herborn, 1593) and to Calvin's exegesis, which offers the same conclusion, in *Commentarius in Petri Apostoli Epistolam Posteriorem.*

[95]Sibbes, *Fountain Sealed*, 5.438.

[96]Sibbes, *Yea and Amen*, 4.132.

[97]Sibbes, *Yea and Amen*, 4.132.

[98]Sibbes, *Yea and Amen*, 4.133.

[99]Sibbes, *Commentary on 2 Corinthians*, 3.467.

[100]Knight, *Orthodoxies*, 96-7. See also, C. F. Allison, *The Rise of Moralism: The Proclamation of the Gospel from Hooker to Baxter* (London: S.P.C.K., 1966), esp. 168f.

Conclusion—Sibbes' and Augustines' Affective Tradition

[pages 261-271]

[1]Muller, "Calvin and the 'Calvinists'", 31: 132, 134 f., esp. 138. Muller tends to ignore Luther throughout his corpus, thus the early Melanchthon (cited instead of Luther in the broader passage noted above) seems to be a surrogate for criticisms of Luther's position.

[2]Paul Blackham, "The Pneumatology of Thomas Goodwin", offers an interaction of Sibbesian concerns with modern theology in a manner that complements the present study. Goodwin was one of Sibbes' most gifted friends (he was twenty-three years younger than Sibbes) and a close supporter—he helped to bring many of Sibbes' works to press after his mentor's death. His own affective theology parallels Sibbes' positions very closely.

[3]Aquinas, *Summa*, Ia2æ. 108.1, *ad* 3: *liber est qui sui causa est.* Cited above in ch. 2, 43.

Selected Bibliography

Primary Sources

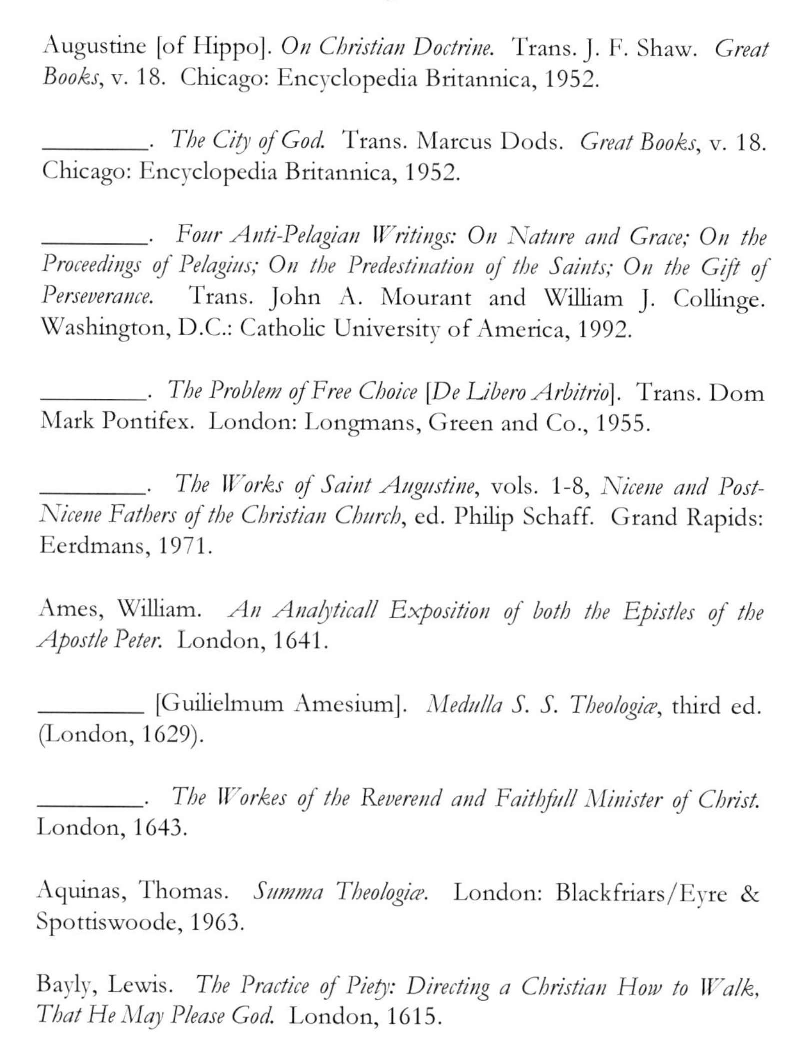

Augustine [of Hippo]. *On Christian Doctrine.* Trans. J. F. Shaw. *Great Books*, v. 18. Chicago: Encyclopedia Britannica, 1952.

________. *The City of God.* Trans. Marcus Dods. *Great Books*, v. 18. Chicago: Encyclopedia Britannica, 1952.

________. *Four Anti-Pelagian Writings: On Nature and Grace; On the Proceedings of Pelagius; On the Predestination of the Saints; On the Gift of Perseverance.* Trans. John A. Mourant and William J. Collinge. Washington, D.C.: Catholic University of America, 1992.

________. *The Problem of Free Choice* [*De Libero Arbitrio*]. Trans. Dom Mark Pontifex. London: Longmans, Green and Co., 1955.

________. *The Works of Saint Augustine*, vols. 1-8, *Nicene and Post-Nicene Fathers of the Christian Church*, ed. Philip Schaff. Grand Rapids: Eerdmans, 1971.

Ames, William. *An Analyticall Exposition of both the Epistles of the Apostle Peter.* London, 1641.

________ [Guilielmum Amesium]. *Medulla S. S. Theologiæ*, third ed. (London, 1629).

________. *The Workes of the Reverend and Faithfull Minister of Christ.* London, 1643.

Aquinas, Thomas. *Summa Theologiæ.* London: Blackfriars/Eyre & Spottiswoode, 1963.

Bayly, Lewis. *The Practice of Piety: Directing a Christian How to Walk, That He May Please God.* London, 1615.

Bayne, Paul. *Briefe Directions unto a Godly Life: Wherein every Christian is furnished with most necessary help for the furthering of him in a godly course here upon earth, that so he may attaine eternall happinesse in Heaven.* London, 1637.

________. *A Caveat for Cold Christians.* London, 1618.

Bernard [abbot] of Clairvaux. *Cantica Canticorum: Eighty-Six Sermons on the Song of Solomon.* Trans. and ed., Samuel J. Eales (London, 1896). Vol. 4 of *Life and Works of Saint Bernard, Abbot of Clairvaux.*

________. *Saint Bernard, His Meditations: or, Sighes, Sobbes, and Teares, upon our Saviours Passion.* London, 1611.

Beza, Theodore. *Master Bezaes Sermons Upon the Three First Chapters of the Canticle of Canticles.* Trans., John Harmar. Oxford, 1587.

________. *An Oration Made By Master Theodore de Beza* [1561; no pub. loc. or date].

Bullinger, Henry [Johann Heinrich]. *The Decades of Henry Bullinger.* 4 vols., ed., Thomas Harding, trans., H. I. [incomplete], Cambridge, 1849 ff.

Calvin, John. *Calvin's Calvinism: The Eternal Predestination of God and The Secret Providence of God*, (Geneva, 1552 & 1558), trans., Henry Cole (1856). London: Sovereign Grace Union, 1927.

________. *Calvin's Commentaries: The Epistles of Paul The Apostle to the Romans and to the Thessalonians.* Trans. Ross Mackenzie; eds. David W. Torrance and Thomas F. Torrance. Grand Rapids: Eerdmans, 1960.

________. *The Institutes of Christian Religion*, 1559 edition., 2 vols. Ed., John T. McNeill; trans., Ford Lewis Battles. Philadelphia: Westminster, 1960.

________. *The Sermons of M. John Calvin upon the Fifth Booke of Moses Called Deuteronomie.* Trans., Arthur Golding. London, 1583.

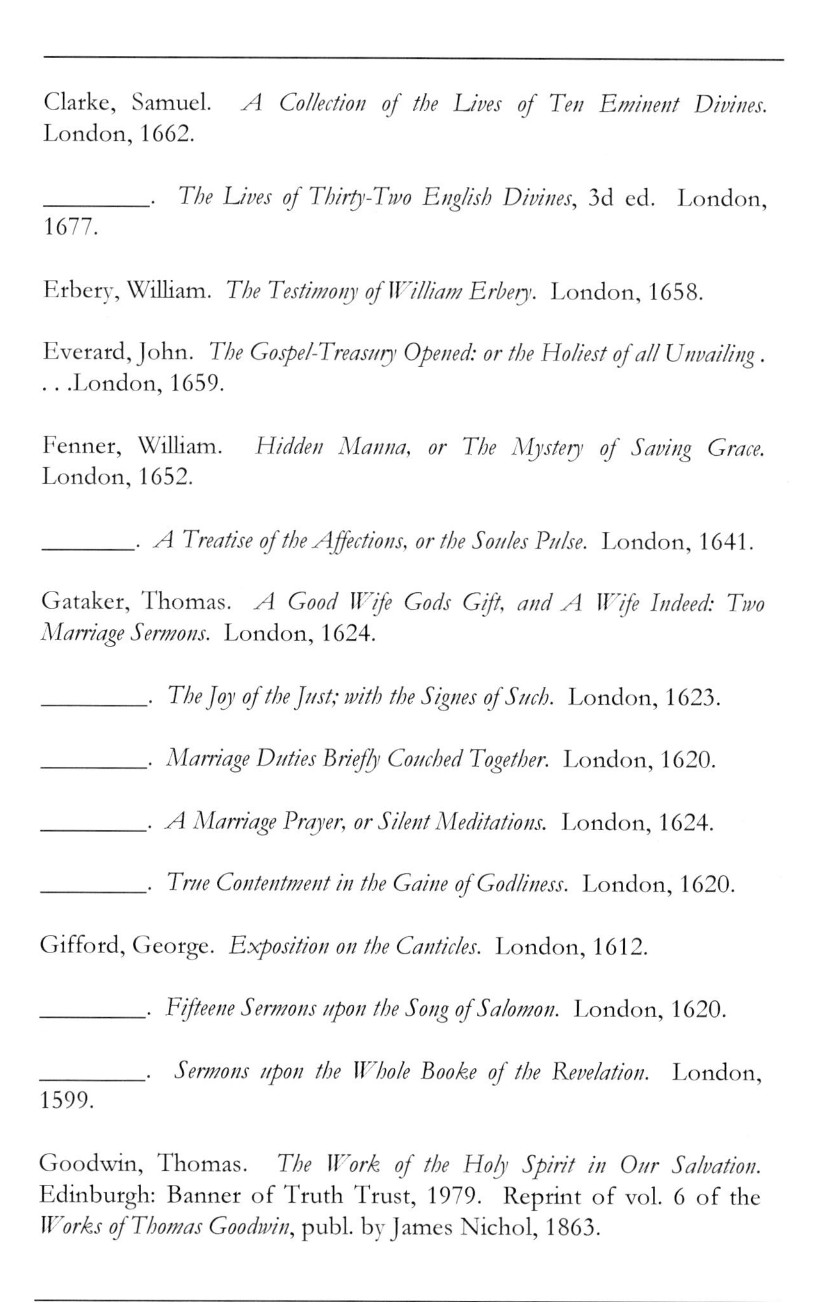

Clarke, Samuel. *A Collection of the Lives of Ten Eminent Divines.* London, 1662.

________. *The Lives of Thirty-Two English Divines*, 3d ed. London, 1677.

Erbery, William. *The Testimony of William Erbery*. London, 1658.

Everard, John. *The Gospel-Treasury Opened: or the Holiest of all Unvailing* . . . .London, 1659.

Fenner, William. *Hidden Manna, or The Mystery of Saving Grace.* London, 1652.

________. *A Treatise of the Affections, or the Soules Pulse.* London, 1641.

Gataker, Thomas. *A Good Wife Gods Gift, and A Wife Indeed: Two Marriage Sermons.* London, 1624.

________. *The Joy of the Just; with the Signes of Such.* London, 1623.

________. *Marriage Duties Briefly Couched Together.* London, 1620.

________. *A Marriage Prayer, or Silent Meditations.* London, 1624.

________. *True Contentment in the Gaine of Godliness.* London, 1620.

Gifford, George. *Exposition on the Canticles.* London, 1612.

________. *Fifteene Sermons upon the Song of Salomon.* London, 1620.

________. *Sermons upon the Whole Booke of the Revelation.* London, 1599.

Goodwin, Thomas. *The Work of the Holy Spirit in Our Salvation.* Edinburgh: Banner of Truth Trust, 1979. Reprint of vol. 6 of the *Works of Thomas Goodwin*, publ. by James Nichol, 1863.

Luther, Martin. *Luther's Works*, v. 26, *Lectures on Galatians, 1535.* Ed., Jaroslav Pelikan. St Louis: Concordia, 1963.

________. *Martin Luther's Basic Theological Writings.* Ed., Timothy F. Lull. Minneapolis: Fortress, 1989.

Melanchthon, Philip. *Loci Communes Theologici* [1521]. *Library of Christian Classics.* Ed.,Wilhelm Pauck. Philadelphia: Westminster, 1969.

________. *Loci Communes Theologici* [1543]. Trans., J. A. O. Preus. St Louis: Concordia, 1992.

Perkins, William. *William Perkins, 1558-1602: English Puritanist.* Ed., Thomas F. Merrill. Nieuwkoop: B. De Graaf, 1966.

________. *The Workes of . . . William Perkins*, 3 vols. London, 1626.

________. *The Work of William Perkins.* Ed., Ian Breward. Appleford: The Sutton Courtenay Press, 1970.

Reynoldes, Edward. *A Treatise of the Passions and Faculties of the Soule of Man.* London, 1640.

Rogers, John. *Ohel or Bethshemesh, A Tabernacle for the Sun.* London, 1653.

Rous, F[rancis]. *The Mysticall Marriage.* London, 1635.

Sibbes, Richard. *Works of Richard Sibbes.* 7 vols. Ed., Alexander B. Grosart. Edinburgh: The Banner of Truth Trust, 1979; originally published 1862-64.

Ursinus, Zacharias. *Commentary on the Heidelberg Catechism.* Trans., G. W. Williard. Phillipsburg, NJ: Presbyterian and Reformed Publishing Company, 1985; reprint of 1852 ed.; original Latin ed., 1585.

The Westminster Standards. [*Confession of Faith; Larger and Shorter Catechisms*] Philadelphia: Great Commission Publications, 1989.

Secondary Sources: Books

Allison, C. F. *The Rise of Moralism: The Proclamation of the Gospel from Hooker to Baxter.* London: S.P.C.K., 1966.

Armstrong, Brian G. *Calvinism and the Amyraut Heresy.* Madison: University of Wisconsin, 1969.

Balke, Willem. *Calvin and the Anabaptist Radicals.* Trans., William J. Heynen. Grand Rapids: Eerdmans Publishing Co., 1981; orig. publ. *Calvijn en de Doperse Radikalen*, Amsterdam, 1973.

Bangs, Carl. *Arminius: A Study in the Dutch Reformation.* New York: Abingdon, 1971.

Baskerville, Stephen. *Not Peace But a Sword.* London: Routledge, 1993

Beeke, Joel R. *Assurance of Faith: Calvin, English Puritanism, and the Dutch Second Reformation.* New York: Peter Lang, 1991.

Bell, Theo. *Divus Bernhardus: Bernhard von Clairvaux in Martin Luthers Schriften.* Mainz: Verlag Philipp von Zabern, 1993.

Berkouwer, G. C. *Divine Election.* Grand Rapids: Eerdmans, 1960.

________. *Sin.* Grand Rapids: Eerdmans, 1971.

Bouwsma, William J. *John Calvin: A Sixteenth Century Portrait.* Oxford: Oxford University Press, 1988.

Bozeman, T.D. *To Live Ancient Lives: The Primitivist Dimension in Puritanism.* Chapel Hill: University of North Carolina, 1988.

Brachlow, Stephen. *The Communion of Saints: Radical Puritan and Separatist Ecclesiology, 1570-1625.* Oxford: Oxford University Press, 1988.

Caldwell, Patricia. *The Puritan Conversion Narrative: The Beginnings of American Expression.* Cambridge: Cambridge University Press, 1983.

Casey, Michael. *Athirst for God: Spiritual Desire in Bernard of Clairvaux's Sermons on the Song of Songs.* Kalamazoo: Cistercian, 1988.

Clebsch, William A. *England's Earliest Protestants, 1520-1535.* New Haven: Yale, 1964.

Cohen, Charles L. *God's Caress: The Psychology of Puritan Religious Experience.* Oxford: Oxford University Press, 1986.

Collinson, Patrick. *The Elizabethan Puritan Movement.* Oxford: Oxford University Press, 1967.

________. *The Religion of Protestants: The Church in English Society, 1559-1625.* Oxford: Oxford University Press, 1982.

Coolidge, John S. *The Pauline Renaissance in England: Puritanism and the Bible.* Oxford: Oxford University Press, 1970.

Costello, William T. *The Scholastic Curriculum at Early Seventeenth-Century Cambridge.* Cambridge: Harvard University Press, 1958.

Coward, Barry. *The Stuart Age.* London: Longman Group, 1980.

Craig, William Lane. *The Only Wise God: The Compatibility of Divine Foreknowledge and Human Freedom.* Grand Rapids: Baker, 1987.

Cross, Claire. *Church and People, 1450-1660: The Triumph of the Laity in the English Church.* Hassocks: Harvester, 1976.

Davies, Julian. *The Caroline Captivity of the Church: Charles I and the Remoulding of Anglicanism.* Oxford: Oxford University Press, 1992.

De Witt, J. R. *Jus Divinum: The Westminster Assembly and the Divine Right of Church Government.* Kampen: J. H. Kok, 1969.

Dowey, Edward A. *The Knowledge of God in Calvin's Theology.* New York: Columbia University, 1952.

Engel, Mary Potter. *John Calvin's Perspectival Anthropology.* Atlanta: Scholars, 1988.

Evans, G. R. *Augustine on Evil.* Cambridge: Cambridge University Press, 1982.

________. *The Mind of St. Bernard of Clairvaux.* Oxford: Oxford University Press, 1985.

Evans, Robert F. *Pelagius: Inquiries and Reappraisals.* London: Adam & Charles Black, 1968.

Fiering, Norman. *Moral Philosophy at Seventeenth-Century Harvard: A Discipline in Transition.* Chapel Hill: University of North Carolina, 1981.

Fincham, Kenneth, ed. *The Early Stuart Church, 1603-1642.* London: Macmillan, 1993.

________. *Prelate as Pastor: The Episcopate of James I.* Oxford: Oxford University Press, 1990.

Finlayson, Michael G. *Historians, Puritanism, and the English Revolution: The Religious Factor in English Politics Before and After the Interregnum.* Toronto: University of Toronto, 1983.

Ganoczy, Alexandre. *The Young Calvin.* Trans., David Foxgrover and Wade Provo. Edinburgh: T. & T. Clark, 1987; orig. publ. as *Le jeune Calvin: Genese et evolution de sa vocation reformatrice*, 1966.

Gerrish, B. A. *Grace & Gratitude: The Eucharistic Theology of John Calvin.* Edinburgh: T&T Clark, 1993.

________. *Grace and Reason: A Study in the Theology of Luther.* Oxford: Oxford University Press, 1962.

Gilson, Etienne. *The Mystical Theology of Saint Bernard.* Trans., A. H. C. Downes. London: Sheed & Ward, 1940.

Greeves, Frederic. *The Meaning of Sin.* London: Epworth, 1956.

Gura, Philip F. *A Glimpse of Sion's Glory: Puritan Radicalism in New England, 1620-1660.* Middletown: Wesleyan, 1984.

Hall, David D. *The Antinomian Controversy, 1636-1638: A Documentary History.* Middletown: Wesleyan, 1968.

Haller, William. *The Rise of Puritanism.* New York: Columbia University, 1938.

Hambrick-Stowe, Charles E. *The Practice of Piety: Puritan Devotional Disciplines in Seventeenth-Century New England.* Chapel Hill: University of North Carolina, 1982.

Helm, Paul. *Calvin and the Calvinists.* Edinburgh: Banner of Truth, 1982.

Heppe, Heinrich. *Reformed Dogmatics.* Transl., G. T. Thomson. London: George Allen & Unwin, 1950; orig. publ., *Reformerte Dogmatik*, 1861.

Hill, Christopher. *Change and Continuity in 17th-Century England.* Revised ed. New Haven: Yale, 1991; orig. publ. 1974.

________. *A Nation of Change and Novelty: Radical Politics, Religion and Literature in Seventeenth-century England.* London: Routledge, 1990.

________. *Society and Puritanism in Pre-revolutionary England.* London: Penguin, 1964.

________. *The World Turned Upside Down: Radical Ideas During the English Reformation.* London: Penguin, 1972.

Hillerbrand, Hans J. *The World of the Reformation.* New York: Scribners, 1973.

Hindson, Edward, ed. *Introduction to Puritan Theology: A Reader.* Grand Rapids: Baker, 1976.

Hughes, Ann. *The Causes of the English Civil War.* London: Macmillan, 1991.

Kelly, J. N. D. *Early Christian Doctrines.* Fifth, revised edition. London: A & C Black, 1977.

Kendall, R. T. *Calvin and English Calvinism to 1649.* Oxford: Oxford University Press, 1979.

Knight, Janice. *Orthodoxies in Massachusetts: Rereading American Puritanism.* Cambridge: Harvard University Press, 1994.

Knott, John Jr. *The Sword of the Spirit: Puritan Responses to the Bible.* Chicago: University of Chicago, 1971.

Lake, Peter. *Moderate Puritans and the Elizabethan Church.* Cambridge: Cambridge University Press, 1982.

Lamont, William. *Godly Rule: Politics and Religion, 1603-60.* London: Macmillan, 1969.

Locher, Gottfried W. *Zwingli's Thought: New Perspectives.* Leiden: Brill, 1981.

McGinn, Bernard. *The Foundations of Mysticism.* London: SCM Press, 1991.

McGrath, Alister E. *The Intellectual Origins of the European Reformation.* Oxford: Blackwell, 1987.

________. *Iustitia Dei: A History of the Christian Doctrine of Justification*, 2 vol.s: v. 1. *From the Beginnings to 1500*; v. 2. *From 1500 to the Present Day.* Cambridge: Cambridge University Press, 1986.

________. *A Life of John Calvin: A Study in the Shaping of Western Culture.* Oxford: Blackwell, 1990.

________. *Reformation Thought: An Introduction*, 2nd ed. Oxford: Blackwell, 1993.

McKim, Donald K. *Ramism in William Perkins' Theology.* New York: Peter Lang, 1987.

Miller, Perry. *The New England Mind: The Seventeenth Century.* New York: Macmillan, 1939.

Morgan, Edmund S. *Visible Saints: The History of a Puritan Idea.* Ithaca: Cornell University Press, 1963.

Morgan, Irvonwy. *Puritan Spirituality: Illustrated from the Life . . . [of] John Preston.* London, 1973.

Morgan, John. *Godly Learning: Puritan Attitudes towards Reason, Learning, and Education, 1560-1640.* Cambridge: Cambridge University Press, 1986.

Muller, Richard A. *Christ and the Decree: Christology and Predestination in Reformed Theology from Calvin to Perkins.* Durham: Labyrinth, 1986.

________. *God, Creation, and Providence in the Thought of Jacob Arminius: Sources and Directions of Scholastic Protestantism in the Era of Early Orthodoxy.* Grand Rapids: Baker, 1991.

________. *Post-Reformation Reformed Dogmatics: Prolegomena to Theology.* Grand Rapids: Baker, 1987.

Niesel, Wilhelm. *The Theology of Calvin.* Translated by Harold Knight. Grand Rapids: Baker, 1980; first published as *Die Theologie Calvins*, Munich: Chr. Kaiser Verlag, 1938.

Nuttall, Geoffrey F. *The Holy Spirit in Puritan Faith and Experience.* Chicago: University of Chicago, 1992; 1st published by Blackwell, 1946; 2d ed., 1947.

Oberman, Heiko A. *The Dawn of the Reformation: Essays in Late Medieval and Early Reformation Thought.* Edinburgh: T&T Clark, 1986.

________. Editor, *Forerunners of the Reformation: The Shape of Late Medieval Thought.* London: Lutterworth, 1966.

________. *Luther: Man Between God and the Devil.* Trans. Eileen Walliser-Schwarzbart. London: HarperCollins, 1993.

________. *The Reformation: Roots and Ramifications.* Trans. A. C. Gow. Edinburgh: T&T Clark, 1994.

Ozment, Steven E. *Mysticism and Dissent: Religious Ideology and Social Protest in the Sixteenth Century.* New Haven: Yale, 1973.

Paul, Robert S. *The Assembly of the Lord: Politics and Religion in the Westminster Assembly and the 'Grand Debate'.* Edinburgh: T & T Clark, 1985.

Pettit, Norman. *The Heart Prepared: Grace and Conversion in Puritan Spiritual Life.* Second edition; introduction by David D. Hall. Middletown: Wesleyan, 1989. First published in 1966.

Porter, H. C. *Reformation and Reaction in Tudor Cambridge.* Cambridge: Cambridge University Press, 1958.

Ridderbos, Herman. *Paul: An Outline of His Theology.* Trans. J. R. De Witt. Grand Rapids: Eerdmans, 1975; orig. *Paulus: Ontwerp van zijn theologie*, 1966.

Rolston, Holmes, III. *John Calvin Versus the Westminster Confession.* Richmond: John Knox, 1972.

Rooy, Sidney H. *The Theology of Missions in the Puritan Tradition.* Grand Rapids: Eerdman's, 1965.

Russell, Conrad. *The Causes of the English Civil War.* Oxford: Oxford University Press, 1990.

________. *The Fall of the British Monarchies, 1637-1642.* Oxford: Oxford University Press, 1991.

Schuldiner, Michael. *Gifts and Works: The Post-Conversion Paradigm and Spiritual Controversy in Seventeenth-Century Massachusetts.* Macon: Mercer University Press, 1991.

Seaver, Paul S. *The Puritan Lectureships: The Politics of Religious Dissent, 1560-1662.* Stanford: Stanford University Press, 1970.

________. *Wallington's World: A Puritan Artisan in Seventeenth-Century London.* Stanford: Stanford University Press, 1985.

Sprunger, Keith L. *The Learned Doctor William Ames: Dutch Backgrounds of English and American Puritans.* Urbana: University of Illinois, 1972.

Stephens, W. P. *The Holy Spirit in The Theology of Martin Bucer.* Cambridge: Cambridge University Press, 1970.

Stoever, William K. B. *'A Faire and Easie Way to Heaven': Covenant Theology and Antinomianism in Early Massachusetts.* Middletown: Wesleyan, 1978.

Strehle, Stephen. *Calvinism, Federalism, and Scholasticism: A Study of the Reformed Doctrine of Covenant.* Bern: Peter Lang, 1988.

________. *The Catholic Roots of the Protestant Gospel: Encounter Between the Middle Ages and the Reformation.* Leiden: E. J. Brill, 1995.

Tennant, F. R. *The Concept of Sin.* Cambridge: Cambridge University Press, 1912.

Thomas, Keith. *Religion and the Decline of Magic: Studies in Popular Beliefs in Sixteenth and Seventeenth-Century England.* London: Penguin, 1971.

Torrance, Thomas F. *Calvin's Doctrine of Man.* London: Lutterworth, 1949.

________. *The Hermeneutics of John Calvin.* Edinburgh: Scottish Academic Press, 1988.

Twigg, John. *A History of Queen's College, Cambridge, 1448-1986.* Woodbridge: Boydell, 1987.

Tyacke, Nicholas. *Anti-Calvinist: The Rise of English Arminianism, c. 1590-1640.* Oxford: Oxford University Press, 1987.

Underdown, David. *Fire from Heaven: Life in an English Town in the Seventeenth Century.* London: Harper Collins Publishers, 1992.

Vandervelde, G. *Original Sin: Two Major Trends in Contemporary Roman Catholic Reinterpretation.* Amsterdam: Rodopi N.V., 1975.

Von Rohr, John. *The Covenant of Grace in Puritan Thought.* Atlanta: Scholars, 1986.

Wakefield, Gordon. *Puritan Devotion: Its Place in the Development of Christian Piety.* London: Epworth, 1957.

Wallace, Dewey D. Jr. *Puritans and Predestination: Grace in English Protestant Theology, 1525-1695.* Chapel Hill: University of North Carolina, 1982.

Watt, Tessa. *Cheap Print and Popular Piety, 1550-1640.* Cambridge: Cambridge University Press, 1991.

Weir, David. *The Origins of the Federal Theology in Sixteenth-Century Reformation Thought.* Oxford: Oxford University Press, 1990.

White, Peter. *Predestination, policy and polemic: Conflict and consensus in the English Church from the Reformation to the Civil War.* Cambridge: Cambridge University Press, 1992.

Theses

Affleck, Bert Jr. "The Theology of Richard Sibbes, 1577-1635." Ph.D. dissertation, Drew University, 1968.

Beck, Stephen Paul. "The Doctrine of *gratia praeparans* in the Soteriology of Richard Sibbes." Ph.D. dissertation, Westminster Theological Seminary, 1994.

Blackham, Paul. "The Pneumatology of Thomas Goodwin." Ph.D. dissertation, University of London, 1995.

Brauer, Jerald Carl. "Francis Rous, Puritan Mystic, 1579-1659: An Introduction to the Study of the Mystical Element in Puritanism." Ph.D. dissertation, University of Chicago, 1948.

Dever, Mark Edward. "Richard Sibbes and the 'Truly Evangelicall Church of England': A Study in Reformed Divinity and Early Stuart Conformity." Ph.D. dissertation, Cambridge University, 1992.

Farrell, Frank E. "Richard Sibbes: A Study in Early Seventeenth Century English Puritanism." Ph.D. dissertation, University of Edinburgh, 1955.

Frost, Ronald N. "Richard Sibbes' Theology of Grace and the Division of English Reformed Theology." Ph.D. dissertation, University of London, 1996.

Godfrey, William R. "Tensions Within International Calvinism: The Debate on the Atonement at the Synod of Dort, 1618-1619." Ph.D. dissertation, Stanford University, 1974.

Gründler, Otto. "Thomism and Calvinism in the Theology of Girolamo Zanchi (1516-1590)." Th.D. dissertation, Princeton Theological Seminary, 1961.

Higgins, John Robert. "Aspects of the Doctrine of the Holy Spirit During the Antinomian Controversy of New England with Special Reference to John Cotton and Anne Hutchinson." Th.D. dissertation, Westminster Theological Seminary, 1984.

Hoyle, David M. "Near Popery Yet No Popery: Theological Debate in Cambridge, 1590-1644." Ph.D. dissertation, University of Cambridge, 1991.

Lillback, Peter A. "The Binding of God: Calvin's Role in the Development of Covenant Theology." Ph.D. dissertation, Westminster Theological Seminary, 1985.

McGrath, Gavin J. "Puritans and the Human Will: Voluntarism Within Mid-Seventeenth Century English Puritanism As Seen in the Works of Richard Baxter and John Owen." Ph.D. dissertation, University of Durham, 1989.

Mcphee, Ian. "Conserver or Transformer of Calvin's Theology? A Study of the Origins and Development of Theodore Beza's Thought, 1550-1570." Ph.D. dissertation, Cambridge University, 1979.

Rosenmeier, Jesper. "The Image of Christ: the Typology of John Cotton." Ph.D. dissertation, Harvard University, 1965.

Rossall, Judith. "God's Activity and the Believer's Experience in the Theology of John Calvin." Ph.D. dissertation, University of Durham, 1991.

Schaefer, Paul R., Jr. "The Spiritual Brotherhood on the Habits of the Heart: Cambridge Protestants and the Doctrine of Sanctification from William Perkins to Thomas Shepard." D.Phil. dissertation, Oxford University, 1994.

Shelly, Harold Patton. "Richard Sibbes: Early Stuart Preacher of Piety." Ph.D. dissertation, Temple University, 1972.

Tamburello, Dennis E. "Christ and Mystical Union: A Comparative Study of the Theologies of Bernard of Clairvaux and John Calvin." Ph.D. dissertation, University of Chicago, 1990.

Tipson, Lynn Baird, Jr. "The Development of a Puritan Understanding of Conversion." Ph.D. dissertation, Yale University, 1972.

Weisiger, Cary N., III. "The Doctrine of the Holy Spirit in the Preaching of Richard Sibbes." Ph.D. Dissertation, Fuller Theological Seminary, 1984.

Woolsey, Andrew A. "Unity and Continuity in Covenantal Thought: A Study in the Reformed Tradition to the Westminster Assembly." 2 vols. Ph.D. dissertation, University of Glasgow, 1988.